THE SPIRIT ABOVE THE DUST

Herman Melville

Portrait by Asa Weston Twitchell
painted between 1845 *and* 1847

The Spirit
Above the Dust

A STUDY OF

HERMAN MELVILLE

by

Ronald Mason

New Foreword

By Howard P. Vincent, Ph.D.

Second Edition

PAUL P. APPEL, *Publisher*

MAMARONECK, N.Y.

1972

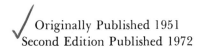Originally Published 1951
Second Edition Published 1972

Published by PAUL P. APPEL
By Arrangement with Ronald Mason

Library of Congress Catalog Card Number — 70-162496
ISBN 911858-19-9

To
My Wife

What is the price of Experience? do men buy it for a
    song?
Or wisdom for a dance in the street? No, it is bought
    with the price
Of all that a man hath, his house, his wife, his children.
Wisdom is sold in the desolate market where none come
    to buy,
And in the wither'd field where the farmer plows for
    bread in vain.

WILLIAM BLAKE, *The Four Zoas*

Acknowledgments

A VERY little of the material in this book has already appeared in the form of articles in literary periodicals. The chapter on Melville and Hawthorne is an expansion of a piece which appeared in *The Wind and the Rain* (autumn, 1947); I have also incorporated passages from an essay entitled *Symbolism and Allegory in Melville* which was printed in *Penguin New Writing No.* 22. I acknowledge with thanks the permission of the editors of these publications to make use of this material.

Similarly I would like to acknowledge the kindness of the following publishers in allowing me to make use of copyright material in their possession : Jonathan Cape, Ltd., for a passage from T. E. Lawrence's *Letters*; Mrs. Frieda Lawrence and William Heinemann, Ltd., for an extract from D. H. Lawrence's *Letters* and for several passages from *Studies in Classic American Literature*; and Macmillan & Co., Ltd., for quotations from John Freeman's book on Melville in the English Men of Letters Series.

The copyright in the frontispiece portrait of Melville is vested in the President and Fellows of Harvard University, Cambridge, Massachusetts; and for permission to reproduce it here I am indebted to them and to their American publishers, the Harvard University Press, and to their English publishers, Messrs. Cohen & West, Ltd.

I am strongly conscious of many other occasions for gratitude. I am indebted to Mr. E. L. Grant Watson for much interest and encouragement, as well as for friendly advice, inadequately followed; to Mr. John Lehmann for valuable suggestions and for the timely loan of unprocurable books; to my friend Stanley McKay for going to great trouble and expense when in America to find me editions which I could not obtain over here, and to my friends F. V. and M. M. Checksfield, and my sister-in-law Dorothy Coles, for similar kindnesses. To my friend and fellow-Melvillean T. F. Evans, who at my request read nearly all the book in manuscript and has assisted me throughout with pertinent (and impertinent) comment, I owe a special word of acknowledgment and thanks. Lastly I would like to record my gratitude for the co-operation and forbearance of my wife, who at the cost of much of her own leisure contrived both time and space for me to write this book in comfort.

RONALD MASON

Contents

Foreword To Second Edition

An Anglophile himself, like most of his countrymen, Herman Melville has long experienced in return the admiration and affection of discriminating Englishmen, against the long-respected orders of Sidney Smith not to read an American book. The names of W. Clark Russell, Henry Salt, Alice Meynell, E. L. Grant Watson, and John Middleton Murry have an admirable pioneer status in the history of Melville studies. Furthermore, during Melville's lifetime he found the book reviewers of England often more discerning and generous than those of his own country.

The publishers did well by him, too. John Murray first published his first book, *Typee* (1846), and five years later Richard Bentley published *The Whale,* that three-volumed fastfish which preceded the American printing of *Moby-Dick* by a month. Constable published in the early 1920's the first collected edition of Melville's writings, at a time when Melville's books were almost unobtainable in the United States, a condition scarcely remedied, such the lack of interest by readers, for several decades.

Constable also included in that memorable set the first publication of *Billy Budd* (1924), instantly recognized by the *London Times Literary Supplement* for the masterpiece it is. Remembering this, and remembering the Forster-Crozier-Britten opera of *Billy Budd,* and further remembering what Peter Ustinov did to bring out the film of *Billy Budd,* and, finally, remembering that the novel deals with the British Navy, then it might also seem that Melville is partly an English author. Maybe this is what the publishers of the English Men of Letters Series meant when they dared contradiction by including John Freeman's *Herman Melville* in that series.

In this tradition of critical intelligence transcending national boundaries and biases, Mason's *The Spirit Above the Dust* is distinguished. Mason undertook this book from sheer love of the subject, an authorial drive far more honorable than the expectation of promotion which motivates most literary criticism. Mason was then a Civil Servant, a novelist, and was just starting his career, now well established, as a commentator on cricket, where his devotion to that game is as pure and ecstatic as was his ardor for the American writer. Mason himself has a spirit much above the dust.

Mason was marooned on the island of England. Without the then-emerging scholarship from the American presses, without a body of enthusiasts in his own country to talk with, save for the encouragement of E. L. Grant Watson and of Tom Evans, a Welshman with Celtic insight into the mystery of whales, Ronald Mason wrote alone with somewhat the same aloneness and the same fever displayed by Melville during the last weeks of composing *Moby-Dick,* an obsessed man trying to harpoon a mighty subject.

Mason's pages are humbling to scholars and critics who today do not study the author so much as they study the studies of authors. Uncontaminated by scholarship and criticism, Ronald Mason boldly confronted Melville's writings, to arrive at criticisms and conclusions which now, twenty years later, have continuing freshness and illumination, all conveyed in a style which leaps like light from page to page. Ronald Mason, long after Doctor Johnson and Virginia Woolf, wisely acted as the Common Reader, no uncommon task, so that his book is free from eccentricity, from striving for novel effect. He is intelligence studying intelligence and speaking intelligently to intelligence.

Which brings us to Ronald Mason's *The Spirit Above the Dust,* 1951. Early in the 1950's John Lehmann adventurously dared to include *Billy Budd, The Confidence-Man,* and *White Jacket* in his Chiltern Library, these at a time when even Melville's own country did not have these titles available. Lehmann was therefore in a receptive mood when Mason's manuscript of literary criticism came to his attention. He published it, and then, alas, foundered on the financial rocks so that all of these books disappeared from print, with only occasional copies turning up in secondhand book stores. *The Spirit Above the Dust* became a waif; very few American libraries as yet have copies of the book. Now the lack is remedied.

November

1971   Howard P. Vincent

CHAPTER I

Introduction

THE ACTUAL events of Herman Melville's life, except in so far as they are directly recorded or reflected in his books, are not of very great interest or importance, and it is possible to extract a coherent meaning from the body of his writing without having much recourse to biographical narrative. This study is accordingly cast in the form of a critical estimate of his books, and not as biography proper. Such events and incidents as affected the shape and temper of his work will naturally find their place; but in Melville, as in Shakespeare, Blake and similar writers whose perceptions were oftener dependent on spiritual and imaginative than on physical adventure, it is the embodiment of those perceptions in the written word that is the crucial action, not the incident that may have suggested it. I do not believe that this principle applies to Melville any less on account of the unusually adventurous nature of his formative years. By his own confession his imaginative life began where his physical vicissitudes ended; his artistic development was an activity entirely independent of the sequence of his early travels.

The truth is that Melville's travels are still allowed a disproportionate importance in proper critical judgment. In his own lifetime he won popularity by his two narratives of life in the South Seas, and for a few years he sold his books on the strength of that initial popularity alone. A little later his angry criticism of the Navy in *White-Jacket* increased his authority to the status of a popular social reformer. Yet the book which followed was a failure, although it is now universally, and rightly, regarded as his masterpiece; and he never regained public favour. He lapsed into obscurity before his life was half over; and died at seventy-two forgotten except as the author of those promising travel-books and a novel about whaling that was too much like an encyclopaedia to succeed as fiction, and too pretentiously poetic to suggest reliability as fact. He was remembered, if he was remembered at all, as an interesting failure; *Typee* and *Omoo* remained longer in the public memory than any of his other books, and in right of these he would find his way into footnotes in literary histories. Many studies of nineteenth-century American literature continued to ignore him.

He died in 1891. Thirty years later most of the spade-work of rehabilitation had been done. Professor Raymond Weaver deserves the bulk of the credit for this comparatively rapid revival; and in 1921 his *Herman Melville: Mariner and Mystic* sought for the first time to allot to this unusual writer the serious consideration he deserved. In 1924 a Collected Edition of his works was published, with the incidental addition of a manuscript novel (written in the last few years of Melville's life) whose existence had been for thirty years unsuspected.

By this time *Moby Dick* had emerged from obscurity to take its place beside *Typee* and *Omoo* in the catalogue of survivors. It was not long before it was recognised, finally accepted, allotted a place among the classics. Critics began to talk of it in terms of *King Lear* and *Faust*. Together with the perennial travelogues, it was admitted to popular reprints: it was even filmed, with Barrymore as Ahab. A life of Melville by John Freeman appeared in the English Men of Letters series, which had already admitted the American Hawthorne (though excluding Emerson, Longfellow and Thoreau) and which was also to let in Whitman and, much later, Poe. By the end of the nineteen-twenties Melville was being discussed by a wider public than ever before except at the very height of the immediate success of *Typee*.

The critics began to develop their impressions. There was a sympathetic essay by Mr. Middleton Murry in the *Times Literary Supplement* in 1927; Mr. E. M. Forster's celebrated Clark lectures at Cambridge in the same year gave close and perceptive treatment to *Moby Dick* and *Billy Budd*; D. H. Lawrence wrote two charac-teristic pieces in his studies of American literature. In 1929 Mr. Lewis Mumford completed and published the first considerable critical biography of Melville. It was issued in America and had a fairly wide circulation in this country. Detailed, enthusiastic, at times deeply sympathetic and illuminating, it was marred only by a tendency to dramatise, to infuse spurious emotion into a character already possessed of sufficient of his own. The potency of its criticism suffered a serious dilution, and with the later access of Melville scholarship its accuracy became challengeable.

Since 1929 study of Melville by American scholars has been steadily increasing in assiduity. All evidence points to a body of close and detailed research which has not yet been significantly sifted. The colleges and universities attract theses upon every aspect of Melville's life and work: many of them, to judge by the references in such books as have percolated into this country, being of great interest as contributions to a subject barely surveyed as yet, much less examined in detail. New editions of the works are being prepared; one valuable full-length study by the late Mr. William Ellery Sedgwick, entitled *Herman Melville, the Tragedy of Mind*, has achieved a preliminary correlation of results of research and criticism; Newton Arvin's biography in the American Men of Letters series effects a useful balance between the life and the works; and the late Professor F. O. Matthiessen's impressive *American Renaissance* contains perhaps the most penetrating examination of Melville's purpose and achievement yet made.

Yet the tale of Melville's popularity in this country is disap-pointingly meagre. Much of the early response to the publications and discoveries of the early 1920s originated, as we have seen, on this side of the Atlantic; but after 1929 and the appearance of Mr. Mumford's book British readers seemed to lose the initial impetus of their interest. By 1939, it is true, many of the novels had been reissued in cheap reprints, but, as before and as always, the two South Sea stories and *Moby Dick* were still the most accessible. The very limited Standard Edition of 1924 was dispersed among libraries; and even now many of his most important books are unobtainable except by the most assiduous search. Enterprising publishing of recent years has made *Billy Budd* and *The Confidence-Man* once more available—the latter, to judge by the bookstalls, over-available; but *Pierre*, that difficult, much-maligned, and extremely important novel, is still scarcer than gold. The ordinary reader with fewer opportunities of access to specialist libraries is all but prohibited from seeing a full set of Melville, much less possessing it; in my own case, nearly half of my collection reached me through the tirelessness and kindness of friends in America, who gave up valuable time and dollars to scour the bookshops on my behalf. It is not really surprising that a writer barely accessible in his own country should find it difficult to acquire a merited reputation in another; and in spite of an appreciable quickening of interest in Melville, the British public have not as yet responded very widely to him.

It is perhaps unfortunate for his present reputation that the leading English critics are inclined just now to concentrate on the moral and social implications of literature rather than the purely imaginative. For them Melville's untidy spontaneity accords insufficiently with a correlated moral or intellectual system, and he is in consequence left out of contemporary discussion. This is not intended as a criticism of modern schools of appreciation; it is merely a comment on Melville's illfortune in arriving at recognition at a time when his particular qualities have temporarily exhausted all the discussion that this generation felt could be given to them. The consequence is that Hawthorne, a writer of lesser powers but of clearer-cut principles, who harnessed his myth to the moral rather than to the spiritual problem, is now in the process of a profounder analysis than Melville has ever been accorded on this side of the Atlantic.

It is in the hope of redirecting the interest of English readers and critics back to the swarming complexities and relevances of Melville's unusual art that I have attempted in this book to give him the close consideration that is long overdue. Even such a study as this has to be pruned if it is not to be unwieldy; and I am conscious that for every implication that I have tried to examine and relate to the main structure of his achievement, I have let a dozen others escape me. From this I am convinced that only a generation or so of detailed critical examination will extract from the bewildering mass of Melville's life's work something approaching an adequate critical judgment. It should be the work of a succession of scholars; a single critical book, even if it is followed in due course, as I hope it may be, by a set of detailed studies on more particular aspects of his work, can do no more than plot the ground over which better-equipped parties may carry out more elaborate surveys. I am convinced, too, that the ultimate critical verdict will not quarrel with the more spontaneous emotional conviction that a reader fascinated by Melville cannot help expressing: that this writer has been unduly withheld from universal recognition as one of the foremost poetic imaginations in the world's literature. He is a compelling force, with whom a considered reckoning can no longer be honourably avoided.

Melville's own personal history may be sketched briefly enough. He was born on 1st August 1819 in New York, the son of an active and prosperous merchant who could trace his descent back to a Scot knighted by James the Sixth, and grandson of a Major Thomas Melville who took part in the Boston 'Tea-Party'. His mother, like so many distinguished American figures, was of Dutch origin; and there was a certain national pride on her side of the family as well, for her father had achieved distinction against Burgoyne in the American War of Independence. A normal childhood and undistinguished school life was interrupted by a sudden, permanent decline in the family fortunes; and the death of his father in 1832 left the novelist's mother and her eight children in a condition in which family pride had to struggle hard to retain the appearance of respectability. There is some resemblance in these unfortunate beginnings to the almost contemporary misadventures of the Dickens family; and though Herman Melville never suffered the humiliations which the English novelist conceived himself to have undergone, it is clear that his spasmodic employments as bank clerk, shop assistant, farm worker and teacher, left him insecure and unhappy, cherishing an adventurous spirit on the memories of an idyllic childhood that had vanished for ever. When he was eighteen he cut loose and went to sea.

His travels did not in themselves occupy a very large slice of his youth, but they determined the lines on which his creative imagination would develop in the future. In about seven years fortune gave him an unusual variety of seafaring experience, from the merchantman on which he first took ship for Liverpool to the whalers on which he cruised among the South Sea archipelagoes and the man-of-war in which he eventually returned home. These voyages were varied by a short interlude during which he jumped ship at the Marquesas and lived for some months as the enforced guest of a cannibal tribe; and on his retirement from seafaring at the age

B

of twenty-five it was this unusual episode that first matured in his mind as material for the imaginative writing to which he now determined to devote his life.

For the next ten years his output was exceptionally prolific. His early books, *Typee* and *Omoo*, narratives of his life in the South Seas, encouraged him by their popularity first to settle down and found a family and next to develop his literary art along rather more original lines than his eager public bargained for. The failure of his first really ambitious novel *Mardi* drove him back upon plainer reminiscence in *Redburn* and *White-Jacket*, and to his one wholly successful blend of reminiscence and philosophical symbolism, *Moby Dick*. Unhappily for his popularity, his increasing assurance and tautening control over his craft were accompanied by a deepening preoccupation with metaphysical issues as well as by the onset of a spiritual crisis in his own life; factors which tended to distort the narrative clarity of his books and to make them less valuable as individual productions than as illuminating evidence of the imaginative progress of an exceptional poetic mind. It is no surprise to find his popularity filtering away, his publishers becoming chary, even the quality of his work reflecting a bitterness not wholly attributable to his response to universal suffering. After a time it became necessary for him to look elsewhere for a living. He tried a little farming, he tried a little lecturing; neither with much success. He made attempts, lasting over a dozen years in all, to obtain a position in the Government service; and after the Civil War, when for ten years he had written no prose whatever and had the publication of one book of verse only to his name, he managed to scrape an appointment as district inspector of Customs in New York. Here, virtually in retirement as a writer, he lived and went about his routine business for nineteen years; one long narrative poem, *Clarel*, being his only publication during that time. After his retirement in 1885 he collected and published, in severely limited editions, two volumes of lyric verse; and occupied the last two years of his life in the composition of the remarkable short novel, *Billy Budd*, that was not published until more than thirty years after his death.

His importance, as I have already remarked, went almost unnoticed in his lifetime; and what popularity he acquired seems in a century's perspective to have attached very largely to his less valuable work. The obscurity in which the greater part of his life was passed has projected itself over his posthumous reputation; he has not yet been considered in proportion to his own exceptional achievement and that of his contemporaries. An isolated phenomenon of uneven quality, he is perfunctorily accepted for his superficial successes and as perfunctorily dismissed for his (no less superficial) failures.

He arrived upon American literature at the moment of its most self-conscious expansion. His own essay on Hawthorne witnesses to his awareness of this, and he himself was as integral a part of the great national uprising of American letters as any of his more renowned contemporaries. The unspoken, perhaps only partially realised aspirations which coloured his most significant writing contained, as I shall show, a strong vein of national consciousness and national ambition which render any consideration of the development of the American genius lame and lopsided without him. Yet his genius was so individual that his national importance can be overlooked. Of the five great writers whom Matthiessen chose to illustrate his impressive account of the American renaissance of the mid-nineteenth century he seems perhaps the obscurest and most wayward; certainly, in spite of his exhaustless eloquence, the least articulate. Emerson's orderly and luminous expositions seem to diffuse an instant intellectual clarity quite beyond Melville's power either to apprehend or to communicate, while Thoreau and Whitman, so utterly different in all essentials save integrity, each contrived to apprehend a significant unity, the one in natural beauty, the other in human society, that made their individual witness the more readily acceptable and their contribution to the country's culture unchallengeable. Hawthorne, too, by declining to venture outside the limits of a native reticence, and binding a strong imagination to the service of a vigorous Puritan tradition, gave the appearance of a moral certainty the lack of which seemed in Melville a disastrous eccentricity. Melville's chartless voyages, rewarded as often with frustration as with discovery, did violence to the natural desire of a young and virile nation for early reassurance. It is no wonder that it finally grew impatient with his dissatisfactions and preferred material certainties that were ultimately to betray it into materialist hands that have never relaxed their hold since.

Yet no one who studies the rich flowering of the American genius into the memorable literature which the second half of the nineteenth century produced can have any doubt of the worth of Melville's own contribution to it. It is not my intention to institute comparisons; it is enough to remark that the sheer vitality of his imagination makes every one of his illustrious compeers look sluggish beside him. Thoreau seems tenuous, Emerson arid, Whitman garrulous; while Hawthorne, just as in life he shrank from Melville's urgent friendship, shrinks by his side to the dimensions of a brooding and irresolute moralist whose vision is limited by an ingrained timidity. The paradox of the tardy recognition of Melville lies in his failure to limit himself to the accepted moral confines which the precise moment of national renaissance appeared to demand. Because he was far in advance of the common imaginative understanding he appeared inadequate to the requirements of a self-conscious community. He courted misunderstanding by his refusal, or even his inability, to limit his context. It is in fact not an exaggeration to describe Melville as the only American writer of genius effectively to sink the confining consciousness of nationalism in the wider context of the human soul. Without ever losing his awareness of race or his comprehension of the crucial part it had to play in history, he contrived, unlike his contemporaries, to subordinate it to the profounder purpose. A common sailor home from a hard seafaring, he used the symbols of the sea to illustrate a quest that is the prerogative of no single nation but of every sensitive individual—the search for the rediscovery of that innocence in the human soul of which contact with worldly experience has deprived it. Of this search his books make up a single, deeply impressive record. So courageous is his attack upon his theme, so comprehensive and untiring his development of it, that he speaks to the universal condition of man as no other of his countrymen has ever spoken.

CHAPTER II

Typee and the Statement of Innocence

"UNTIL I was twenty-five," wrote Melville to Hawthorne, "I had no development at all. From my twenty-fifth year I date my life." This is true of his spiritual and imaginative development; from a stolid and backward small boy and a youth of physical courage and initiative but to outward appearance no unusual dower of imagination Melville blossomed suddenly and late into a vital creative artist of extreme nervous energy. As he went on to say in the same letter: "Three weeks have scarcely passed, at any time between then and now, that I have not unfolded within myself." We can take that as reliable evidence; Melville chronicling his inner development speaks directly and factually, in contrast to his practice of embellishing his record of actual incident with imaginative trimmings. He wrote that letter when he was thirty, at the height of his fame and power. Its implied account of his unusually rapid development as a writer is given ample evidence by the list and character of his books published in those highly productive years.

Typee was published when he was twenty-seven; by Melville's own evidence therefore we can allow it to carry at least a little of the quality of his newly awakened poetic imagination. It bears many of the marks that commonly distinguish a young writer's first novel: it is autobiographical, untidy, inflated with a romanticism which was partly genuine, as I shall try to show, but largely conventional and derivative; but it has what few first novels, even of significant writers, can boast of, and that is a consistent readability. And I begin by examining the reasons for the surface attractions of this book because it seems that they may help to indicate not only Melville's technical equipment as it was at the beginning of his writing life but, more important, the original processes by which Melville's own experiences of whatever kind were translated into terms of art.

For Melville may have declared that he had no development at all before he was twenty-five, but he omitted to mention that from the time he was eighteen to the time he was twenty-four he was assimilating experience, and experience of a diverse and violent nature, at a rate far more punishing than most young men are called upon to sustain. In those few but impressionable years he had seen service on a merchant ship, agonised a term or two as a schoolmaster, sailed for a year on a whaler, deserted and roamed for an indefinite period among the cannibals in the South Sea Islands, served a further spell on another whaler, been involved in a mutiny, escaped its consequences, joined the U.S. Navy and worked his passage home on a man-of-war, and all at the age when many senior students are still at the University. There seems little in his own account of himself in any of his phases, either as the passive wanderer in *Typee* or *Omoo*, the raw novice in *Redburn* or the hardened deck-hand in *Mardi* or *Moby Dick* or *White-Jacket*, to suggest that the young man was blessed or cursed with a deeper sensitivity than the common run of his fellows; indeed it is at all times difficult to separate, in Melville's most characteristic work, the imaginative power of the supposed narrator from the actual imaginative power of the novelist recording the scenes. Nevertheless Melville's studied self-portrait is that of a vigorous, forthright, robust character, humane and sympathetic, better-educated than his fellows but not in the creative sense imaginative, and with a broadly humorous rather than an acutely perceptive eye. Yet the man who went through these experiences, or most of them, was unconsciously storing them away in one of the most dynamic imaginations in the history of literature; and the incidents of these crowded half-dozen years became the essential raw material of a formidable body of creative work. The process of assimilation was organic to the ultimate task of re-creation in pictorial form;

Melville's statement that his development began only when he was twenty-five may be regarded as tacitly referring to his active use of the imagination as contrasted with the passive; for the purposes of this letter he ignored the paramount value of the period during which the "negative capability" of his superbly responsive mind selected from experience such material as was necessary and laid it by in his memory until such time as his imagination should mature.

Typee, as the first production of a talent as yet unaware of its own capacities, is valuable as a demonstration of the instinctive use of material. The material at Melville's disposal was, as we have seen, of great variety and scope; his selection, and the manner of his manipulation of it, for his first full-length essay in fiction, is much more interesting and significant than the general topic and framework of an otherwise only moderately distinguished book would lead a casual reader to expect.

The first point to notice is Melville's own proclamation of the literal truth of the facts as he presented them in the book. There is a story that the book was published in London only on Melville's specific guarantee that everything in it was true. Yet recent re-searches have shown that where it suited him Melville drew on his own imagination and the imaginations and reminiscences of other writers, coloured up certain episodes (for example his escape from the island), distorted the actual periods spent in captivity, accentuated certain qualities of the islanders at the expense of others and, in fact, imposed his own creative character upon the book quite as firmly as if what he were writing were wholly fiction. Mr. C. R. Anderson has shown quite clearly in *Melville in the South Seas* that Melville deliberately deviated from the facts whenever and however he pleased. This naturally does not matter at all to the artistic and imaginative validity of *Typee*; Melville's purpose, ostensibly to record a series of personal adventures, is revealed by this valuable research to have been something rather different, and that is why this deviation must be remarked at the start and never forgotten in any consideration of *Typee* and *Omoo*. It shows that masquerade as a literal autobiographer merely masked a more significant being altogether: a conscious artist.

The factual story of *Typee* is easily told. The narrator (it is for obvious reasons misleading to call him Melville, and to distinguish him from his creator I shall refer to him in the South Sea context by his native nickname of Tommo) deserts his whale ship at Nukuheva, an island in the South Pacific group called the Marquesas, and, in company with another defaulting member of the crew, journeys off into the interior in search of a friendly tribe of natives who were reputed to welcome white men. After a number of scarifying adventures among the mountains and watercourses the two deserters decend into a fertile valley inhabited not by the friendly Happars but by their notoriously brutal enemies, the cannibal Typees. With this tribe they are forced to stay; Tommo's leg, injured in the mountains, is seriously enough damaged to prevent him from moving for a while, and his friend Toby, baulked of various attempts to go to the coast for medical help, is ultimately lured away in the belief that help is round the corner and never returns. The rest of the book is given up to the detailed and vivid description of Tommo's enforced but not uncomfortable captivity among the Typees, and culminates in his thrilling dash for escape in a boat that has put inshore from a cruising whaler.

How much of this is the literal truth does not matter; what is important is the accentuation, the firm and positive clarity of Melville's impressions. The action, the temper of the book can leave no doubt of the love and solicitude with which Melville cherished in his mind and in the written expression of it the symbol, visionary or actual, of this native tribe. His first presentation of them is original, and for a time baffling, but it is consistent. He approaches them in a whaler, described in the most disparaging terms.

> "With a very few exceptions, our crew was composed of a parcel of dastardly and mean-spirited wretches, divided among themselves, and only united in enduring without resistance the unmitigated tyranny of the captain.
> "Not only the implied but the specified conditions of the articles had been violated . . . the usage on board of her was tyrannical; the sick had been inhumanly neglected; the provisions had been doled out in scanty allowance; and her cruises were unreasonably protracted."

And when the ship anchors in the bay and the lovely native girls swim joyfully out to welcome the strangers, they climb aboard and entertain the seamen with their wild and graceful dancing.

"Our ship was now wholly given up to every species of riot and debauchery. The grossest licentiousness and the most shameful inebriety prevailed . . . through the whole period of her stay. Alas for the poor savages when exposed to the influence of these polluting examples! Unsophisticated and confiding, they are easily led into every vice, and humanity weeps over the ruin thus remorselessly inflicted upon them by their European civilisers. Thrice happy are they who, inhabiting some yet undiscovered island in the midst of the ocean, have never been brought into contaminating contact with the white man."

This vivid little picture, bitter and unforgettable, presents the imaginative reason, if not the actual compelling one, for Tommo's and Toby's flight. Approached from this pervasive atmosphere of oppression, purposelessness, physical suffering, and inhuman indifference, the idea of freedom and plenty on land is irresistible, and Tommo and Toby make their daring and successful getaway. Yet seasoning their joy at their escape and their anticipation of native hospitality and comfort, there abides at the back of their minds the hideous fear of the cannibal Typees—

"the dreaded Typees, the unappeasable enemies of the other tribes. They inspire the other islanders with unspeakable terrors. Their very name is a frightful one; for the word 'Typee' in the Marquesan dialect signifies a lover of human flesh. It is rather singular that the title should have been bestowed upon them exclusively, inasmuch as the natives of all this group are irreclaimable cannibals. The name may perhaps have been given to denote the particular ferocity of this clan, and to convey a special stigma along with it."

There in plain words is stated Melville's—or perhaps it should be Tommo's—dilemma. On the one hand the degenerate squalor of a sensual and inhuman civilisation; on the other the promise of peace and freedom among surroundings of surpassing natural beauty, only marred by the terrors of a primitive barbarism even more hideous than the life aboard the whaler. Seizing the frail chance that in escaping from the one they may with the help of Providence avoid the other as well, Tommo and Toby strike instinctively into the unknown. Yet Fate holds this paradox over their heads; that the natural beauties of the island visit them on their journey with nearly unsupportable hardships; and when they find shelter and welcome, they find it at the hands of the dreaded Typees. This process was to repeat itself many times in Melville's imagination; and the symbol of the primitive or the elemental, whether it took the form of the sea or native savagery or the desert, was again and again to present itself to the mind of Melville or his hero as a force to be feared while still unknown and to be loved and understood once terror had been overcome and contact made. The most striking and homely of these symbolisms in Melville's maturer work is the encounter of Ishmael in *Moby Dick* with the cannibal harpooner Queequeg: an incident which opens in horror and ripens into close and enduring friendship, the loneliness of the civilised man responding to the innocence of the natural savage.

And this essential innocence is what Melville found among the Typees. Tommo, more instinctive and less sophisticated than his author, fled to the cannibals' valley in disgust at the physical and spiritual servitudes on board his ship; Melville, who had done much the same in actuality, achieved a profounder act of imagination when he sat down to give his recollection of the adventure a significant artistic form. To a reader who knows the later Melville it is clear that *Typee* is more than common popularity and report would label it, a mere tale of adventures among cannibal islanders; it is the first attempt by a writer of a consistently expanding imagination to find a symbol which would adequately express his most intimate obsessions. Therefore the prevailing qualities, the reiterations and insistencies of *Typee* should be carefully watched; for they point to the prevailing imaginative obsessions of Melville's life. The key to the purpose of the book is the innocence of the Typees.

"The easy unstudied graces of a child of nature," says Melville of his particular favourite, the young girl Fayaway, "breathing from infancy an atmosphere of perpetual summer, and nurtured by the simple fruits of the earth: enjoying a perfect freedom from care and anxiety, and removed effectually from all injurious tendencies, strike the eye in a manner which cannot be portrayed." And again he says, taking a wider view of the general atmosphere in which the islanders lived their careless lotus-eating existence. "One peculiarity that fixed my admiration was the perpetual hilarity reigning through the whole extent of the vale. There seemed to be no cares, griefs, troubles or vexations in all Typee. The hours tripped along as gaily as the laughing couples down a country dance." And in the paragraphs that follow Melville breaks out into a vigorous attack, light-hearted enough in form but carrying with it undertones of frustration that were to increase in insistence later, on the distractions of modern civilisation from which the Typees were mercifully immune:

> "There was none of those thousand sources of irritation that the ingenuity of civilised man has created to mar his own felicity. There were no forclosures of mortgages, no protested notes, no bills payable, no debts of honour, in Typee; no unreasonable tailors and shoemakers, perversely bent on being paid; no duns of any description: no assault and battery attorneys, to foment discord, backing their clients up to a quarrel and then knocking their heads together; no poor relations everlastingly occupying the spare bedchamber, and diminishing the elbow-room at the family table: no destitute widows with their children starving on the cold charities of the world; no beggars; no debtors' prisons; no proud and hard-hearted nabobs in Typee; or, to sum up all in one word—no Money! That root of all evil was not to be found in the valley."

It reads like a curiously distorted epitome of Dickens or Balzac; and it helps to point a valuable contrast at the outset between the kind of novelist Melville was going to be, and the other kind of novelist that the world expected him to be and cold-shouldered him for the best part of a hundred years for not being. For the indication implicit in this scornful paragraph is that Melville was not quickened in the creative imagination, as the great nineteenth-century story-tellers were, by the to-fro bustle of contemporary society. The brilliant Liverpool scenes in *Redburn* are too episodic, and the city scenes in *Pierre* too crudely melodramatic, to rank as indications that Melville had absorbed modern civilisation into his creative, as distinct from his intellectual, perceptions. Having limitless sympathy with man, he had dangerously imperfect sympathy with men and their activities; his preoccupations were with the elements, and the terrors and joys, the passions and specu-lations which close contact with those elements provoke. His affinities were with Aeschylus, not Euripides. The fascination and diversity of the *quicquid agunt homines*, which so many novelists have revelled in as their province and much more, repelled Melville and left him fierce and frustrated unless by their very nature or immediacy to his own peculiar experience they led him directly to a deeper understanding of the elemental and universal contradictions which engaged his imagination most deeply. He did not entirely shun them; but he recoiled from them. They barred him from the innocence which he believed to be the essential quality by which humanity could outface evil, resist it and defeat it: the innocence of the Typees, of Jack Chase, of Queequeg, of Billy Budd. Therefore at the outset of his creative life he rejected the civilisation which he felt in some obscure but final way had rejected him. It was a continuing act, culminating a dozen years later in *The Confidence-Man*, the novel in which all his early instincts of distrust found their most sophisticated expression.

Nevertheless the rejection could not be final. D. H. Lawrence, a man much after Melville's stamp, had shared independently many of Melville's own frustrations and had conceived in his turn projects of escapism to which the idealisms of *Typee* and *Omoo* were strangely pertinent even though three-quarters of a century separated them. Yet Lawrence understood the flaw in *Typee* better perhaps than Melville did himself. "It is no good persisting in looking for paradise regained" . . . he says. "The truth of the matter is, one cannot go back. Some men can: renegade.[1] But Melville couldn't go back; and Gauguin couldn't really go back; and I know now that I could never go back. Back towards the past, savage life. One cannot go back. It is one's destiny inside one."

Strip away as much as possible of Lawrence's personal "mystique"; yet it remains clear that he has rightly interpreted Melville's inner dissatisfaction with his own instinctive escapism. The feverish desire to escape from the idyllic life in *Typee*, which haunts the captive Tommo like an illness, is something profounder and more elemental than the natural hankering of a white man for the familiar company and civilisation of white men, or the nostalgia of a wanderer for his home. It is in effect a reaction against the inertia that goes with the innocence, or rather with the elementary innocence personified by the childlike Typees. "The continual happiness," says Melville, "which appeared to prevail in the valley, sprung principally from that all-pervading sensation which Rousseau has told us he at one time experienced, the mere buoyant sense

---

[1] There is one of these "renegades" in *Omoo*; and Melville's treatment of him is a fair indication that Melville acknowledged the truth of what Lawrence goes on to say.

of a healthful physical existence." Melville, even in his youth, at
the very outset of his career, was astute enough to perceive the
limitations of this kind of innocence, and the value of a spiritual
state which would barely survive an indigestion. Instinctively he
fled to the Typees; instinctively he loved them; instinctively he
feared them, not for their anthropophagous tendencies but for the
degeneracy which he knew would sap them fatally in the context
of a modern civilisation; and instinctively he fled back from them
into the very surroundings of squalor and oppression from which
so recently he had made a daring escape. Tommo's dash for safety—
if life aboard a leaky and mutinous whaler is safety in comparison
with life among friendly natives—is the most nervous and dramatic
incident in the book. It foreshadows some of the finest scenes of
taut and desperate physical action in *Redburn* and *Moby Dick*;
with the boat fighting for the open sea but driven by a fierce head-
wind towards the rocks from which the angry savages leap into the
sea to intercept and overturn it, Tommo has as desperate and
difficult a release from his retreat as he had had in his hazardous
entry to it over the nearly impassable mountain ranges. Lawrence
(naturally) sees in the description of the arrival in Typee "a bit of
birth myth or re-birth myth on Melville's part"; and if we stretch
the analogy to include the exit along with the entry, it will serve
to accentuate the deep painfulness of each experience and to relate
the "escape" to Melville's rebirth into modern civilisation just
as his struggle over the mountains was a birth into the idyllic
innocence which he had to experience before he was ripe enough
to discard it.

Tommo escaped, killing a Typee warrior in the struggle. In
violence he discarded immature innocence and returned to the
shoddy sophistication which he loathed. Yet Typee left its mark
on him for the rest of his life; the direction of his life's work was
determined by that preoccupation for which he made Typee stand
as symbol. It served him then as it served him throughout, as a
symbolic representation of the human ideal for which the whole
of his recorded work is a search of progressive complexity. The
innocence of the Typees is elementary enough, as *Typee* the book
is in a literary and artistic sense simple and unsubtle enough; but
it stood as a sufficient, a barely sufficient sign of Melville's purpose
—at this stage probably a purpose hardly realised. Innocence,
at every stage of its universal progress to tragedy, was to be

Melville's constant and (I am going to suggest) central theme; and although the only conclusion to be drawn from *Typee* is that innocence as Melville knew it then could only wither in the atmosphere of contemporary civilisation, that conclusion was a temporary one and marked only the first of a prolonged series of bitter endeavours to reconcile the two conflicting elements. The tragedy of innocence was his theme; and at the end of his life, by a wonderful effort of the imagination, he achieved a vision of a condition in which that tragedy might be turned to triumph. In the days of *Typee*, of course, that was unimagined, unimaginable. In *Typee* he did no more than state his case.

CHAPTER III

Omoo

TYPEE was a success; probably the greatest material success that Melville ever had. It was taken up in all the literary circles of America, besides penetrating into remote territories like the high Sierras. The great names in contemporary American literature were ready and generous with praise; Hawthorne and Whitman in reviews, Emerson and Thoreau in their journals made favourable references to it, Washington Irving and Longfellow went out of their way to read it. The wider and less intellectual public fell upon it eagerly; a contemporary journalist, Donald G. Mitchell, spoke of the "Typee disorder" attacking schoolboys and young ladies. The romantic fact of having lived among cannibals invested Melville's name with an unusual fascination, and he enjoyed for a short while a popularity he was never to know again. Rightly or wrongly *Typee* succeeded with discriminating and undiscriminating reader alike. It is not difficult to understand why, for it is clearly and vigorously written in a prose which as yet has none of the tortuous convolutions which his later reading and conjecturing gave to his style, and the story he tells is modest, direct, adventurous and above all, dramatic. It is shaped and poised with a barely conscious artistry. Although it is unambitious, and, apart from the unusual subject-matter, is in no sense original, it has its own effect of completeness. I have shown how organic its theme and treatment is to the major preoccupations of Melville's later life; but contemporary readers could not be expected to recognise this. All they saw was a romance, supremely readable. The reasons for its readability were only partly accessible to them; with our perspective we can approve their instinctive judgment.

Whether *Omoo* was primarily Melville's own idea or his publisher's, we cannot tell: but it would have been unnatural, if such a success as *Typee* were not followed up after a strategic interval by a sequel, seeing that so much of Melville's journeyings remained untapped. As far as the facts with which it deals are concerned it is almost an integral part of the first book, since the narrative follows directly upon Tommo's escape from the Typees in the whaler's boat and accompanies him on the next rather rambling episode of his travels to and around the island of Tahiti. It ends, much as *Typee* ends, with his departure on a whaler for a destination he barely knows or cares about; which left it open to Melville, it would seem, to go on retailing his adventures by the reel for so long as he found it lucrative to do so in the future. That is the chief structural similarity between the two South Sea Island books; for apart from the fact that they treat of the same hero and somewhat the same geographical area, there is little justification for lumping the two books carelessly together, as is so often done. *Typee*, however simple and elementary in form, is a symbolic record of a stage in an artist's spiritual experience; its successor *Omoo* amounts to very little more than an unco-ordinated series of descriptions of events which no doubt happened to Melville but which do not seem to have awakened any significant response in his creative imagination. The shape of the narrative in *Typee* is clear-cut and economical; the traveller arrives among cannibals, is entertained with friendliness but with just sufficient restraint to make his desire to escape tense and urgent throughout, and finally makes his breakaway in a scene of rapid and nervous action. *Omoo*, on the other hand, though keeping perhaps more closely to the events that really happened, fails to shape or select, and presents merely a chain of incidents of more or less relevance to the rather vague plan of the story. "Omoo" is the Tahitian word for "wanderer"; and the book bears out the title. As *Typee* never does, and as Melville through all his strange individual development was never to do again, it wanders.

This purposelessness may have its significance, seen against the statement of Melville's central obsessions so carefully (though perhaps unconsciously) laid down in *Typee*. *Omoo* is clearly a pot-boiler ventured upon in the hope that as a kind of sequel to the popular *Typee* it would repeat the success of its forerunner. But even a pot-boiler derives its vitality from some source in addition to the natural incentive to sell it in large numbers; and this particular pot-boiler, though failing to tap the deepest springs of Melville's imagination, shares its predecessor's attractive vigour and spirit as well as its immense readability. Therefore the purposelessness of the narrative is to be attributed, not to any failure of inspiration or communication but to the fact that the very physical activity which the book itself chronicles was of its own nature aimless and unprogressive. Technically *Typee* and *Omoo* are much of a piece: imaginatively *Omoo* is a retrogression, a relaxation, a record lacking the intimacy of passion.

Appropriately enough it follows that the chief impression that it leaves is one of degeneracy. Melville had idealised the Typees; even in his fear of them and his escape from them he made them symbolise a spiritual state which he was to hold for the rest of his life to be the most precious and creative of all. But in this second book the escape from the Typees results in an uneasy and shiftless frustration. The actual physical details of the narrative are quickly enough recited. The whaler which had carried Tommo from Typee had been commanded by a sick and incompetent captain and a drunken overbearing mate; the crew, enraged by the prolongation of their voyage, demanded to be put ashore at Tahiti, and on being refused permission to land broke out into mutiny. By force of circumstance the ship was docked; but the men were taken, by the orders of an unsympathetic consul, to a crude and nominal imprisonment inland. It was not long, as it happens, before they were released, and the ship sailed without them; while Melville (or was it Tommo?) with a single companion set off on a journey across the island, partly it seems in search of a change, and partly with the idea of gaining an ultimate freedom more enduring than the one that had delivered him from the Typees. The book ends with him once more taking ship—another stage in that long servitude to the sea which was to end a year or two later as abruptly as it had begun: to be renewed indeed most intensely in the imagination, but otherwise to lapse for ever. And as I have said, the predominating quality in the events and circumstances described in this narrative is degeneracy. Melville is back in the brutal nineteenth-century corruption of Western civilisation, from which he had fled to the Typees and back to which he had been somehow compelled to escape. The contrast between the gay and uninhibited natives and the sodden and incompetent crew is appalling; and it is by no means minimised by the fact that the only tolerable companion whom Melville can find among this unsavoury riff-raff is the dissolute ship's doctor whose irresponsible self-indulgence has ruined an attractive and valuable personality. Yet the contrast is more strongly pointed still: and this is the crux of the relation between *Typee* and *Omoo*: indeed it harbours the real reason for *Omoo's* importance. It is the contrast, not between native and white man, but between one kind of native and another.

Tahiti and Typee are not specifically contrasted in *Omoo*; but nobody who has read *Typee* can fail to do it for himself. The result is powerfully impressive. One of the objects of the book proposed by Melville in the preface was "to give a familiar account of the present condition of the converted Polynesians, as affected by their promiscuous intercourse with foreigners, and the teachings of the missionaries, combined". This he does by carefully amassing, both from his own observation and the journals of recent voyagers, a devastating series of impressions of the natives in their uneasy transitory stage between the primitive and the sophisticated. This is most effectively symbolised in the grotesqueness of their costume. "As for the men, those who aspire to European garments seem to have no perception of the relation subsisting between the various parts of a gentleman's costume. To the wearer of a coat, for instance, pantaloons are by no means indispensable; and a bell-crowned hat and a girdle are full dress." Melville adds the comment that "ridiculous as many of them now appear in foreign habiliments, the Tahitians presented a far different appearance in the original national costume," which is now prohibited by law (contrast Fayaway in the garb of Eden in *Typee*!) on the grounds of its association with some forgotten heathen observance. A similar interdict has been laid on large numbers of their national amusements, and dancing, wrestling, foot-racing, flute-playing, archery and other entertainments were all described by Melville as punishable offences, forbidden by missionary decree because of their heathen or immoral associations.

"Doubtless," he comments, "in thus denationalising the Tahitians, as it were, the missionaries were prompted by a

sincere desire for good; but the effect has been lamentable.
Supplied with no amusements in place of those forbidden, the
Tahitians, who require more recreation than other people, have
sunk into a listlessness, or indulge in sensualities, a hundred
times more pernicious than all the games ever celebrated in the
Temple of Tanee."

Striving to be fair, Melville sets out at chapter-length such
benefits as he believes the advent of the missionaries to have
conferred on the native: taboos and idolatries have many of them
been removed, schools and churches established, the Bible translated into Tahitian, friendly contact made with foreign travellers
and traders. This is admittedly good; but over against it has to be
set the restrictive nature of the Christianity taught them, which
leads inevitably to ignorance and hypocrisy: the innate idleness
of the natives which makes it impossible for them to practise with
industry any development in manufacture or cultivation which
civilisation may bring to their island; and the deplorable fact that
as a race they are physically unsuited for steady employment, and
the coming of Western methods would most certainly decimate
the remainder whom drunkenness, smallpox and virulent venereal
disease had not already removed.

"In view of these things," Melville concludes, "no one can
remain blind to the fact that so far as mere temporal felicity is
concerned, the Tahitians are far worse off now than formerly;
and although their circumstances, on the whole, are bettered by
the presence of the missionaries, the benefits conferred by the
latter become utterly insignificant when confronted with the
vast preponderance of evil brought about by other means. Their
prospects are hopeless."

And although in this summing-up he contradicts Darwin, who
had landed in Tahiti from the *Beagle* in 1835, and in a ten days'
stay found nothing in the islanders' morals to warrant the charges
that previous travellers had made, yet R. L. Stevenson forty years
later was to agree emphatically with Melville from an experience
that lasted even longer than his. And against this desolate picture
of the decline and fall of a naturally attractive people Melville
ironically sets the figure of a servant at the Tahitian Queen's Court,
one Marbonna, a Marquesan from the very same island upon which
Tommo had lain a captive of the Typees. "Large and muscular,"
Melville calls him, "well made as a statue, and with an arm like

a degenerate Tahitian's thigh . . . I found him a philosopher of nature—a wild heathen, moralising upon the vices and follies of the Christian court of Tahiti—a savage, scorning the degeneracy of the people among whom fortune had thrown him." The civilised man joined hands with the savage in condemnation of the race who had come to grief in the process of artificial civilisation. This man Marbonna marks another significant point in Melville's extended commentary upon his age. It was corrupt and evil, and even the savage recognised it to be so; moreover at the other end of the scale it would not do for the European or American to go native in search of the prim innocence of which his age had deprived him. Melville's comment on that is the incident of the *renegado* Lem Hardy, the deserter whom the whaler's crew met at Hannamanoo: who had signalised his final abrogation of any distinctive superiority which the civilised man may pretend to possess over the savage by allowing his face to be tattooed from ear to ear. "Far worse than Cain's," says Melville, polishing that eloquent Biblical imagery which he was to use so effectively in later life, "—the tattoo was a mark indelible, which all the waters of Abana and Pharpar, rivers of Damascus, could never wash out."

Melville turned his back on Polynesia in the end; but in the first stage of his adult development it had symbolised for him the extremes of good and evil in human life, its innocence and depravity, its beauty and its corruption. In Polynesia he found for the time his most helpful artistic symbol; that which he sought and shunned was there, man's final lore, as he was to say later of Shakespeare when the problems of existence had attained a complexity before which the black-and-white contrasts of *Typee* and *Omoo* shrunk to crude superficialities. Satisfactory as it was for his purpose at this early stage of his work, it is easy in the light of his later career to see how little use he would be able to make of it once his truly creative imagination had begun to work. Primarily the symbolism is static: it represents a state of grace (or later, degrees of failure to achieve it) through the image of a certain primitive state of nature. Since Melville's whole purpose became directed to the penetration of philosophic problems and the resolution of philo-sophic conflicts, he would have been mistaken had he dwelt any longer on the elemental data which he expressed once and for all in these two first volumes of his career. His symbols, to reflect the incessant flux of his conjectures, had necessarily to become dynamic, and it is interesting to see how the realisation of this necessity was to overtake him almost in the act of composition.

"Three weeks have scarcely passed," we remember him writing to Hawthorne, with special reference to the sudden birth of his imaginative awareness, "that I have not unfolded within myself." It is possible to corroborate this statement by exact reference to his next work, and to agree and approve its inevitability. As I have already sought to show, *Omoo* itself marks a significant variation on the theme of *Typee*; a variation that in itself requires a study of its successors before its importance is fully understood.

Therefore *Typee* and *Omoo* should not be underrated in the broad study of Melville's life and work. There is a danger that their realistic nature may relegate them to a class of production which the critic fascinated by the subsequent complexities may be tempted to ignore altogether. He would probably have a greater incentive to do so since their relative readability has attracted to them a popularity and a low-level acceptance which no other of his works, not even *Moby Dick* itself for all its wide prestige, has been able to do. Even now *Typee* seems to be the oftenest reprinted of Melville's books. It is a lucid and lively curiosity: a man's life among cannibals in a romantic and escapist setting: a travel and adventure story vividly enough told to give it the status of a minor classic. *Omoo* tags on behind it, its only less readable sequel; together they make a picture of ideal vagabondage irresistible by the modern city-dweller thirsty for action that he may never share except vicariously through books of travel-memoirs. Yet the reader who has understood, however dimly, the potentialities and actual achievement of the later Melville would be mistaken in assuming that, because these two early books are accepted and enjoyed at their face value by readers to whom the later Melville matters nothing, therefore they can be discounted in a valuation of Melville's whole career. It should be evident that Melville is here setting out—without necessarily knowing it, for much of creation is an unconscious and an involuntary process, and Melville if a great artist was far from being a sophisticated one—the bases, the preliminary positions, from which his maturer creative actions were to be deployed. As yet he was in the infancy of his art: but the clues which he lets drop in these two books are vital to the prosecution of the maturer principles that were to guide his later and far more important work.

CHAPTER IV

Mardi: the Transition

MELVILLE published *Typee* in 1846 and *Omoo* in 1847. The next five years were to be the most crowded and productive of his life. An astounding unfolding of his creative powers, demonstrated through *Mardi*, *Redburn* and *White-Jacket* (the first two of which appeared in 1849 and the third in 1850) culminated in 1851 in his masterpiece *Moby Dick* and was extended in the following year in the ambitious *Pierre*, the partial failure of which put a significant check on this remarkable productivity. From a purely artistic point of view these years produced the best results of his life. The recollection of those apparently aimless years of action underwent an imaginative transformation in a mind unusually gifted with the power of universalising personal experience, whether through realistic narrative, as in *Redburn* and *White-Jacket*, or in allegory, as in *Mardi*, or in a remarkable blend of the two, as in *Moby Dick*. There is an immediacy, a personal urgency, about the productions of these five years that is absent from his later work (is present, indeed, in *Billy Budd*, but even there in a much-modified form) and which is partly the cause of the systematic underrating by the majority of critics of anything Melville wrote after *Moby Dick*, and the mistaken classification of Melville as nothing but an unusually powerful writer of sea and travel stories. These books are undeniably of great importance; but they are not, even *Moby Dick* itself is not, the last word either of or about Melville. They mark a stage, and a vital one, in a complex and profound development. With Melville it is essential to keep in view the progressive continuity of his imaginative activity from 1844, his twenty-fifth year from which he "dated his life", until 1891, the year of the completion of *Billy Budd* and Melville's death. The climax of these remarkable five years of continuous creative excitement was *Moby Dick*: but it cannot be too often insisted that *Moby Dick* was not the climax of his life.

Just as *Typee* and *Omoo*, collectively, form Melville's statement of a human condition from which modern civilisation compels a deviation for better or worse, so the books which follow them reveal in bulk Melville's intricate chronicle of such movement. *Typee* and *Omoo* represent inertia; the books following represent, in one form or another, vitality, an exploration of the potentialities of life, experiment and experience. And that Melville at the outset of these five years was aware to some extent of the nature of his task is clear from the quality of the first book in which he broke away from the limited territory of literature in which he had made himself a name. In *Mardi* he showed for the first time a desire for spiritual adventure; and he accentuated this sudden expansion of his horizon by placing it in the setting with which he had so familiarised his readers that they had already "typed" him like a character-actor: the South Seas.

The author's own preface to *Mardi* is more interesting for what it omits than for what it reveals.

"Not long ago," he says, "having published two narratives of voyages in the Pacific, which in many quarters were received with incredulity, the thought occurred to me of indeed writing a romance of Polynesian adventure and publishing it as such; to see whether the fiction might not possibly be received for a verity; in some degree the reverse of my previous experience. This thought was the germ of others, which have resulted in *Mardi*."

Now this tells us precisely nothing. If we read this preface before the book, it will not be long before the book destroys our anticipation of a counterfeit of actual experience by skating off into obvious fantasy; and if we read it, as some readers do prefaces, after we have finished the story, the ostensible explanation will be so painfully inadequate as an illumination of the author's purpose or achievement that the only sentence in it to remain at all valuable is the last (referring to "other" unspecified thoughts), and that is too vague to be useful. Nevertheless it is corroboration for the internal evidence of the book itself; that *Mardi* developed out of commonplace conventional narrative into something of a different quality altogether, and did so under the writer's hand. The simple explanation in the preface is so naïve and irrelevant that we have to look behind its overt statement to discover any good reason why Melville thought it necessary to write it at all; and indeed there can be only one sufficient reason—which is that Melville himself was somewhat bewildered by the curious portent that had grown under his fingers and, feeling some explanation due, uttered the first apology that came into his head and made that do, concealing the real reason because at that stage he did not know what it was himself. Like Dickens' famous "I thought of Mr. Pickwick", it tantalises without illuminating; the mind switches uneasily and ironically forward from the hint dropped in the one evocative word "germ" to the almost equally tantalising prefaces of Henry James, whose elaborate lucidity is as suggestive and as baffling as Melville's evasive simplicity.

Whatever the process that transformed *Mardi* from just another *Omoo* into a remarkable and unique survey of the whole contemporary world, the book is a striking witness to Melville's rapacious reading and capacity for assimilating the beliefs and superstitions of the society of his day. The theme of *Mardi*—at least of the later and greater part of it, once the allegory is got under way—is more ambitious than anything Melville had ever tried before and had a far wider scope than anything he was to try again, *Moby Dick* and *Pierre* included. It amounts to an exhaustive search for the true philosophy; it is complicated by an infinite number of inner allegories; the confusion nowhere resolves itself into any very tangible lucidity. Yet in the course of the long narrative of nearly six hundred pages Melville contrives to pass under review all the contemporary prevailing philosophies and intellectual theories and all the various nations of the world, with comments, very often self-contradictory, on all of them in turn.

Mardi began as the story of a voyage: and so perhaps, but for the mysterious access of creative insight that, reinforced by no comparable technical advance, descended on Melville while he was

part way through it, it would have ended. It began as his other
books had begun—on board a whaler, a setting in which Melville
always seemed particularly at home; and the opening of *Mardi* is no
less realistically convincing than the opening of *Typee*. Nevertheless there is a difference in pitch; the prose of the narrative is
pitched higher, the cadence of the paragraphs reads more his-
trionically, than in the deliberately prosaic tone of the two books
of travel. Melville seems to remember the whole time that he is
specifically engaged upon a romance.

"We are off!" it begins. "The courses and topsails are set; the
coral-hung anchor swings from the bow: and together, the three
royals are given to the breeze, that follows us out to sea like the
baying of a hound. Out spreads the canvas—alow, aloft—
boom—stretched, on both sides, with many a stun' sail: till like
a hawk, with pinions poised, we shadow the sea with our sails,
and reelingly cleave the brine."

There is here a sedulous effort to force the pace, to charge every
scene with dramatic tension. If we set beside this opening paragraph
a short passage from the early part of *Omoo* describing an exactly
similar incident we can compare the relative virtues of the penny
plain of the old prose style and the twopence coloured of the new.

"Upon the boat's return, we made sail again, and stood off
from the land. There was a fine breeze; and notwithstanding my
bad night's rest, the cool, fresh air of a morning at sea was so
bracing, that as soon as I breathed it my spirits rose at once."

It is not for their relative quality that I quote these two passages.
It would perhaps be unfair to make the comparison *in vacuo*,
although there can hardly be any disagreement over the strained
note of the *Mardi* passage and the crisp economical effect of the
description from *Omoo*. What is more significant is the deliberate
enrichment of the texture; the copious use of metaphor and simile;
the conversion of the orthodox form into a mixture of the lyrical
and the dramatic. That this has affected the prose, as prose, for the
worse is probable, but not for the moment the whole of the truth;
the importance of the transformation is in its intentions, not in its
result. The deliberate dramatisation of the mood indicates that
Melville's prose is now to be used for a new purpose; a purpose

evidently not yet clearly comprehended by Melville himself. All
he was aware of at the beginning of *Mardi* was an unusual access of
excitement, unspecific and undirected, and this is all that the
opening succeeds in communicating. His "Polynesian romance"
differs so far from his other two Polynesian romances in this
intensified excitement alone. Moreover Melville displays, even in
such an evident effort to escape from the common courses of fiction,
what seems at first sight a surprising lack of originality in the
selection of incident; for just as *Typee* began with a secretly
contrived escape from a whaler, and *Omoo* in its later chapters was
concerned with the ultimate break-away of the hero and Doctor
Long Ghost first from the captivity of shipboard and later from the
more orthodox captivity of a land-prison, so *Mardi*, conventionally
opening with a lyrical presentation of a ship at sea, moves with a
sure inevitability to yet another secretly contrived escape, this
time by a stealthy push-off from the ship's side in the middle
watch.

This preoccupation with the symbolism of escape is clearly
stamped on all Melville's early work—and indeed, in a lesser form,
on important incidents in books of his later development (for
example, the whole manner and circumstance of Pierre's flight
from Saddle Meadows to the city is impregnated with this same
reminiscence). The recurrence of the symbol denotes a subconscious dissatisfaction. The actual form which the immediate
symbol took is closely connected with the young Melville's own
early history, and with his hurried departure at eighteen from the
ordinary security of a townsman's life to the adventure and
brutality of his first voyage, which he was to describe later in more
specific and realistic form in *Redburn*. There are not sufficient
facts available to speak with certainty: but there are hints that his
first voyage was the culmination of a runaway dash to sea. Whether
or not his flight was secret is not so important as the undoubted
fact that it was conceived in a hurry and conceived as a kind of
liberation—a liberation of both himself and the Melville family
from the intensified poverty and insecurity in which his father's
death some years before had left them. The disillusion was to come
later, but Melville could absorb that; he never seems to have
outgrown or outfaced the sense of restriction that his flight had
sought to break—and that restriction and the struggle for liberation
were worked in these later years, painfully and repetitively, into

the first dynamic symbolic act of his writing life: the symbolism of departure, of escape, of liberation.

Liberation is perhaps not the word; it suggests too spacious a quality for the world of experience. Melville's temperament and imagination did not find experience a liberating force. For one who had, partly by his youthful intuition and partly by an untutored but genuine intellectual argument from first principles, arrived at an idealistic conception of a primal state of innocence, a transmutation of that state could never ennoble the human spirit and had every chance of debasing it altogether. That is the central lesson, if any lesson there be at all, that can be understood from *Typee* and *Omoo*. Nevertheless there is an implication in those books, and an even stronger implication in *Mardi*, that experience must be faced. Ingrown innocence will only breed degeneracy. Therefore the escape lets in a kind of chaos; a chaos which it is the whole of human destiny to subdue. *Mardi* is Melville's immature realisation of his own duty as a creative writer to take part in that conflict. Imaginatively, though not artistically, he has increased immeasurably in stature since completing *Omoo*.

This realisation and this immaturity together help to account for the curious confusion of *Mardi*. The form of the book is crude and chaotic, an ambitious but inexpert attempt to achieve with inadequate resources the expression of new intellectual and philosophical comprehensions. It is not very often in the history of prose literature that an experiment of genius has floundered and stumbled so clumsily among half-realisations and imperfectly assimilated symbolisms. The narrative, apart from the heightened tone that has already been remarked, begins normally enough with the boat's escape from the whaler, its lonely voyage with the narrator and the impressive Skyeman Jarl, its chance encounter with the derelict *Parki* with its two Polynesians for crew. These two, the noble savage Samoa and his wayward wife Annatoo, are realised with a sympathetic and perceptive humour new to Melville's capacity as novelist; for Fayaway had been little more than a projection of his early romantic idealism, and his other major creation, Doctor Long Ghost, a character whom critics of Melville have praised very highly, seems on closer reading to be merely a static portrait of eccentricity, built up observantly, it is true, but lacking the informing vitality that distinguishes a character who can make a narrative stir with the quality of his individuality.

Samoa and Annatoo, being primitives, are cruder than the depraved Westerner Long Ghost but are originally more alive than he; their courage and resource, their domestic quarrels and subterfuges, are sketched in with the liveliness of pure humorous realism in which for a time the novelist's sedulous purpose is forgotten and the prose becomes temperate and relaxed again. In fact the whole sequence of descriptive passages connecting the first escape from the whaler with the final sinking of the *Parki* and the violent death of Annatoo is in Melville's most vigorous manner, where his prose is cleared for action and he leaves himself no time to be encumbered with the metaphysical conceits which he was always to find irresistibly seductive. Up to this point the narrative is nervous and rigid, a well-controlled tension giving a poise and direction which *Omoo* had certainly lacked.

Yet at this very point an important change comes over the book. It is possible almost to isolate the passage in which the transition occurs. As for the transition itself it is the central paradox of Melville's life; for here on this almost identifiable page he spoiled his book and realised himself as an artist. Here for the first time his aspiration seemed consciously to reach beyond the limits that his earlier works had set and that his admirers seemed content that he should keep; for the first time his flat realistic picture of the South Seas was to be expanded into the dimensions of a larger vision. This purpose his intuition apprehended clearly enough; that he did not match this profounder vision with a corresponding advance in technique was the ruin of *Mardi*; but the ruin of *Mardi* matters very little beside the compensating intensity accruing to the creative art of Melville.

Briefly, he side-steps into fantasy. Of the nature of this fantasy it will be necessary to say much more later, since Melville's use of myth, allegory and symbol is fundamental to his work and the relative importance of his later novels tends to vary with his different use of these three elements. At the time when the early realism of *Mardi* merged unexpectedly into allegory Melville's touch was so uncertain and his handling of his unfamiliar medium was often so clumsy as to obscure his purpose altogether. What must be remembered at the *Mardi* stage is that none of his later and greater work could have come to its satisfying stature had it not been for the tentative beginnings scattered through *Mardi* like ruins. For the last five hundred pages of *Mardi*, scrappy and absurd though they may seem in the light of the realism preceding them, contain Melville's statement of experience, just as *Typee* and *Omoo* together had contained his statement of innocence. Taji's allegorical voyage is chaotic (though there are remarkable constants among the chaos), because Melville's mature experience was chaotic and he had not yet the imaginative power to resolve chaos into order; nevertheless, it is his first published record of the impact of experience upon innocence. It has been argued, particularly by M. Pierre Frédérix in his recent biography, that it reflects the sudden expansions of Melville's awareness of contemporary thought as a result of his introduction to the New York literary salons; and more directly, the impact upon him of the Mexican War of 1847 with all its implications. This theory is a very likely one.

The transition comes at the point where the shipwrecked voyagers encounter the strange canoe with its high priest and attendants and its romantic captive maiden Yillah. This unreal and shadowy creature, who lacks reality in spite of all Melville's passionate attempt to create in her the power and mystery that the central figure of his invented myth had to convey if it were to retain its magic throughout the long-drawn tale, is introduced with elaboration; as the first of Melville's symbolic (as distinct from realistic) creations, she must be regarded as a concentration of his idealisms, and the meaning of the story must centre in her. She is not of the savage stock, being fair-skinned and, at least remotely, of Taji's own people; she is alone among wild and uncertain folk, and at the moment of meeting with Taji is in fact, though this does not appear until later, bound for sacrifice at the hands of the high priest who has her in his charge. In the spontaneous rescue carried out by the three travellers the high priest is slain and Yillah saved from his attendants; and in this abrupt act of violence the whole dramatic and philosophical direction of the novel finds a common origin.

Melville's world has broadened now to include passion; of an undefined vagueness still, but nevertheless dynamic. The flat adventurousness of *Typee* had produced nothing but Fayaway to approximate to the realisation of this first assault upon innocence; and she is nothing more than a decorative concession to the presence in nature of the female form. Yillah is conceived with less charm and realism than Fayaway; but she generates tension in the story, even though its quality is derivative and inorganic.

Melville is mature enough, even in this imperfect attempt, to suggest in all Yillah's actions and behaviour and fate more than a hint of tragedy. The death of the priest at Taji's hand coincides with her rescue; that is a good tragic beginning. If the death of the Typee warrior during Tommo's escape from the cannibals was a historical rather than an imaginative fact, it may not be too extreme a conjecture to trace in the repetitions of the symbolism here an outcrop of suppressed guilt determining Melville's tragic development. The elaborate Yillah-myth, trailed wearisomely through an endless variety of allegorical scenes, leads off with this admirable contradiction of opposites—the good and the evil uniting at its birth. Without the good there would be no idealism and beauty for Yillah to personify; without the evil there would be no sense of doom attending the pursuit of that idealism and that beauty.

For after a brief idyllic companionship on the isle of Odo, Taji loses Yillah, spirited mysteriously from him by an elusive Queen Hautia who, continually throughout the tale, claims and reclaims a strange allegiance from Taji through the medium of three damsels bringing flowers. The story resolves itself (ostensibly) into an endless pursuit of the lost Yillah with an equally steadfast reiteration of his refusal to accept the dominion of Hautia, whose silent heralds weave in and out of the incidents of the journey like ritual dancers, scattering symbolic blossoms as they sue for allegiance and are refused it. Thus the pursuit is complex at the start; the pursuer, in the quest for his ideal, is himself constantly at the call of a second fateful follower. But this is not yet all the story; Hautia's heralds are mysterious and ominous enough, the spiritual dominion they seek being clearly a maleficent one, but their visits are alternated throughout the long voyage through Mardi by either the rumour or the actuality of the three fierce sons of the murdered high priest bent on avenging on Taji the death he had dealt their father. To the pursuers seeking to enslave the mind are added the pursuers out to destroy the body; in embryo a fine dramatic theme, with the central heroic figure bound the while on his own enthralled quest of the beauty he had once achieved but which now seemed lost to him for ever.

This theme is admirably stated, and it runs through the tenuous texture of the remainder of the book like a tough recognisable thread on which the rest of the woven pattern depends. It forms the constant of which I spoke earlier, that redeems the second part of *Mardi* from chaos; it would have gained by a more studied isolation from its confusing context. For with the departure of Taji and his companions on their long search for the lost Yillah, Melville's speculative ardour breaks all reasonable bounds and he ambitiously tries to crowd into his novel not only this subtle and dramatic theme of the pursuer doubly pursued but also a far vaster and less immediately relevant consideration of the whole scope of contemporary thought, philosophical and political. The great glittering chain of islands forming the imaginary archipelago that Melville calls Mardi, through which Taji and his friends go journeying, is the symbol under which he loosely unites his considered impressions of the world as he awoke to it, and makes a statement, coherent if confused, of the problems of modern life which he considered most vital. Again it is significant that early in the transition stage the story sheds virtually all the flesh-and-blood characters in whom realism had been preserved during the first hundred pages. Annatoo had been lost at sea even before the canoe bearing Yillah had been sighted; while the search for Yillah is hardly begun in earnest before first Samoa and then the Hebridean Jarl meet summary ends. It is true that they are killed by Taji's revengeful pursuers; but any sense of appropriateness in their deaths is offset by the almost laconic abruptness with which Melville sweeps them from the scene to clear away realism and make all fit for the high symbolism he seems to have felt it his duty to pursue. Their departure removes yet more of that vital verisimilitude without which Melville's high flights of fantasy were always dangerously uncertain.

It is enough to have indicated the unwieldiness of Melville's handling of his theme, or rather his confusing set of themes. The confusion is to be deplored; but the sudden expansion of technique which caused it, and made such a pastiche of *Mardi*, reflects a far more important expansion in Melville's creative consciousness. Before we examine the later part of *Mardi* in detail it would be wise to consider that expansion of consciousness as a vital stage in Melville's development unhappily obscured by the deficiencies of a craft not yet flexible or powerful enough to express it. *Mardi* is in essence the bold attempt of an untrained but voracious reader and thinker, coming late to the feast after a long period of exhausting travel and action, to marshal the bewildering impressions of his new maturity into a shape that would serve to contradict an over-whelming sense of chaos. It was the answer of an untried innocence in the face of hostile experience, and it was the answer of an artist—in Blake's words, to make a Heaven in Hell's despite; to defy chaos by creating an instinctive work of beauty to deny it. Like Blake, Melville had too little hold on tradition to find any comfort there. He had only his own irresponsible imagination out of which to build his defiance. Blake's *Prophetic Books* and Melville's *Mardi* share a common heroism and a common failure.

CHAPTER V

Mardi: the Power of the Symbol

B
UT IN his search for simplification he laid conscious hold
for the first time on a symbol; and to symbolism, conscious
or unconscious, he was to turn again and again in later life
with much profit. The germ of Melville's symbolism is in the confusion of *Mardi*. It remains the most valuable discovery of his life:
though it was not until some time later that he was to understand
how it could best be used. In *Mardi* he found it almost by accident,
and used it blindly. With a wisdom that must have been partly
instinctive he chose for his central symbol one most familiar to
him in actual experience, which he could charge at will with every
kind of emotional or conjectural allusiveness—the symbol of a
voyage. He had used travel and adventure in one form or another in
Typee and *Omoo*, but merely as realistic background for his main
statement of mood and incident. In *Mardi* he set out similarly;
but at a crucial point in the narrative the real voyage shaded off into
a symbolic one; the individual adventurers became representative
of mankind; the islands they sailed among became the whole world.

The symbolism of a voyage or journey satisfied Melville very
well; he was to use it again many times—in *Redburn* and *White-
Jacket* (more realistically it is true, but after *Mardi* all realism with
Melville must be suspected of a secret symbolism), in *Moby Dick*
and *Israel Potter*, in *The Confidence-Man*, where the voyage is not

at sea but down a river, and in the long poem *Clarel*, where the journey is entirely by land. It is not a complex symbol but it admits of unlimited possibilities, and Melville found it so adaptable that only one of his major novels (*Pierre*) lacks this symbolism altogether, and though admittedly it is not prominent in *Billy Budd* the idea of a voyage is at least subconsciously present to the mind during the action of that story.

To transpose a given object from the realistic to the symbolic plane is, if done with effect and significance, the act of a poetic artist. By effect I mean the creation of a deeper understanding both of the object itself and the abstraction which it is intended to represent; by significance I mean the illuminating relation of both to the rational idea which engendered the image; that idea being conceivably anything from a simple piece of reasoning to an ordered philosophy of life. Such a use of symbol is essential to the finest art; for it is the function of art to abstract from general observation a particular image or symbol which the artist represents in a new relation to universal principles. Melville's first major act of symbolism represents therefore a new awareness of his capacity, and even of his duty, that he had not attained at the time of *Typee* and *Omoo*. The "epic-tragedy" of *Mardi* is centred chiefly round the rescue of Yillah and the death of her guardian priest. It is followed by the loss of Yillah and the long search for her by Taji, who is plagued simultaneously by the pursuits of Hautia's heralds and the three avengers. The fact that this sequence began more than a hundred pages after the start of *Mardi* and can be detached altogether from the realistic preamble, supports the suggestion that Melville grew to this new poetic stature after *Mardi* was well in hand; and accounts, at least in part, for the curious transition that cuts the work in two and has put many of Melville's critics at pains to explain it, and at least one to confess that he could not.

The power of the symbol was at first unrealised by Melville; or at least if he realised it he did not control it very effectively. He split it for his present purpose into two; and two sides of his creative imagination impelled him in two directions at once, one to the prosecution of the Yillah-myth, the other to the elaboration of the Mardi-satire. The first engaged his profounder passions, the second his critical and speculative faculties. At no point in the book do these impulses appear to co-ordinate; and this failure to unite is the ruin of a promising experiment. He was divided, in fact, between symbolism and allegory.

In allegory the material and spiritual worlds are presented, implicitly or explicitly, in a set and ordered alignment. The action on the material plane is tidily and deliberately representative of the action on the spiritual plane, which the writer has apprehended first and translated into concrete symbols for the benefit of readers whose imagination is less ready to accept abstract reasoning. Bunyan in the *Pilgrim's Progress*, Jesus in the parables, Aesop and Tolstoy in their fables, have realised the large truths first and have distilled them with great skill and beauty into stories whose detail is as attractive as their implications are plain. In the author's mind there is no doubt about these truths and there is no ambiguity about the symbols representing them, for they are expressive of the certainties grasped by the author's own peculiar vision. It follows that allegory is the product either of a great spiritual clarity or (which is commoner) of an ingrained or accustomed certainty. It is seldom the immediate result of a conflict or of a spiritual bewilderment; its use is to provide illumination and not to express, however sympathetically, the discord which is so frequently active at the root of creative inspiration. For this reason great allegory can only be the work of men deeply convinced of the rightness and stability of their own ideals, with a firm hold upon the ultimates.

The symbolism to which Melville's visionary dissatisfaction drove him was the converse of this. Where the great allegorists worked backwards from settled abstract principles, and made flesh and blood of spiritual and divine attributes, Melville worked forward into unknown territories of speculation from the bases of real and solid fact which he knew as the chief and abiding experiences of his life. From eighteen to twenty-five he had made travel by sea and land the main fact of his existence; therefore when he came to adult stature as a writer the symbol he instinctively chose was the symbol of the voyage. Living among ships as he had for seven years, he knew and experienced every detail of life on board with unusual intensity; flesh and blood of sailors, harpoon-line and whale's blubber, sperm oil and ships' nails, existed in his imagination as living and palpable images instinct with a larger suggestiveness. Seeing these concrete symbols first, Melville reversed the sublime certainties of the allegorists, and relied on the resources of his imagination to force him through to a dimly-perceived understanding of their larger significance. In this way he found himself, before he was half-way through *Mardi*, engaged upon an attempt to deduce intuitively the spiritual truths from which the allegorists began. The allegorist expresses his certainty of the greater truth by imaging the less; the symbolist uses his familiarity with the less to guide him to experience the greater. Heaven inspired Bunyan to imagine trumpets; a wild flower inspired Blake to imagine Heaven. And it is one of my purposes in this study to show that Melville's imagination was of the same order as Blake's.

At the beginning of his development, he was naturally unaware of the implications of this newly-discovered quality in his creative processes. Indeed this particular quality is as often involuntary, unguessed at by its author, as it is realised and fostered. Blake himself, Emily Brontë, Dickens, Dostoevsky, are examples of writers of incalculable creative power whose complex resources are often revealed through crudities and simplicities that indicate very clearly the instinctive nature of their use of the symbol; yet no one can deny the power and range of those unsuspected instincts and involuntary experiments. Melville is of their kind; his half-awareness, part way through his first considerable work, *Mardi*, of a broad purpose to which he felt himself compelled, is testimony to the passive nature of his imagination. "Oh, reader, list!" he cries towards the end of the story, which has clearly bewildered him by its variety and scope nearly as much as it has since bewildered all his readers—"I've chartless voyaged. So if after all these fearful, fainting trances, the verdict be, the golden haven was not gained; yet, in bold quest thereof, better to seek in boundless deeps, than float on vulgar shoals; and give me, ye gods, an utter wreck, if wreck I do."

Mardi is the product of this bewilderment. His new awareness compelled him to voyage; his spiritual uncertainty deprived him of any chart but his own imagination. Part of his creativeness lent him a right instinct; part of it allowed his speculative intelligence to lead his artistic sense astray. The first, and right, impulse impelled him to the symbolisms of the voyage and the dramatic three-fold pursuit; the second, and faulty, impulse betrayed him into the complex and shapeless allegory-satire of the journey through the islands of Mardi. This duality of purpose, together

with his immaturity of technique, imposed a paradox on the
result; which is that while the conception of the pursuit is moving
and impressive, the details of its realisation are too often otiose,
tawdrily romantic and repetitive: and conversely, most of the
memorable and significant passages in the tale are part of the
variegated satire under cover of which Melville runs the whole
range of contemporary thought and superstition. The two halves
of the book are badly stitched together; yet it cannot be questioned,
after studying the book itself and its relation to the work that was
to follow it, that the imaginative power in the book is concentrated
in the personal epic-tragedy of the pursuit and that the rest, for
all its incidental value, is merely an intellectual embellishment.

Significantly, the book merges from straight realism into the
realms of allegory and symbolism through a lyrical prose passage
of arresting beauty. At this stage in his development Melville's
hold on his eloquence was uncertain; like a Welsh preacher in his
hwyl, he was released at times of exaltation from the necessary
restraints of prose art. Yet there is a palpable increase of tension
as the key point of *Mardi* is approached; it is as if he paused
expectantly in the knowledge that the transition was at hand. And
the passage through which the dream-world of the symbolic
imagination is approached for the first time in Melville is the
description of the phosphorescence of the sea at night, troubled
and appalled by the fiery spoutings of the great shoal of whales.
Unerringly Melville has found his symbol. His world for nearly
all of his life was to be the world of the sea; therefore he chooses
to signalise his new intensity of mood by a new experience of a sea-
change of great rarity and beauty; and with the unearthly brilliance
of the revelation, he unites the figure, only half-perceived as yet
and wholly unrealised as a significant image, of the greatest of all
sea-monsters. In this beautiful chapter ("The Sea on Fire") he
tries over and lets drop the themes of his greatest work. His
instincts are true; he has handled the material and put it for the
moment aside, but it remains unforgotten in his imagination.

That is the first significant landmark that must be noted in
Mardi; and a hundred pages on, when the journey through the
islands has begun, there is another that rises out of the narrative
with an arresting air of soliloquy. From time to time the flow of the
story is broken for the author's own comments and instructions;
and the chapter called "Faith and Knowledge" enunciates in

deliberate paradox the power of the human imagination to comprehend the universal truths. And the power of the intuitive imagination that understands all, he calls faith: which he believes to be the only knowledge. All other knowledge is equivalent, he infers, to credulity.

"The greatest marvels are first truths; and first truths the last unto which we attain. Things nearest are furthest off."

This is acceptable enough; things nearest, material things, are furthest off the substance of one's intuitive perceptions. He goes on:

"Man has a more comprehensive view of the moon, than the man in the moon himself. We know the moon is round; he only infers it. It is because we ourselves are in ourselves, that we know ourselves not. And it is only of our easy faith, that we are not infidels throughout; and only of our lack of faith, that we believe what we do."

This is not a simple passage: at one moment he seems to be using "faith" as synonymous with credulity, and at another as antipathetic to it. Yet he must mean that materialist conceptions result from a failure to understand with the eye of faith; that faith, as he advocates it, contradicts human knowledge as it is generally accepted. "In some universe-old truths," he goes on, "all mankind are disbelievers. Do you believe that you lived three thousand years ago? That you were at the taking of Tyre, were overwhelmed in Gomorrah? No." The cold material eye of common knowledge denies him. All mankind stand by the obvious facts, all but he:

"But for me, I was at the subsiding of the Deluge, and helped swab the ground, and build the first house. With the Israelites, I fainted in the wilderness; was in court, when Solomon outdid all the judges before him. . . . I, it was, who originated the conspiracy against that purple murderer, Domitian; I, who in the senate moved that great and good Aurelian be emperor. I instigated the abdication of Diocletian and Charles the Fifth; I touched Isabella's heart, that she hearkened to Columbus. I am he, that from the king's minions hid the Charter in the old oak at Hartford: I harboured Goffe and Whalley; I am the leader of the Mohawk masks, who in the Old Commonwealth's harbor, overboard threw the East India Company's Souchong; I am the Vailed Persian Prophet: I, the man in the iron mask: I, Junius."

He proclaims against all possibility his complete identity, by faith, with the whole of mankind. Only by faith, by creative understanding, by (as he will find out much later) love, can that impossible identification be made complete: and he proclaims his passionate identity here with the great names and great events primarily associated with progress, with justice and benevolence, with the replanning of civilisation and the abdication of tyrants, with the foundation of liberty and the concerted attack on monopoly and injustice. At the end of his incantation of honour come his strong sense of nationality, his family pride (for his grandfather, we remember, was at the Boston Tea Party), his love of mystery and ambiguity, his love of independence; all of great importance in his character and his work, but rightly subordinate here to this major pronouncement, so characteristically ambiguous, of the poetic creed by which from that moment on he meant to live. And this proclamation of the power of faith, of intuitive comprehension of all that is valuable in the quality and history of mankind, is only an oblique proclamation of the power of the symbol which was to rule him and which he was to rule. For to express true poetic insight it is necessary to speak in the language, not of cold material common sense, but of faith; and for the artist the language of faith is the symbol.

In the light of this somewhat oracular introduction, Melville voyaged out in the guise of Taji, seeking truth. On the plane of symbol he sought it personified as Yillah; on the plane of allegory he sought it in the philosophical, religious and political systems of the islands of Mardi. In the curious chapter on "Dreams"—a comparison in kind to the interlude on "Faith and Knowledge", but less obscure because his strain in it is not after paradox but after lyric intensity—he lists what is in effect a catalogue of the spiritual resources upon which he can draw. Embedded in an exalted incantation in which sea-images and music-images predominate, Melville pours out the names of the poets and philosophers whose energies are united in him—twenty and more, from Homer to Waller, united indistinguishably with the Mississippi and the great American rivers in his turbulent imagination as authors of his eloquence. Professor Matthiessen has described this chapter as a parable, not merely of the birth of his inner life, but of the way in which this fresh consciousness demanded new ranges of language for its expression. This is true: and I would place even more insistence on the "demand" to which Melville's mental and physical resources were subjected at this important moment of his life. I have already quoted his record of his sense of helplessness ("I've chartless voyaged"). The concluding passage of this chapter on "Dreams" adds a graphic note on the compulsion of his inspiration.

"My cheek blanches white while I write: I start at the scratch of my pen; my own mad brood of eagles devours me; fain would I unsay this audacity; but an iron-mailed hand clenches mine in a vice, and prints down every letter in my spite. Fain would I hurl off this Dionysius that rides me, my thoughts crush me down till I groan; in far fields I hear the song of the reaper, while I slave and faint in this cell. The fever runs through me like lava; my hot brain burns like a coal: and like many a monarch, I am less to be envied, than the veriest hind in the land."

It was under the oppressive sense of this creative urgency that Melville, as Taji, went into Mardi: dazed with speculations, eager with desire to image them in a form which would illuminate them both for his readers and himself, and bolstered with the inherited eloquence of a score of poets and philosophers, whose wisdom was of better value to him than the clutter of their unassimilated styles.

Taji voyages through Mardi with four companions: Media the autocratic native king, Mohi or Braid-Beard his ancient counsellor, the philosopher Babbalanja and the poet Yoomy. Melville passes each topic, each island-country in turn, through the test of these four temperaments. Taji himself reserves his energies mainly as chronicler of fact and incident, concentrating his emotions upon the symbolic chase and pursuit which is the other half of the story. He is Melville's imagination, keen and minutely observant yet hag-ridden by inexplicable hungers; his four companions personify broadly four of his chief intellectual or imaginative characteristics. Mohi is a sketch of antique conservatism, Yoomy an even rougher sketch of the most conventional and ineffective kind of poet. Babbalanja is by far the most important of these characters; Melville's acute intelligence, his broad and sensitive humanism, are revealed in this figure as in no other of his full-length characters in all his literary career, and in his soliloquies and in his search for an ideal philosophy are embodied Melville's own close-knit speculations and his own earnest pursuit, through the intellect, of the same truth that Taji was following, through the instincts, in the symbolic form of Yillah. King Media acts up to his name; flavoured with cynicism and a touch of the epicurean, he 'mediates' between the extremes represented by the other three, tempering the transports of Yoomy with raillery and the philosophic flights of Babbalanja with an irony which is sometimes salutary. Media is worldly wisdom, benevolent unless crossed, autocratic and ruthless in the face of opposition. Five-in-one and one-in-five, this compact little expedition sees unrolled before it the panorama of contemporary life.

The satire is easy, varying little from what, knowing Melville, we should already have learnt to expect; thorough and outspoken in places, though never so savage as Swift nor so bitterly devastating. Readers of *Typee* and *Omoo* will be prepared for the full-scale onslaught on Roman Catholicism, with the blind priest Pani in the island of Maramma taking contribution from the pilgrims and rejecting all those who will not follow him on his own terms, and the mysterious Pontiff whose inmost secret holds nothing for the seeker, a riddle without any answer. Pausing, on the way from this disillusion, to deal a friendly whack at antiquarianism, Melville proceeds to trounce the fetish of social order and convention in his account of the island of Pimminee whose inhabitants sacrifice all for meaningless ornament and ceremony. Perhaps the most lively and interesting of the chapters at this intermediate and somewhat static stage of the voyage round the known world are those in which contemporary nations are recognisably held up to criticism in passages of real humour and insight. In the realm of King Bello, Lord of Dominora, whose rapacity extends to a desire to possess the whole world of Mardi, are reflected the impressions of an American, with experience of the early nineteenth century and with roots in the late eighteenth century, of the Imperialist expansion of a commercially covetous Great Britain, intriguing with and against her turbulent neighbour Porpheero (which is Europe) for the exploitation of the young and proud republican state of Vivenza. This latter nation, being part of the greater island of Kolumbo (the continent of America) represented in Melville's eyes "a fresh start in the Mardian species, requiring a new world for their development".

"Like a young tropic tree she stood, laden down with greenness, myriad blossoms, and the ripened fruit thick-hanging from one bough. She was promising as the morning."

And again

> "Childlike, standing among the old robed kings and emperors
> of the Archipelago, Vivenza seemed a young Messiah, to whose
> discourse the bearded Rabbis bowed."

Yet with all his native and natural pride, Melville imputes in the
very next paragraph the main source of Vivenza's greatness and
potentiality to its origin in Dominora. "What isle but Dominora
could have supplied thee with that stiff spine of thine? That heart
of boldest leaf?" It seems that for all his admiration for the sturdi-
ness of racial and national individualities, Melville even thus early
mistrusted fundamentally the tendency to pride and braggadocio
engendered in too enthusiastic nationalism. Perhaps significantly,
Taji seeks Yillah first in Dominora, Melville possibly regarding King
Bello's outbursts of chauvinism as rooted in a tougher and finer
stock than those of the Vivenzans could by then be expected to be:
and there are moving accounts of the revolutionary idealisms of the
exploited Dominorans, oppressed by their rulers and ultimately
betrayed by their leaders. This passage was written in the year of
the abortive Chartist rising, and is eloquent with the liberality and
sympathy of an enlightened seeker after social stability; and in the
light of this chapter it is interesting to turn to the later chapters in
which Vivenza itself is visited, again with the same critical and
discriminating eye and again with the same distrust of the dangerous
emotions implicit in patriotism.

For Melville's humanism was sceptical of democracy, as Shakespeare's had been. (Indeed this is the first sign in Melville's work of
an influence which was soon to possess him more profoundly than
any other, and to make Melville one of the most Shakespeare-
intoxicated creative writers in literature.) His pity for mankind
was instinctive and he spoke it at every opportunity; but it never
led him so to idealise the capacity of the ordinary man to order his
own government as to rely on the democratic principle that was the
watchword and the catch-cry of every prominent Western social
philosopher since the Declaration of Independence. His scepticism
came out strongly in his chapters on Vivenza, in which national
enthusiasms are finely tempered with a dash of warning good sense
and a dark glance at the negro slaves. The anonymous proclamation
which challenges the youthful idealisms of Vivenza is full of pregnant
and provocative declarations: "Civilisation has not ever been the

brother of equality"—"It is not the prime end and chief blessing to be politically free. And freedom is only good as a means: is no end in itself." "That all men should govern themselves as nations, means that all men be better, and wiser than the wisest of one-man rulers." And again he points to the more modest, less trumpeted, yet as genuine liberty enjoyed in the despised monarchical Dominora. And in the far south of Vivenza the travellers shake their heads gloomily over the slaves. "This is freedom, when heaven's own voice is throttled: and were these serfs to rise and fight for it; like dogs they would be hunted down by her pretended sons." And, grimly—writing in 1848—Melville comments "These South savannahs may yet prove battlefields."

The chapters on Vivenza should not perhaps be built too pretentiously into a foundation for a full statement of Melville's political creed. If he ever had one, it should only interest us so far as it illuminated or inspired his imagination; and we shall extract far more value from his later-expressed views and visions of the destiny of individual men than from set topical essays, however attractively presented, on set national themes. What is valuable in these roving sketches, for they are not much weightier than that, is their indication of Melville's vigorous independence, his refusal to join in the popular catch-cries. Like *Typee* and *Omoo* before it, *Mardi* in these passages is still little more than a tentative statement of a case, a deployment of the resources of a remarkable mind with which he proposes to attempt more important ventures when he has his premises clear. The admirable chapters on Vivenza link with later work of his in a manner which we can examine more advantageously later. Meanwhile, they register his awareness, which with Melville harbours both a promise and a warning.

Yillah is not in Vivenza; and the travellers are driven on, by the power of Melville's as yet half-recognised symbolism, to further search. As the book nears its end the satiric, allegorical intermission is overtaken once more by the recurring hints of tragedy; the regular cries of Taji upon his lost Yillah, which had punctuated, not very effectively, even the episodes of detailed political satire, merge again into the haunting ritual that had almost been lost sight of—the pursuit by the three inexorable avengers, accompanied inevitably by the silent heralds of Hautia. Melville, even in the excitement of philosophical and political argument, has remembered that the vitality at the heart of *Mardi* is essentially tragic.

Apart from the reintroduction of the symbolic episodes of pursuit, the deepening of the narrative is closest reflected in the mounting eloquence and tormented preoccupations of the sage Babbalanja. "I am intent," he had said earlier, "upon the essence of things, the mystery that lieth beyond . . . that which is beneath the seeming." His vision of the ambiguous perplexities, concealed behind other men's absolute convictions is intensified by his "possession" by the prophetic demon Azzageddi, who utters through his mouth fierce and provocative protests against accepted standards. He becomes, philosophically, a sceptic and a rebel, where prior to experience he had been content with an urbane acceptance. "I but fight against the armed and crested lies of Mardi, that like a host assail me. I am stuck full of darts; but tearing them from out me, gasping, I discharge them from whence they came." Compact with Melville's richly increasing store of speculation on every kind of intellectual and imaginative topic, Babbalanja is at the same time harried by all Melville's insistent agonies of doubt Taji's emotional tragedy is paralleled in him by the intellectual one, and if there is any co-ordination at all between the two uneasy blocks into which *Mardi* is split, it is in this rough parallelism of the two kinds of innocence submitted and submitting to the two kinds of experience.

Nevertheless the ways of Babbalanja and Taji divide before the end. The travellers reach the island of Serenia, where the ideals of the essential truths of Christianity are realised in a chapter of moving and unsentimental intensity. Babbalanja, whose increasing powers of perception and penetrating scepticism were rendering him progressively less reconcilable with their successive hosts, and whose vision of truth was making him an outlaw in Mardi, is captivated by the precepts of Alma (Jesus) and finds in complete acceptance the delicious resolution of his doubts. "In thee at last I find repose. Gone, gone are all distracting doubts. Love and Alma now prevail. Reason no longer domineers; but still doth speak." And with him the whole boatload of distracted travellers, with Taji himself a significant exception, kneel and renounce "all that wars with Alma's precepts". Yoomy the minstrel finds in Alma the answer to his quest for beauty; Mohi the old courtier a rest and reward in his old age: the pagan and demi-god King Media a new humility and a less barbarous principle of government. Babbalanja refuses to continue the voyage; knowing in the clarity of his new vision that Taji's search is illusory, that Media will face greater trouble in his own land when he returns to it, as it were Christianised, than ever he faced before, he dismisses his friends with a blessing. In Alma he had found himself completely; reason and faith are reconciled. The triumphs of Alma, the almost magical resolution of Christianity, remove tragedy from Babbalanja.

And here Melville parts company with him. Melville, intellectually, may have been Babbalanja; but emotionally, imaginatively, he knew himself to be Taji. On the first appearance of *Mardi* this might not have been so clearly evident; but in the light of Melville's later work there is no doubt that he had not yet reached Serenia in his own mind. Tenderly he left Babbalanja, an attractive figure in his independence and humanity, to the comfort of a religion that he himself could only postulate intellectually, though into his conjecture he infused a warmth born possibly of his longing for an identification with it that as yet his instincts denied him. It is significant that his picture of Serenia is flatly allegorical—a reflection of a set of principles conceived outside the author's own creative imagination. At this stage of his life it is the compulsion of the symbol that points Melville's direction. His intellect, and perhaps all his inclination, urged him towards the haven of Serenia; his imagination denied him that comfort.

For his imagination was a surer guide than his intellect or his inclination. The escape to Serenia would have obliterated tragedy; but Melville's awakening vision, springing to self-realisation only after *Mardi* itself had got well under way, recognised a deeper and more prolonged tragic conflict implicit in the contact of innocence with experience than could at this early stage be realised by the Christian solution. Melville's instinct could not renounce tragedy. To renounce tragedy would have been to renounce art, for art of a tragic temper which nevertheless ignores tragedy is worthless unless it has been great enough to overcome tragedy in the imagination. There will be time enough later in Melville's life to consider whether he ever succeeded in doing this: in *Mardi*, at twenty-nine, he had barely fledged himself, and his supreme tragic creation was still two years away in the future.

Mardi is not a serene book; it would not have been appropriate to have ended it in Serenia, though to indicate that Serenia existed was surely right. But since Melville never faces tragedy in *Mardi*, but only suffers from its implacable pursuit at his back, his hero

Taji does right to contract out of the tempting refuge. He turns from it to the terrible realities that demand immediate action; Hautia's insistent heralds, Hautia's island and Bower of Bliss, on the one hand; the spectral avengers, on the other; ahead the visionary gleam of the departed presence of Yillah. Renouncing Serenia, he has renounced everything but his passion; the complex passion, it must be remembered, for a Yillah who represents qualities of spiritual as well as fleshly perfection. The quest is not entirely sensual.

In fact the quality of spirituality in his passion preserves him from the squalid fate of those who had blindly followed Hautia and met destruction. This Siren-Circe-Lorelei figure charms him seductively to her island at last, with veiled promises of Yillah at hand, so near and yet so far. Here, it is clear, the myth differentiates strongly between the two, whether Yillah may be taken to represent the spirit and Hautia the flesh alone, or whether, as Professor Matthiessen has suggested, the implications are not confined only to the moral question, but Hautia is experience to Yillah's innocence. This fits with Melville's broad preoccupation and his battle with the evil implications of experience, now closely engaged. Whichever be the solution, and it will not do to regard them as alternative or mutually exclusive, Taji's singleness of purpose and fanatical intentness on the vision of Yillah operate to defeat Hautia's power to dominate him, and in the crescendo of emotional action in which the book concludes she abandons him to the grimmer pursuit of the avengers. "Go—go and slay thyself; I may not make thee mine."

In a transport of frenzy, Taji beholds the drowned form of Yillah in Hautia's hidden lake. He plunges to rescue it, but the currents baffle him and the half-seen vision eludes him. Back on the seashore he hears from Mohi and Yoomy the tale of Media's hostile reception in his own land, his almost certain doom and his injunction to the rest to flee for safety to Serenia. On Mardi's outer reef the storm is rising; Yillah is lost, Media doomed, Taji desperate. Here the prose, in spite of excursions into turbid Elizabethan blank verse, rises to a controlled height of suggestiveness. The symbol, here on the last page, is superbly in control again. The sophistication of the allegory, the tedious elaboration of the romanticised figures of Yillah and Hautia, the involved speculation, all are forgotten. Melville, like Taji, is alone with the elemental symbol; the voyage become a desperate flight, the epic become a tragedy, the passion thwarted by death and loss, the pleadings of his few friends irrelevant and unheard. The pervasive sea, always in Melville a character of potency, sounds in every syllable of the magnificent ending.

"In trumpet-blasts, the hoarse night-winds now blew; the lagoon, black with the still shadows of the mountains, and the driving shadows of the clouds. Of all the stars, only red Acturus shone. But through the gloom and on the circumvallating reef, the breakers dashed ghost-white.

"An outlet in that outer barrier was nigh.

"Ah, Yillah! Yillah!—the currents sweep thee oceanward: nor will I tarry behind. Mardi, farewell!"

"Nay, madman! Serenia is our haven. Through yonder strait, for thee, perdition lies. And from the deep beyond, no voyager e'er puts back."

"And why put back? Is a life of dying worth living over again? Let *me*, then, be the non-returning wanderer. . . . Now, I am my own soul's emperor; and my first act is abdication! Hail! realm of shades!"—and, turning my prow into the racing tide, which seized me like a hand omnipotent, I darted through.

"Churned in foam, that outer ocean lashed the clouds; and straight in my white wake, headlong dashed a shallop, three fixed spectres leaning o'er its prow; three arrows poising.

"And thus, pursuers and pursued fled on, over an endless sea."

Thus Melville abandons all in his final desperation. His hero has cut himself adrift from all the civilisations through which he has passed; has lost the guiding object of his passionate existence, has thrown aside his friends, his helpers, his hope of safety and consolation, and entrusted himself alone to the impersonal ferocity of the elements and the malevolence of his sworn pursuers.

Even the momentary photographic "shot" on which the climax of *Mardi* fades out is so vivid as to be productive of both pity and terror, those two authentic companions of great tragedy. Innocence has been overwhelmed by the evil implicit in Experience: and utterly alone, the soul of man is swept out upon a racing tide beyond the known world, the Eumenides howling in his wake. At that time there was nothing more that Melville's symbolic imagination could do; out of the rich chaos of his speculations, he had contrived this dramatic disaster at the compulsion of his intuitions.

For the moment he could carry it no further. The closing moments of *Mardi* have an elemental horror that were to be paralleled later only by the consummation of *Moby Dick*. In the later novel they are commensurate with the whole massive creation which they complete; in *Mardi* the final impression is profounder than the vast structure that precedes them wholly warrants.

Mardi will never attract readers. It is too long, its lack of co-ordination is both baffling and boring, it suffers from every fault of the ambitious amateur, from facetiousness to obscurantism. Its allegory, though pointed and penetrating enough, is at times superficial, and fails on the whole to reflect either an ordered attitude to existence or a solution to the complexities it records; its symbolism, even at its most powerful, is encumbered with a set of images and personifications too derivative and decadent to illuminate their material counterparts with any conviction. It is at most a callow and pretentious effort to do far more than the unity of a single book can usefully contain between its covers. It attempts at least two separate tasks—the stabilisation of Melville's intellectual development, and the expression of his spiritual and imaginative dilemma—and does neither of them adequately. It succeeds merely in being a fantastic and incredible story of the Polynesian islands, a curious romance that started promisingly and went wrong; a romance as inept as its unilluminating Preface; by all standards a failure, and, at a key period of Melville's development, rather a serious one.

Yet it embodies qualities of power and urgency which are inseparable from greatness. Physically the effort of composition must have been colossal; as a work of intellectual and imaginative force alone it is, in spite of its many faults, deeply impressive. The reader is *released* at the end from a compelling experience, as he is released at the end of *King Lear* or *The Brothers Karamazov*. It has neither the scope nor the stature nor the insight of either of those masterpieces, but it is recognisably of a kind with them; and in the chronological recital of Melville's work this is a new experience to record. The depth of his conjectures, and the power of the tragic symbol that he here uses (or that here uses him) for the first time in his life, prepare the reader for the quality and the stature of his very greatest achievement. Melville has by this book alone put himself out of the class of travel-romances and into a fraternity of writers who strike none too easy a balance between the transports of the imagination and the perceptions of the intellect. It is easy enough to dismiss *Mardi* as a technical ruin. So it is: but it is an unmistakable sign that its author has attained that unusual state in which allowances have to be made for the great gaps in the technique on account of the manifest power of a spirit too vigorous for normal techniques to contain. As early as *Mardi* it must be faced that faulty construction, obscurity, defects of presentation in Melville are to be related neither to failure of inspiration nor paucity of invention. Mr. Van Wyck Brooks has acutely observed that Melville was one of those writers who prove that the rules of an art are of small importance when the mind and the grasp of life are large enough. *Mardi* is proof of all these things—of the hap-hazard relations to the rules as well as of the power of mind and the grasp of life. Leaving the rules, and his infringements of them, momentarily aside from a consideration of this book, we have to recognise its cardinal importance as a factor in his expansion towards greatness. Embodied in *Mardi* is not only his fullest statement yet of the theme of the conflict between Innocence and Experience, that topic common to all his past and future writing, but what is more important than this, the emergence of the tragic vision. That he had not at this stage all the tools of tragedy at his command is the reason for his partial failure of communication, but for this lack Melville cannot be held wholly to blame; his active inheritance was a cribbed and limited tradition, without which he could get nowhere and within which his superb imagination moved in fetters. Nevertheless, far and away above the imperfection of his art stands ranged in importance his discovery of the symbol. Conjecture and fantasy might allure and bewilder him; but in the presence of the familiar concrete symbol Melville's precision did not fail him. Provided that his chosen symbols were active, dynamic, representative of a life and vigour to which his imagination could instantly respond, there was no end to Melville's evocative power. The last nervous paragraphs of *Mardi* are compact of this new mastery.

"But through the gloom and on the circumvallating reef, the breakers dashed ghost-white." "Turning my prow into the racing tide, which seized me like a hand omnipotent." "Churned in foam, that outer ocean lashed the clouds." "Headlong dashed a shallop, three fixed spectres leaning o'er its prow; three arrows poising."

E

The picture is supremely sketched; imagery, suggestiveness, mystery, vitality, unite at the height of tension. Unerringly Melville's instinct closed the book on that high pitch, left it vibrating, its images alive and haunting. Once and for all he has set the tragic theme that was to inform his life and his work in unforgettable forms: the symbolism of action, the pursuit, the sea. Until in due time a greater symbol rose out of the sea to meet him, he was to play for a while detailed variations on this very theme. The mastery which he had found incidentally in the great endeavour and partial failure of *Mardi*, he was to use less ambitiously, but to consummate effect, in the next two books he was to write.

CHAPTER VI

Redburn: the Assault upon Innocence

MELVILLE himself in later years spoke slightingly of *Redburn*. Even at the time of writing it he accentuated its limitations. "I have now in preparation," he writes to his publishers in July 1849,

"a thing of a widely different cast from *Mardi*—a plain, straightforward, amusing narrative of personal experience—the Son of a gentleman on his first voyage to sea as a sailor—no metaphysics, no cosmic sections, nothing but cakes and ale."

And his recorded remarks after its appearance are even harsher. "The wonder is," he wrote in the journal of his voyage to Europe in the late autumn of 1849,

"that the old Tory [meaning *Blackwood's Magazine*, which had spread itself on a review of the book] should waste so many pages upon a thing which I, the author, know to be trash, and wrote it to buy some tobacco with."

That entry is of early November 1849; a month later he was writing to Evert Duyckinck, back in America, on the same topic.

"The book *Redburn* to my surprise (somewhat) seems to have been favourably received. I am glad of it—for it puts money into an empty purse. But I hope I shall never write such a book again—tho' when a poor devil writes with duns all round him, and looking over the back of his chair—and perching on his pen and diving in his inkstand—like the devils about St. Anthony— what can you expect of that poor devil?—What but a beggarly 'Redburn'! And when he attempts anything higher—God help him and save him! for it is not with a hollow purse as with a hollow balloon—for a hollow purse makes the poet *sink*— witness *Mardi*."

It is clear that Melville in *Mardi* had tasted blood—that he had seen, though he had hardly yet been successful in realising, the potency of the symbol, and was dissatisfied from that time forward unless he could find better ways of exploiting it. *Redburn* to him seems to have represented a regrettable retrenchment; a return to methods which he felt had been worked out to the full in *Typee* and *Omoo*; a partial acknowledgment of *Mardi's* failure. Cherishing *Mardi* more, as typifying a far wider spiritual experience than he was yet able to put into a cogent form, he visited his disappointment upon its successor. "I, the author, know it to be trash, and wrote it to buy some tobacco with." It is quite true that it was a pot-boiler; he needed the money, for he had married in 1847 and his first child was born as he was finishing *Mardi*; but the restrictions that the discipline of realism imposed upon the style and form of his new book, combined with the surprising access of maturity that had come upon him part way through *Mardi*, impregnated *Redburn* with an intensity of feeling quite outside the range of his early realist fictions. Mr. Ellery Sedgwick, in his thorough and perceptive book on Melville, refers rather unexpectedly to *Redburn* as presenting a "dingy, poor-relation's appearance among Melville's books of this period", but later qualifies his own and Melville's dispraise by calling it "perhaps the most charming of all his books . . . a combination of liveliness and wistfulness." It is difficult to agree with either of these views. For the first, it is so full of the surprise of fresh experience that "dingy" is about the least appropriate adjective that could have been chosen for it; and for the second, it is stripped entirely of that quality in *Typee*, mingled delight and regret, that comes nearest to charm in a writer who never made a feature of it, and presents rather a new, but increasingly characteristic, quality of bitterness—the lost desperation of the last page of *Mardi* being infused in a less violent but still recognisable form into the more realistic actions of the new book.

On the material plane, it was true that after finishing *Mardi* Melville needed money, so wrote a straightforward account of a green boy's first voyage at sea. On the imaginative plane the sequence was even more compulsive, and in the light of Melville's total development far more significant; the fact being that Melville instinctively recognised the inadequacy of the symbol in *Mardi* and set about constructing a sure factual foundation on which a maturer symbolism might more profitably raise itself at some time in the future. His instinct was perfectly right as well. He returned, with his new imaginative assurance and his surprisingly lengthened vision, to the episode in his own life which had most nearly moved his earliest development; his first voyage. Most wisely, as he was essaying experiment, he chose to write of his earliest experience; time enough later, when his control had matured, to treat of his profoundest contacts with life aboard the whaler. For the present his young art is admirably bent to the delineation of his young self. The happy-go-lucky Tommo of the Typees had grown out of a callow and shrinking past; and Melville, fresh from a world-wide voyage of speculation, overcasts the picture of his boyhood with the predominant mood with which experience, personal and vicarious, of actual human suffering, had left him for ever. *Redburn* is yet another conclusive statement of the fate of the innocent soul in face of the dispassionate enmity of experience. Blake in *The Book of Thel* had imagined the virgin soul listening in horror to the accents of sorrow that greet her on her entrance into the world—

" *Why cannot the Ear be closed to its own destruction . . .*
Or the glistening Eye to the poison of a smile? . . .
Why are Eyelids stor'd with arrows ready drawn,
Where a thousand fighting men in ambush lie,
Or an Eye of gifts and graces show'ring fruits and coined gold? . . .
Why a tender curb upon the youthful burning boy? . . ."

Blake's metaphors are hideously apt: poison, arrows, fighting men, ambush, coined gold, burning. The snares hidden in experience utter a frightful destructive purpose. *Redburn* is the product of an identical phase in the expansion of Melville's consciousness. The onset of experience is half-heard and half-felt in *Typee* and *Omoo*, expounded more theoretically than directly in *Mardi*, and

proved upon his pulses and his active fertile memory in *Redburn*.
With less subtlety of course than Proust but with no less poignancy
and immediacy, he takes the memory of his own boyhood and
entwines it with tragic and bitter irony with the present consciousness of his disillusion. His imagery is less compact than Blake's,
because his medium is prose narrative and not lyric poetry; but
expanded into episodic form it is no less evocative and no less true
to its authentic origin in the responses of a youthful mind.

That *Redburn* is an imaginative fiction I have no doubt whatever.
It is certainly based on a series of episodes that Melville had himself, in one way or another, experienced; but to regard it, as Mr.
Lewis Mumford would seem to do, as a piece of autobiography to
be abstracted like a journal for the authentic record of Melville's
physical adventures on board his first ship, is to underestimate its
imaginative quality and misunderstand its peculiar value. It will
perhaps serve my purpose better if I sum up my view of this
particular question by declaring that in considering the quality of
Melville's work it is of no importance whatever to determine
whether or not any one recorded incident did or did not occur to
Melville in person, and that moreover it will often be found on
closer examination that the record of an incident that never happened to him at all is of profounder importance than the record
of an incident known to be entirely authentic. (The classic instance
of this apparent anomaly is the astounding description of the fall
from the mast-head in *White-Jacket*: a piece of violent action so
vividly realised that it has always been assumed that Melville
himself underwent the actual experience as and when he said he
did, until the joint researches of Mr. Anderson and Professor
Matthiessen have lately proved beyond any possible doubt that
not only did the incident as described certainly not happen to
Melville, but equally certainly the incident as described happened
to somebody else, from whose printed narrative Melville stole it
long after, with the artist's unquestioned licence to use as he
pleased anything he happened to come by.)

Therefore the incidents of Wellingborough Redburn's first
voyage must depend for their authenticity less upon historical
research than on the genuine responses that they evoke in the mind
of the sympathetic reader; for on that reader's acquiescence, which
it is the author's task to demand and receive, is constructed the
enduring value of a book like *Redburn*. If the chosen symbols—

in *Redburn* they take the form of a chain of new characters and episodes—are accepted, then the book is a true record of experience, whether Melville lived through the incidents or merely thought them out for himself. In point of fact *Redburn* for almost all its length compels acceptance; only for a few scattered episodes does Melville relax a tact and control unusual in such a spontaneous and ebullient writer; and some few characters and some few episodes are charged with an unforgettable power. In the figure of Jackson there is presented for the first time in Melville a character of outstanding dramatic quality; and in the episode in the Liverpool slum where Redburn tries in vain to bring help to the dying beggar-woman and her children, Melville does in five pages of quiet narrative what even Dickens could not have done in five hundred— stirs the human marrow with hot pity and anger while coming near to freezing it with horror. Nineteenth-century literature, in protest against the indifference of a ruthless industrialism, is prolific of such passages, and there is hardly a humane writer in that great age of humanitarians who has not provided his or her chapter of outraged realism. Yet I would set this passage at the head of them all. Dickens and de Maupassant, Balzac, Mrs. Gaskell, George Eliot and Zola between them never attained the pity and the poignancy of that soberly written account.

Redburn's pity and Jackson's evil must be accentuated at the forefront of any discussion of this book, since in these two are realised Melville's new awareness of these two dramatic and dynamic opposites. Jackson is not just another shipmate of Redburn's; he is personified iniquity, a force in the universe that Melville had newly discovered—perhaps in the universe to which Taji was driven by the tide that swept the outer reef of Mardi. The scene in Launcelott's Hey in Liverpool is not just another incident that a curious youth happens upon in his travels; it is the moment of the casting of his innocence, when the sight of extreme human suffering rends a youth with pity and anger, and makes him on the instant a man for whom there can still be danger in evil, but no longer any surprise or terror. These two striking elements in the book are both introduced casually, undramatically; both force their way into the consciousness; both after they have accomplished their task are dismissed, Jackson to his death, the Liverpool incident to apparent oblivion, for it is never once referred to again; but both sign themselves indelibly upon the story.

Jackson is realised with only that minute and loving faithfulness that the fascination of fear and hatred can prompt: and of all the forces that harass the unhappy greenhorn he stands out as the most malicious and implacable. The stagey bullyings of the captain are conventional enough; so is the insolent indifference of the rest of the crew, and even the sometimes over-elaborate innocence of Master Wellingborough himself, with his shooting-jacket and teetotalism and longings for his mother. In all these there are echoes of other writers, Dana and Marryat in particular; and whether Melville had read the latter or not, *Redburn* often reads strangely familiar to a reader who remembers his *Midshipman Easy*, published the year before Melville went to sea. But neither Dana nor Marryat, dead serious although the one was and vividly imaginative the other, could have electrified his book with the direct malignity of Jackson, the sick malingering tyrant of the forecastle, with the squint-eye—

> "I would defy any oculist to turn out a glass eye half so cold and snaky and deadly. It was a horrible thing; and I would give much to forget that I have ever seen it, for it haunts me to this day . . . going in and out, very quick, as if it were something like a forked tongue."

Clever and cunning and dexterous in malice, Jackson lorded it over his shipmates. Melville saw even as early as this that there was a controlled quality of power in the utmost evil that could awaken even a certain admiration; that even at the heart of depravity there was both a greatness and a fascination. "All the time Jackson seemed to have even more contempt than hatred for everybody and everything," says Melville, realising that in the innermost recess of the wicked man's heart is a chill loneliness which freezes even the power of his own hate. It is a clear and subtle study of an element in life which was to become from this time onwards a deep emotional preoccupation with Melville. From Jackson to Claggart the personifications stretch with barely a break; yet Jackson, the earliest of Melville's Iagos, is the most significant of them all, for in his person is announced to the young Redburn-Melville the theme that was never to leave him.

> "I could not avoid Jackson's eye, nor escape his bitter enmity. And his being my foe set many of the rest against me, or at least they were afraid to speak out for me before Jackson; so that at

last I found myself a sort of Ishmael in the ship, without a single friend or companion, and I began to feel a hatred growing up in me against the whole crew—so much so that I prayed against it that it might not master my heart completely, and so make a fiend of me, something like Jackson."

The boy has perceived evil, and evil has begun to work upon the boy: a cosmic spiritual process most skilfully suggested here in Melville's unpretentious realism; a completely organic expression of the larger and more ominous expansion of Melville's own profounder preoccupations. For the moment, Redburn and Jackson are instinct with tragic vitality, removing the book *Redburn* once and for all from the bounds of commonplace potboiling narrative. The tension is not sustained; but the threat remains, and there is more than one renewal.

Coincident with Redburn's awareness of the power of evil comes his perhaps even more poignant recognition of loneliness. This is partly attributable to the baneful Jackson, but not wholly. Experience attacks the novice not in single isolated blows, but cumulatively from all sides, in small things as well as great. Jackson's malevolence permeated the ship, the harsh unfamiliarity of the routine, the ship's discipline understandably severe but more than understandably heartless—all wore away, along with the natural buffetings of the Atlantic weather, the pathetic and half-defiant self-confidence with which the boy had come aboard. His high artificial romantic enthusiasms—symbolised most neatly in his love for the glass ship on the corner-table in the parlour at home—are violently, and valuably, transformed into a virile resilience characteristic of Redburn—and the young Melville—but not necessarily common to every member of the human species whose early illusions are submitted to a sudden shattering. Struggling with the skysail-yard at night, in a new and fearful isolation from every security that he had ever known, the young Redburn is at the centre of his loneliness.

"I seemed all alone, treading the midnight clouds, and every second expected to find myself falling—falling—falling, as I have felt when the nightmare has been on me. I could but just perceive the ship below me, like a long narrow plank in the water; and it did not seem to belong at all to the yard over which I was hanging. A gull or some sort of sea-fowl was flying round the truck over my head, within a few yards of my face; and it almost frightened me to hear it—it seemed so much like a spirit, at such a lofty and solitary height."

His fear, which is powerful enough, admits of no self-pity and no decline in observant curiosity; Melville as Redburn accepts the inevitability of loneliness and danger, and for himself saves enough of his self-possession to store away that sea-fowl for the crowning moment of his matured art, when it reappears at the sinking of the *Pequod*, nailed to the mast with the flag in Tashtego's death agony, the bird of heaven with archangelic shrieks dragged down to destruction with the doomed ship of Ahab.

That is a taste merely of the essential loneliness of which Melville when writing *Redburn* seemed so constantly aware; the intensification comes when he lands at Liverpool with his father's old guidebook, eagerly seeking to follow the same wanderings that his father had followed thirty years before. The life of the great city has enormously expanded in the interval; the variety of the bustling crowds, the sailors' boarding houses, the German emigrants, pour themselves bewilderingly into Redburn's astonished consciousness until the whole picture of Liverpool comes alive in his imagination and he sucks in each new impression with a new delight. In brilliant contrast to the grim confinement of the voyage, the roar and rabble of city life with its Irish labourers and balladmongers, Custom house underlings and shady jewellers, jaunty negro seamen and braggart English Chartists, release in Redburn a response that had been stifled as yet by the sea. Melville's manipulation of these Liverpool scenes is most dexterous: he plies the reader with catalogue and fact until his instinct warns him that the interest will slacken unless revived with an anecdote; and his unresting eyes dart and peer brightly as the narrative quickens and slackens, lighting up a splash of colour here and a murky corner in shadow there, until the whole town hums with a vitality that only Dickens of his contemporaries knew how to give to a city. Mr. Plomer described the treatment as "cinematic", and in so far as it is detailed and factual and photographic as well as being in certain passages lit up from within by sheer imaginative vitality, this description is effective and apt. Yet Melville has not quite forgotten the reality of which Redburn himself and Liverpool are even now only the dim simulacra: his purpose is just so much more than documentary as will retain a muted hint of symbolic suggestion. Accordingly Redburn's anticipated ties with this city are snapped in a memorable sequence of disappointed realisation that the city his father knew has long been swamped in the new city in which he himself is now cast up: "The guide book", he says, "was nearly half a century behind the age! and no more fit to guide me about the town than the map of Pompeii."

Mr. Ellery Sedgwick regarded this realisation as the crucial episode in *Redburn*. It is true that it is important, for it signalises Redburn's (and Melville's) plain understanding of the paramount value of personal experience in contrast to the derivative romanticism of adolescence that had idealised the roving life and made the ship of glass represent the essence of the glamour of the sea. Nevertheless the emotional effect of the disappointment does not, on close examination, appear to have been vital. Redburn shuts up the guide-book with the wry remark out of his new-found wisdom that "every age makes its own guide-books, and the old ones are used for waste paper", and plunges with undaunted eagerness into his new experiences. The episode has given him a valuable stimulus, correlative to the emotional loneliness that he had felt up at the masthead at sea; but it cannot be compared in imaginative value with the horrible scene in Launcelott's Hey, which follows a few chapters later. With this episode the bright cinematic liveliness of his method narrows down to a grim and deliberate realism, in which without obtrusiveness and without obvious intent the emotions are challenged and seized. In this short chapter Redburn becomes adult, understands the silent and deadly indifference of contemporary society that is more to be feared than all the bullyings of Captain Riga or even the malevolence of Jackson. In that chapter society becomes a hundred Jacksons. Redburn, who could never stand up to Jackson, stands up to society with the instinctive armament of pity. In Launcelott's Hey society slays the beggar-woman and her children with Redburn powerless to save them; yet in that very experience Redburn learns how to save society. He has discovered pity.

It is this quality that leaves the most distinct mark on *Redburn*, in spite of its rambling and diverse narrative. The slant of Melville's adult mind across the adolescence and innocence of Redburn's results in a stereoscopic complexity, a vitality attributable to far more than the vigour and speed of the action. The depth imparted to the picture bears a direct relation to the depth of the emotion engendered by the older man's ironic contemplation of his younger self—an emotion communicated, like David Copperfield's in the very same year, by a blend of humour and pity; less well blended, because cruder and more spasmodic, than Dickens' masterly re-creation of his childhood and youth, but ultimately as complete and as convincing as a portrayal of the maturing of an innocent. The further that Redburn sails from his old home into new experience, the less does Melville recur to farcical incident, and the surer is his capacity to observe and transmit impressions; therefore, though he starts with a preponderance of irony, he ends with an almost complete transformation in favour of pity. After Launcelott's Hey and the dock-wall beggars he had little alternative but to shelve his irony altogether, lacking Dickens' power to fuse his humour and pity and to produce living art out of the fusion.

Thus his attitude towards his unhappy young shipmate Harry Bolton, who with Redburn himself and Jackson makes one of the great central trio of the book, avoids every crying opportunity for satire and remains almost uniformly compassionate. Harry is a representative figure enough, but realised perhaps only half-successfully—the shiftless and airy youth whose elegant posturings concealed an experience as profound as Redburn's own and far more dangerous since he had but a sapless character to withstand the inevitable disillusion. The fanciful and unconvincing London episode belongs to the early stages of Redburn's acquaintanceship with Harry—a melodramatic and rather confused picture of what Melville presumably thought was a typical scene of night-life among the well-to-do. It is curious how the imaginations of so many great nineteenth-century novelists failed before a convincing portrayal of London society. Dickens had to bend it to his satire before it would answer; and Thomas Hardy is another whose adventures into high life are disastrous. Melville is no luckier in his effect; the London episode is the result of pursuing Harry Bolton into Harry's own original context, where his creator barely understood him. But bring Harry Bolton into Melville's own context (which he speedily did, since the poor fellow shipped aboard the *Highlander* for the voyage back to America) and Melville's understanding eye is grim and unerring. In the face of the tyranny and indifference that in the upshot had braced Redburn, Harry Bolton is summarily crushed. Indeed his decline is pitiful to watch.

Carrying with him a certain fineness of quality which is absent
from all Redburn's other shipmates, he nevertheless fails utterly to
withstand the unfamiliar onset. The sea that makes Redburn
breaks Harry Bolton; his jaunty self-confidence is stripped off him,
he funks the climb to the masthead and is driven there with
ruthless contempt by the mate, and yields himself, completely
broken in spirit, to the luxury of passive misery. At the end of the
voyage he departs hopelessly to seek a fortune that even he knows is
illusory; and years afterwards Redburn hears that he has met an
unhappy death on board a whaler. Sketchy as the character of Harry
is, there is a certain poignancy latent behind the conventional
trappings of romantic rake in which Melville dresses him; and his
story and his fate contain just sufficient of undeserved severity to
lend a tragic twist to a tale that might otherwise have been merely
romantic commonplace. His is the darker side of Redburn's own
story: the death of the innocence against which experience prevailed all too easily. Like Ignorance in The *Pilgrim's Progress*, who
seems to meet a fate disproportionate to his transgressions, Harry
had erred in daring a contest that by the very nature of things was
bound to be unequal. To fail to submit to the discipline of your
pilgrimage is the unforgivable sin. Ignorance and Harry failed,
and it did not cost them less dearly that their failure was
unwitting.

But Redburn's survival is a challenge to the destructiveness of
experience, and the transformation of his (and Melville's) attitude
in the process affirms the creative nature of Melville's imagination.
At the end of Redburn we are taken further than Blake, for example,
took us in *The Book of Thel*. *The Book of Thel* is a retreat, but
Redburn is something far more positive than that. It is an education
and a conversion at once. Thel, though she is not denied the comfort of the lesson of love offered her by the Clod of Clay, retires in
distress from the harshness of her vision; Redburn, who is denied
everything but the invigoration of the experience itself, finds himself on the other side of it transmuted by a strange alchemy into a
creature of finer substance. Because Redburn has been able to pity
the beggars in the Liverpool slum, Melville himself in the detachment of maturity is enabled to pity Redburn; and both can extend
the resulting imaginative charity to cover even the instruments of
the hatred that called it forth. "But there seemed", he comments on
the detested Jackson,

"even more woe than wickedness about the man; and his wickedness seemed to spring from his woe; and for all his hideousness, there was that in his eye at times that was ineffably pitiable and touching; and though there were moments when I almost hated this Jackson, yet I have pitied no man as I have pitied him."

The access of pity does not mitigate the horror; but the horror is converted into material for pity, and gains in significance though it does not lose in severity. The unremitting harshness of the routine is enlivened by sudden intensifications; just as the voyage out had led off with the suicide of a delirious drunkard, so the voyage home leads off with the ghastly discovery of the corpse of the impressed sailor, which flames into phosphorescence when a light is held to the face. Last of all, the day before the ship makes its home port, comes Jackson's fall from the yard and his instant death before the eyes of the helpless crew, drowned and vanished in the boiling sea while the sail still dripped with the blood that had burst from his lungs. And though Jackson had, as near as anything might, personified evil, there is no melodramatic relief at his end. The lot of man is no better for his death; there is even a spontaneous comradely sense of kinship with him as he falls that makes his alienation from his mates for the moment less marked. His death has as tragic an effect as Harry Bolton's or the beggar-woman's. Like every other incident in the book, it is creative. All the assaults upon innocence and self-confidence that had subtracted from Harry Bolton's personality, added to Redburn's. They built up out of his callow inexperience a resilience that at the time was little more than a healthy instinctive reaction in face of the threat of negation, but which contained in principle the answer (that Melville had not yet grasped with the whole of his imagination) to all the perplexities in which a profound and adventurous habit of speculation was later to involve him.

There is priceless value in this unpretentious book. It did not satisfy the author, but his readers cannot withhold their admiration on that account. Obsessed with the growing power of the symbol and yet reluctant for the moment to venture further into experiment, he wrote his two realistic chronicles of sea-life grudgingly but with the thoroughness that deep sympathy and familiarity with his topic impelled. Babbalanja in *Mardi* had spoken like Melville in two voices—one his own, the voice of reason, one the voice of his

demon Azzageddi, who spoke through Babbalanja's lips the seemingly inconsequent ravings of a madman who yet seemed, like
Lear's Fool, to speak stronger sense in his extravagant wanderings
than all the same characters in their pedestrian argument. The
discovery and recognition of Azzageddi was a major critical event
in Melville's exploration of the imaginative mind; and in *Mardi* he
had ambitiously experimented with his own Azzageddi. In *Redburn*
he deliberately suppressed him; he was not yet under control, and
(what was perhaps more to the point at the time) he did not pay.
Nevertheless he could not entirely obliterate his traces; for, it
would seem against his own will and without his own knowledge,
this plain, straightforward, amusing narrative that he knew to be
trash, and wrote to buy tobacco with, held a host of hidden but
potent symbols through which can be traced even more clearly than
in the outward recorded facts the journey of an untried youth from
innocence through hardship to a state of imaginative illumination.
The journey has been made by most great artists; but it is not often
that we have it so powerfully and suggestively chronicled.

CHAPTER VII

White-Jacket and the Abandonment of Isolation

IN 1843 Melville had shipped home from the South Seas as an ordinary seaman on the frigate *United States,* rounding off a seven-year-long series of irresponsible journeyings with the most disciplined voyage he ever undertook. Early in the following year the frigate made port at Boston and Melville left sea-voyaging for good, never venturing off-shore again except as a passenger. This last voyage home marked the close of the active experiences which for the next six or seven years were to mature so finely into vivid narrative. In his twenty-fifth year Melville left the sea and began, as he declared to Hawthorne, his significant life—that is, the absorption into his creative imagination of what had passed in the crowded years where there had been no leisure to create but only to accept. *White-Jacket* is the record of this last voyage.

It is of a piece with *Redburn,* in that it was written directly after it and did not attempt any symbolical or experimental flights of the imagination. Like *Redburn,* it isolates one distinctive phase in Melville's own youthful experience and presents it in systematic detail and with a maturer emotional control than the young man who went through the actual experiences would have been likely to command. Again as in *Redburn* the ironic slant of the perceptive author lends impressive depth to the flat conventional picture of a young sailor's life on board ship. But it bears a profounder relationship to *Redburn* than can be simply explained by the superficial likeness in their themes; for whether Melville had the intention in his mind or not, there is an instinctive appropriateness in their juxtaposition, *Redburn* is the record of his first voyage and *White-Jacket* is the record of his last; the pair complement each other in such a way as to provide an admirable epitome of a sailor's life seen first from the point of view of the lonely tyro and next from the point of view of the experienced seaman who understands perfectly his function in the intricate and disciplined routine of the ship. The sense of assurance and maturity that pervades *White-Jacket* did not descend miraculously upon Melville the writer after he had finished *Redburn*; it represents,—and so does the contrasting atmosphere of isolation and experiment so characteristic of the earlier book,— the fulfilment of the apprenticeship and education of Melville the sailor, embodied years afterwards in these two excellent narratives, the heads and tails of the same coin.

But the difference is also a difference of approach; *Redburn* is an examination of the spiritual and imaginative growth of a single man, whereas *White-Jacket* shows the scope of Melville's study immeasurably widened. He subtitles it "The World in a Man-of-War", and it is in this world, rather than in the matured sailor, that he is interested. The Liverpool beggars and the steerage-passengers in *Redburn* are of course clear evidence that *White-Jacket's* broader scope does not represent a new departure; but they are incidents that disturb an individual, and we are led to concentrate on the manner in which they repel and re-form his character. In *White-Jacket* he examines, in his own way, the systems that had made these abominations inevitable.

I say "in his own way" deliberately: at no time in his writing life was Melville primarily quickened by any sense of the economic or sociological forces at work to disturb or distort the character of the individual. He was not, conspicuously, a student of history or of politics; for a man so prone to speculation in the regions of the creative or the philosophical mind, social and ethical abstractions interested him surprisingly little. The reason was the essentially practical nature of his training; as he said himself, the whaling-vessel had been his university; and he learned his experience by the direct method, not needing postulates. Therefore he formed a habit of mind which agonised first of all at the concrete human manifestations of injustice and suffering, and only by a

F

sophisticated effort of the intelligence did he bring his imagination to contemplate the system at whose door much of that injustice had to be laid. Imaginatively, Melville saw each human being as a man on a lonely quest for his destiny, unhampered and unaided by any other. It is the primitive, or Aeschylean, view, that man is essentially impervious to local or accidental vicissitudes. His fate is ordained, tragic, noble. Yet Melville's intelligence, schooled in whalers and frigates, realised that only in a very primitive society (like Athens before Aeschylus) could such a view of human destiny provide a satisfactory answer to human problems. A whaler, perhaps, or a South Sea Island, might furnish a community sufficiently unsophisticated to correspond with its semi-barbarity. The Liverpool chapters in *Redburn* are an indication that he is himself past that stage, though *Redburn* itself does no more than hint at the implications of a wider view. It is characteristic of Melville that when he became, intellectually, fully aware of the importance of the right relations between an individual and the society in which he has to exist, he should have chosen to symbolize that awareness in a detailed study of the only kind of society which he thoroughly understood from top to bottom—a ship's crew: and moreover (and this was probably involuntary) he should most appropriately have chosen, for his most sophisticated and intricate study yet of man's relationship with life, the most sophisticated and intricate of all shipboard routines—life on a man-of-war. Perfectly at home in his familiarity with the symbol he selected, he could make it emblematic of a still more complex society with which he could not hope to deal with any authority. Within his known confines, his authority was easy and supreme.

"Wrecked on a desert shore," he says, "a man-of-war's crew could quickly found an Alexandria by themselves, and fill it with all the things which go to make a capital. . . . In truth, a man-of-war is a city afloat . . . or rather, a man-of-war is a lofty, walled, and garrisoned town, like Quebec, where the thoroughfares are mostly ramparts, and peaceable citizens meet armed sentries at every corner. . . . Or it is like the lodging-houses in Paris, turned upside down . . . or with its long rows of port-hole casements each revealing the muzzle of a cannon, a man-of-war resembles a three-story house in a suspicious part of the town, with a basement of indefinite depth, and ugly-looking fellows gazing out at the windows."

The insistence is too marked to be overlooked. Melville is under-lining, and concentrating his interest upon, the analogy between life on the man-of-war and the landsman's familiar life among city streets.

With this always in mind, he gives in *White-Jacket* perhaps the closest and most detailed account that even he ever gave of day-by-day life aboard ship. The descriptions in *Moby Dick* of the complex and fascinating routine aboard a whaling-vessel constitute a greater and more convincing achievement, since there the close-packed documentation is saturated through and through with the dramatic urgency of the great story. The background vibrates with a movement communicated to it by the electric vitality of the drama played out against it. In *White-Jacket* there is, organically, no such drama. The ship is homeward bound to Boston and the sailor White-Jacket is homeward bound in her. There is danger and there are adventurous moments, but there is neither drama nor tragedy. In isolated incidents, which have important parts in the action and which call for detailed comment in their turn, Melville's imagination tears open the surface of his subject and astounds by its per-ceptiveness, its tragic and dramatic vision. But the incidents are isolated, arbitrary even; they bear but a slender relation to the main theme of the book, which in itself lacks a propulsive cogency too. It is the detail he is after, and this is for the moment important, for in these remarkable intermediate books which he wrote between *Mardi* and *Moby Dick*, between the experiment with the symbol and the control of the symbol, Melville is doing more than he is willing to admit to himself. He blasts and sneers at *Redburn* for beggarly trash and seems to have no higher opinion of *White-Jacket*, for after the imaginative flights of *Mardi* it seemed small beer indeed to chronicle mundane sea-voyages to bring in the money; he need not have been so harsh. For the accumulated detail of *Redburn* and *White-Jacket*, pedestrian and artless as it may have seemed at the time (and to Melville himself more than any-one) was being used unwittingly but inevitably to build up a sure and sound foundation on which the immense ambitious symbol of *Moby Dick* could rest.

And he packs into the narrative the ritual and routine of virtually every creature on board; from the Commodore in his cabin to the sailmaker's gang sewing shrouds, from the angry tyrannical Captain Claret to the seamen flogged at the gratings, foretopmen, purser's steward, midshipmen, master-at-arms—the whole pullulating city-state is anatomised with a conscientious thoroughness. The details might have overweighted the book; but it is redeemed from tedium partly by the liveliness of the narrative and partly by the rare flashes of humanity with which the whole compendious chronicle is again and again illuminated. The pity with which Melville at twenty-nine looked back upon the green youth of Redburn is extended in *White-Jacket* to the great mass of his shipmates. With a moving anger and compassion Melville sets out his accusations against those in authority who could not only permit but enforce the degradations inseparable from life in a man-of-war upon human beings powerless to resist them. For although *White-Jacket* is not a tragic or indeed an unhappy book, being conceived in a mood of quite unusual forbearance, its absence of rancour does not disguise the blunt scorn of the indictment against naval commissioners and naval officers whose precepts and practices alike directly contradict the principles of equality which the ships themselves are expressly manned to defend.

For the reason I have already given, it is not possible to say with accuracy how many of the experiences chronicled were Melville's own; but whether or not the sensation was at first or second hand, the incident when White-Jacket comes near to a flogging seems of central importance. It touched off his anger and indignation to a point where he had to be articulate or burst; it inspired Melville to half-a-dozen chapters in which the practice of flogging on board naval vessels—and in particular the barbarous ritual of "flogging through the fleet"—is ruthlessly attacked; it concentrates against this one practice all the anger and compassion induced in an unusually imaginative sailor by all the varied barbarities, major and minor, in the naval system. In the imaginative form in which he expressed it in the passage referred to, the concentration came near to the act of murder.

> "I but swung to an instinct in me—the instinct diffused through all animated nature, the same that prompts even a worm to turn under the heel. Locking souls with him, I meant to drag Captain Claret from this earthly tribunal of his to that of Jehovah, and let Him decide between us. No other way could I escape the scourge. . . . The privilege, inborn and inalienable, that every man has, of dying himself and inflicting death upon another, was not given to us without a purpose. These are the last resources of an insulted and unendurable existence."

In this degradation of an unusually ready and docile sailor into a potential murderer, Melville epitomises the brutal heartlessness of the disciplinary system under which he and his mates served. His constant sense of injustice prevails over all his other moods, so that as the narrative progresses every incident, every described routine, is liable without warning to be pervaded by Melville's up-standing indignation. The sick-bay, the operating-table, the Articles of War, a burial at sea, a rest in the maintop on the fore-chains, the routine of meals, the routine of watches, the marines and the pressgangs, the swabbings of the decks and the slinging of hammocks—every one of these and of a dozen other incidental topics draws Melville's tireless eloquence and heaps up to the cumulative effect of one of the most powerful broadsides upon a restrictive and inhuman system that any man of specialised experience has ever delivered. "I let nothing slip, however small," he says in one of the later chapter, perhaps a little appalled at the enormous mass of detail which his uncompromising and retentive observation has collected,—

"feeling myself actuated by the same motive which has prompted many worthy old chroniclers, to set down the merest trifles concerning things that are destined to pass away entirely from the earth, and which, if not preserved in the nick of time, must infallibly perish from the memories of man. Who knows that this humble narrative may not hereafter prove the history of an obsolete barbarism? Who knows that when men-of-war shall be no more, *White-Jacket* may not be quoted to show the people in the Millennium what a man-of-war was? God hasten the time! Lo ye years, escort it hither, and bless our eyes ere we die."

It is easy to dismiss that hope to-day as hopeless; just as it is easy to puff aside Melville's repeated declarations in *White-Jacket* of the essential anti-Christianity of war and warships as vain and untimely kickings against the necessary pricks of an imperfect civilisation. Yet timeliness is never the chief virtue of prophets; and there is enough vision and profundity in Melville's clear observa-tion of his selected society to allow him a prophetic role more potent than any of his predecessors or contemporaries. Dana, Smollett, Marryat, all realised the petty barbarities of seagoing routine: only Melville related them convincingly to the larger moral issues which were the proper province of the religion that was daily being professed and profaned.

"Are there no Moravians in the moon," he shouts "that not a missionary has yet visited this poor pagan planet of ours, to civilise civilisation and christianise Christendom?"

"How can it be expected that the religion of peace should flourish in an oaken castle of war? . . . And when it is provided by the Articles of War that the chaplain shall receive two-twentieths of the price paid for sinking and destroying ships full of human beings, how is it to be expected that a clergyman thus provided for should prove efficacious in enlarging upon the criminality of Judas, who for thirty pieces of silver betrayed his Master?"

"Soldier or sailor," he concludes in a later chapter, "the fighting man is but a fiend; and the staff and bodyguard of the devil musters many a baton. But war at times is inevitable. Must the national honour be trampled under foot by an insolent foe?"

"Say on, say on; but know you this, and lay it to heart, war-voting Bench of Bishops, that He on whom we believe *himself* has enjoined us to turn the left cheek if the right one be smitten. Never mind what follows. That passage you cannot expunge from the Bible; that passage is as binding upon us as any other; that passage embodies the soul and substance of the Christian faith; without it, Christianity were like any other faith. And that passage will yet, by the blessing of God, turn the world. But in some things we must turn Quakers first."[1]

Melville wrote this before ever war had come to his doorstep; and the *Battle-Pieces* of later years show that the Civil War came to modify this judgment; yet there is no escaping the insistence of the ice-cold common sense at the heart of his fiery idealism. It is in *White-Jacket* that this universal compassion first lends him this eloquence, repetitive, sometimes clumsy, but inescapable and never irrelevant. Concentrated principally upon the one practice of flogging, this urgency carried a copy of *White-Jacket* to the desk of every Congressman in the nation; and we have the evidence of an American Rear-Admiral that there may be attributed to its sole

[1] Cf. Melville's reiteration at the end of his life in a well-known passage in *Billy Budd*: "A chaplain is the minister of the Prince of Peace serving in the trust of the God of War—Mars. As such, he is as incongruous as a musket would be on the altar at Christmas."

evidence the law that was passed soon afterwards abolishing flogging in the Navy absolutely, without substituting any other mode of punishment in its stead.

But the power of *White-Jacket* is not wholly, nor indeed even primarily, in these trenchant inset paragraphs of reasoned protest. For long stretches of the book Melville's preoccupation with these insistent injustices diverted him from his prime narrative function. Granted that the book is not designed as fiction, yet it is sustained patently, even in the heats of its special pleading, by the vividness of those scenes in it which are presented in fictional form; Melville's writing assumed its greatest cogency when he gave his poetic and dramatic imagination fullest play. Confined to reason and argument, he was inclined to prose; faced with an incident to symbolise his preoccupation, he transferred his theme instantly into a scene of haunting vitality. This scene would remain in the memory for longer than the admirable introductory thesis, and expressed in a far more valuable and enduring form the profundity of the impact of experience upon the mind and sensibility of this unusual sailor. Of these incidents the scene of White-Jacket's arraignment before the mast on a charge of dereliction of duty and his narrow escape from the lash is perhaps the most important; but others stand out as conspicuously in the memory, and in examining them the chief preoccupations of the book can be traced beneath the apparently complete pervasiveness of the prime sense of injustice.

Outstanding among them for its realism and satiric power is the superb set-piece of the surgical operation. The character of the ship's surgeon himself, Cadwallader Cuticle, M.D., with his glass eye and his artificial teeth and his peremptory and pedantic manner, is a crisper and bolder essay in the Smollett manner. The name might have been taken from *Peregrine Pickle*; the delineation gains in irony, in polish, even in savagery—Melville succeeding, where Smollett often failed, in disguising the bitterness of his feelings under an uncharacteristic, but highly effective, economy of expression. The whole scene—the assembled surgeons, the model skeleton at the foot of the operating-table, the scared patient, the pompous prolixity of Cuticle himself—is presented with an acid humour unusual in a writer in whom wit too often relaxed into jocularity; and the pungent comedy of the vivid little incident is no less effective for its dangerous affinity to tragedy.

"Please, sir," said the steward entering, "the patient is dead."
"The body also, gentlemen, at ten precisely," said Cuticle, once more turning round upon his guests. "I predicted that the operation might prove fatal; he was very much run down. Good morning"; and Cuticle departed.

If that scene has affinities with Smollett, the curious little incident of the two old sailmakers stitching a shroud for their dead shipmate might, in another context, have been worthy of Thomas Hardy. The gnarled gritty dialectic of the argument between the two as to whether to observe the superstitious custom of threading the last stitch through the dead man's nose is another brilliant example of Melville's wayward poetic talent, seizing out of pedestrian narrative a moment of enduring drama and adding yet another recognisable link to this living chain of incidents by which the chief preoccupations of this book can be traced.

With these vivid and moving pictures are alternated character-sketches that provide their own vitality without calling upon the dramatic method to supply it. Three in particular stand out, apart from Surgeon Cuticle and the fierce unstable captain. One of these characters is not a man at all, but a harbour; worthy of mention in this place only since the description of the great harbour of Rio called out Melville's finest prose set-piece to date, a magnificent Miltonic record of all the navies of history that might honourably anchor there together.

"Amphitheatrical Rio! in your broad expanse might be held the Resurrection and Judgment Day of the whole world's men-of-war, represented by the flagships of fleets"—

then follows the superb resounding roll-call, from the Phoenician galleys of Tyre and Sidon to Nelson's seventy-fours and (tribute to Melville's own friends) the war-canoes of the Polynesian Kings Tammahammaha and Pomaree—

"aye, one and all, with Commodore Noah for their Lord High Admiral—in this abounding Bay of Rio these flagships might all come to anchor, and swing round in concert to the first of the flood."

This vein of pure lyrical happiness is a delight and a surprise against the sombre background of Melville's commoner moods. After *Typee* it was always a fleeting and insecure possession, but when he commanded it, as he did here, it is a rich testimony to his unfailing love of the element that he chose for his greatest symbolic expression and made supremely his own in his best work. Injustice and oppression seem evanescent beside this abiding loyalty and love of the sea and ships; and Melville, sensing the quality of goodness that is as much a part of the sailor's life as the enduring evil that was his simultaneous obsession, chose to personify it in this book by the second of these three characterisations which call for special attention. To one man aboard the *Neversink* White-Jacket gave his deepest loyalty and admiration, as Melville himself must surely have done aboard the *United States*—Jack Chase, captain of the top, an Englishman by birth, a figure of romantic panache, the idol of his shipmates and terror of his superiors. Melville adored him so that his prose grows flatulent with hero-worship whenever he mentions his name or chronicles his deeds; with the result that dramatically he fails to bring him to life, and the huge fair-bearded form moves awkwardly, his eloquence and his capacity for quoting the epic poets falling like a flat affectation upon our ears attuned by Melville's happier satire to the harsher accents of the more ordinary characters. Yet although he is an artistic failure, he succeeds in conveying poignantly enough the genuine response that he called out from the aloof and sensitive man who served with him and (perhaps unknown to him) worshipped him for the rest of his life. Melville's imaginative development dated itself from the day he left the sea and said good-bye to Jack Chase; and for nearly half a century he voyaged through stranger seas of thought alone than ever he had voyaged in his company; yet at the very end of his life Melville set at the head of his last prose work an acknowledgment of the pre-eminence that that unusual sailor still held in his weary and disillusioned soul. He dedicated *Billy Budd* ''To Jack Chase, Englishman, wherever that great heart may now be, here on earth or harboured in Paradise.'' *Billy Budd* stayed in manuscript until 1924, so Jack Chase himself could never have known of the tribute; and as it is not known whether he or Melville ever heard more of each other after the end of that solitary voyage in 1843, the delight of that great lover of poetry and romance at having befriended all unknowing one of the greatest writers of the sea in the history of literature will have to be left to the imagination.

Yet Melville like Milton before him failed to portray goodness as brilliantly as evil; and Jack Chase remains a shadow beside the active vitality of, say, Mad Jack the drunken officer who could countermand his captain's order and go unpunished, or the grim silky Bland the master-at-arms. Bland is the third of the character-studies which represent important elements in Melville's development of thought, and of all the characters in *White-Jacket* he is perhaps the most subtly and truly observed, although in sum he does not amount to much more than an extended sketch. In Bland is expressed the uneasy paradox which was to trouble Melville more and more intensively as his conjecturings carried him further into the mystery of evil; the paradox that had made young Redburn pity Jackson, and was in the distant future to call out a word of sympathy for the torment in the soul of Claggart. "Bland was no vulgar, dirty knave," says Melville.

"In him . . . vice seemed, but only seemed, to lose half its seeming evil by losing all its apparent grossness. He was a neat and gentlemanly villain . . ."

and there is talk of his "fine polish", his "pliant, insinuating style of conversation," so that save for Jack Chase, "he proved himself the most entertaining, I had almost said the most companionable, man in the mess." Melville goes out of his way to insist upon the dexterity and assurance with which this man deported himself, both towards his superiors and his inferiors, when, found guilty of misusing his office for the furtherance of a wide-spread conspiracy for smuggling liquor, he was relegated with ignominy and reduced to the ranks. So fearlessly did he move among the messmates over whom he had tyrannised, so heroically did he face the degradation which must have been desperately wounding to his pride, that White-Jacket, who had earlier summed him up as "an organic and irreclaimable scoundrel who did wicked deeds as the cattle browse the herbage, because wicked deeds seemed the legitimate operation of his whole infernal organisation," came to regard him with "mixed feelings of detestation, pity, admiration, and something opposed to enmity." "I could not but abominate him," says Melville, "when I thought of his conduct; but I pitied the continual gnawing, which under all his deftly-donned disguises, I saw lying at the bottom of his soul."

Here appears once again that fascination with the problem of evil, and the examination and anatomisation of its essence, that occupied

Melville, emotionally and intellectually, for much of his life. Here, in the portrait of Bland, a slight sketch only is attempted; yet the figure is strangely convincing, the superficial self sufficiency and competence of the man being rendered in very striking contrast to the destructive spirit within him while in no way conflicting with it. The result is that although we are presented, through the generous eyes of White-Jacket, with the picture of a man in some sort heroic, yet we can also firmly echo the judgment of the captain of the foretop that Bland was "the two ends and middle of the thrice-laid strand of a bloody rascal." Melville was to broaden his experience of evil considerably in his later work, though only once more did he attempt such a careful and concentrated analysis of the subject. In *Moby Dick*, where every element is dynamically adapted to drama, the element of evil is distilled through all the significant episodes and never isolated; in *Pierre* it is represented melodramatically and is not sufficiently controlled to be important; in *The Confidence-Man* Melville plays extravagant fantasies upon certain aspects of it without doing more than suggest its power. Only in the character of Claggart in *Billy Budd* does Melville once again submit the problem of evil to a process of objective reasoning.

And so, in this or that piece of characterisation, in this or that incident or symbol, Melville marshalled the powers of evil. The forces of good he had taken for granted as any healthy and active young man takes them for granted; the primal innocence of *Typee* was merely a statement of the hearty simplicity in the virgin soul Tommo, of the young and untried Herman Melville. Experience struck him most potently with the other side of the question; and the waves of experience assailing the adolescent Redburn or the harder-bitten White-Jacket were almost all dynamic with iniquity, some mildly enough, others less so. Whenever anything happens on board the *Neversink*, it has its roots in one kind or another of cruelty or indifference; the small comradeships, the enduring goodness even of a character like Jack Chase, are lightweight beside the overpowering onset of the negative principle which was becoming Melville's obsession. The legal heartlessness of the Articles of War, the pedantic heartlessness of Surgeon Cuticle, the brutal heartlessness of the captain, the scheming heartlessness of Bland, accumulate upon Melville's sensibility until every incident, and every reasoned argument that it calls out, drives home with increasing intensity the insistent awareness of the presence of crude evil at the heart of human society. *White-Jacket* is Melville's first attempt at a studied microcosmography of humanity; where *Mardi* avoided a detailed view of society in activity and concentrated upon the panoramic presentation of one man's imaginative voyage through ideas and ideals, *Redburn* and *White-Jacket* turned inwards to chronicle, first the immature personal adventure, next the reasoned attempt to get to grips with man as a social animal. Melville did not recoil; he absorbed the bitterness and coloured his future imaginative ventures with it, keeping it by him for an essential element in the dramatic presentation of the cosmic problems that he sensed before him at the end of his preparation. In *Redburn* he represented the massacre of innocence; in *White-Jacket* the power of indifference and unjustice.

He seems to have made a curious attempt to embody this awareness in a piece of symbolism that fails to communicate a conviction complete enough for his purpose. This is the recurring theme of the Jacket itself, the White Jacket manufactured for himself out of odds and ends by the hero of the narrative. Botched and stitched together in an effort to keep out the wet and the cold, it fails largely of its function and only succeeds in making the wearer conspicuous among his shipmates. The results are embarrassing; he is singled out for the dirty jobs, and by very reason of his 'difference' from the others he attracts to himself an irrational distrust and suspicion. Thus by his very self-consciousness and attempt at self-protection he acquires nothing but an undeserved ostracism, incommensurate with what seems due to a character presented modestly enough as a handy and willing sailor with no desire to shirk his duties or advance himself at the expense of his fellows. Indeed it is only the protective sympathy of Jack Chase that keeps him out of permanent Coventry; and the accursed Jacket is more than once apostrophised as the secret of all his discomforts and distresses. In so far as it symbolises (as without doubt it must) the possession by Melville of some rare quality of character which his ship-mates recognised but, because they could not understand it, distrusted and cold-shouldered, it does not offend probability. Moreover its whiteness, allied perhaps sub-consciously with the theme of innocence, is a suggestive attribute which he was later to develop in detail. Nevertheless the extent of his ostracism seems disproportionate with the actual degree of resentment which a mere jacket, unaccompanied by more positive qualities or intentions, would be likely to arouse in a hard-headed ship's company, and it is difficult to feel with Melville in his treatment of the constant jacket theme that he has hit upon a truly convincing symbol or treated it luminously once he has chosen it. Admittedly he follows the subject into all its ramifications, to the ultimate point of the Jacket being twice the near-cause of a fatal accident, the second of these two occasions being the deservedly famous episode of White-Jacket's fall from the yard, with the consequent loss overboard of the offending Jacket itself, which, like Christian's burden or the Ancient Mariner's albatross, leaves behind it a supreme sense of liberation.

Throughout *White-Jacket* Melville's sense of symbolism is alive, though the very nature of the book made it difficult for him to co-ordinate that sense with his use of his material. The Jacket was only a partial success; and the two great pervasive symbolisms never far from his mind, the voyage and the State, are too vast and too detailed for him to introduce them with any effect without seeming didactic and prosaic. He does not avoid these faults. There are several scattered similitudes in which the voyage-theme is stated again, chief among which is the wonderful passage in ''the Pitch of the Cape'' in which it is interesting to contrast the tingling nervous prose description of the experience of weathering the Horn with the final otiose morality—''but sailor or landsman, there is some sort of a Cape Horn for all.'' They culminate in the final chapter of pretentious rhetoric in which nothing is left to the imagination. ''As a man-of-war that sails through the sea, so this earth that sails through the air, we mortals are all on board a fast-sailing, never-sinking world-frigate of which God was the shipwright,'' etc. etc. There are other chapters in which the affinities between life aboard a man-of-war and life in a modern land-community are stated eloquently and exhaustively, but not in such a way as to illuminate the comparison unexpectedly. It is perhaps enough at this stage that he is aware of the affinities and aware of the power of the symbol. Confidence in the management and co-ordination of the two will come in good time.

And in spite of the imperfection of his control, one of the most powerful impressions left on the mind by a reading of *White-Jacket* is that of the supersession of Redburn's sense of isolation by White-Jacket's sense of community. It may be a community unjustly and erratically governed; that is not denied. But it is a community in which man, though maltreated, is not maltreated alone; a common suffering unifies as strongly as a common purpose. The system may be in one sense an imposition, like the Articles of War, in another a defence-mechanism, like the feverish activity at the weathering of Cape Horn; but whatever its cause, the effect is to construct a temporary civilisation, where beforehand in loneliness there had been only fear and withdrawal. Contrast the two views of the ship from aloft—the first Redburn's, when he ascended alone to the truck for the first time and saw the ship below him "like a long plank in the water, it did not seem to belong at all to the yard over which I was hanging"—and the second White-Jacket's, at violent combat with the Cape Horn gale, furling the mainsail in a surge of tempestuous foam and spray, with the sail flapping madly beneath the numbed hands of the sailors as they struggled with the frozen yard—"Below us," he says, "our noble frigate seemed thrice its real length—a vast black wedge, opposing its widest end to the combined fury of the sea and wind." There is no mistaking the exaltation in that passage, nor its source in the common endeavour that is so conspicuous an advance upon the shrinking isolation which it supersedes.

And it is in a few pages scattered here and there about *White-Jacket* that it is possible to recognise for the first time Melville's awakening consciousness of his place in his own country's history. He had imagined Vivenza in *Mardi*; the theme makes an important reappearance here. To most Americans of Melville's day, and especially of the decade in which he had begun to write, it was given at one time or another to voice more or less deliberately an irrepressible national pride. This had its origin in part in a legitimate satisfaction with the expressed democratic ideals of the United States that were still less than a century established, but even more in a haunting fear that the promise of this youthful nation was being vitiated by a rootless culture, a literary and artistic tradition unworthy as yet of the aspirations the community was daring. Melville, coming a little late into the field, with experience only of the shipboard and primitive peoples, vented his identification with this common uneasiness very modestly and slowly. In the next chapter I shall examine at some length how his art came ultimately to be as deeply absorbed in the national problem as even Emerson's had been or as Whitman's was later to be. Here it is enough to point to a section in *White-Jacket* set (significantly perhaps, at the point where his most spontaneous emotion of pity was most eloquently called out) at the end of his longest passage upon the custom of flogging; a section in which the destiny of young America is lyrically invoked, and the realisation expressed that in this rising nation lies the hope of the corrupt world. Ironically, a hundred years later, we may look back and consider his words; ironically, if we please, we may set up against them our own contrasted view of an America still potential for good and evil, and still as much a vision of hope as for others it may be a vision of despair. ''God has predestinated, mankind expects,'' writes Melville in an ecstasy, a century ago, ''great things from our race; and great things we feel in our souls. The rest of the nations must soon be in our rear. We are the pioneers of the world: the advance guard, sent on through the wilderness of untried things, to break a new path in the New World that is ours. In our youth is our strength; in our inexperience, our wisdom . . . And let us always remember,'' he concludes (if I may be forgiven for saying so, ominously) ''that with ourselves, almost for the first time in the history of earth, national selfishness is unbounded philanthropy; for we cannot do a good to America but we give alms to the world.''

Let us pardon Melville for his patriotic extravaganza: for it points even more significantly to his own maturing consciousness. He is coming home from sea; and when he lands from the *Neversink* he says good-bye to it for ever. But he has built up its lessons into an ordered cosmogony which, beginning with innocence and its destruction by experience, drew on to pity and to tragedy, and has now learned the complex principles of democratic community. These reinforcements brought a new assurance into his art. The scepticism we remarked in *Mardi* never disappeared; but his experience and his imagination modified it.

CHAPTER VIII

Melville and Hawthorne

W ITH *White-Jacket* Melville at last found himself integrated in a tradition of which up till then he had been conspicuously independent. His loneliness both at home and on board ship had perhaps been partly unrealised; but the salient significances in the episodes of the callow and ignorant Redburn, the irresponsible footloose Tommo, the willing but unacceptable White-Jacket, leave as unmistakable a savour of isolation as the fantastic adventures of Taji leave a sense of unreality. The loss of home and friends, the onset of hostile experience, in the autobiographical romances, are balanced by the uncertainty of control of the symbol in the imaginative prose-poem. Melville in his shipboard university was learning by hard rule of thumb; his physical absence from the contact of his native land, and his more intelligent and sensitive countrymen, deprived him, at a particularly formative period of his writing life, of just that awareness of the national imaginative atmosphere as is necessary to a man if his contribution to the national culture is to have any lasting relevance. Accordingly, for the first and most impressionable period of his life, Melville built his myth and his symbol out of his own restricted personal adventures. Because his search for the primitive societies of the South Seas happened to coincide with a popular intellectual demand for simplicity of life to counteract the complexity of modern materialism—a demand that was answered by Emerson out of Concord, by Thoreau out of Walden, by Whitman out of Brooklyn —*Typee* and *Omoo* had seemed more to accord closely with tradition than the author could ever have realised. The erratic symbolism of *Mardi* made it plain both to Melville and to his public that he depended on nothing but an eccentric inventiveness for the power of his symbol. For *Redburn* and *White-Jacket* Melville retreated to the safe lodging of his own minute observation of hard fact, revealing in the process an unexpectedly enhanced capacity for isolating the significant detail and, if necessary, inventing it.

By the time he wrote *White-Jacket* he had been on shore for five years and had had time to absorb the 'feel' of the age. He had married a daughter of the Chief Justice of Massachusetts and made his home in New York, where he seems with characteristic vigour to have read as copiously as he had written and made several valuable contacts in the publishing world, as well as making a voyage to England and Europe. Later, in 1850, he moved out with his family to Pittsfield in the Berkshires, where in an old farmhouse which he named Arrowhead he wrote *Moby Dick*; but during the important five years in which he tried out and established his individual symbols, he was set firmly in an alert and bookish society teeming with the current preoccupations, the fashionable jargon, the ideas and ideals common to a society aware that it had survived a dangerous transplantation and must now set about justifying it.

It was only natural in the 'thirties and 'forties of the last century that this awakening civic consciousness of the American people should, after over half a century of admirable speechifying about democracy and the rights of man, have become articulately aware of the need for a national creative literature. Sydney Smith in 1820[1] had distinguished himself in the *Edinburgh Review* by the tactless question "In the four quarters of the globe, who reads an American book?" Emerson,[2] the most illustrious of the following generation of American thinkers, was well aware of the nature of the imaginative crisis at which his country (and he particularly, one of its acknowledged leaders) now found itself. "In history," he wrote, "the great moment is when the savage is just ceasing to be a savage . . . that moment of transition." He added a warning that other contemporary writers omitted; that "the foam hangs but a moment

---

[1] Quoted by F. O. Matthiessen, *American Renaissance*, p. 372.
[2] Quoted by F. O. Matthiessen, op. cit.

on the wave: the sun himself does not pause on the meridian, literature becomes criticism, nervousness, and a gnawing when the first musical triumphant strain has waked the echoes."

In this crowded formative hour when American literature was struggling into self-consciousness, Melville read Shakespeare through, apparently for the first time. This had far-reaching consequences not only in his style, his breadth of allusion and his ironic acceptance of the most diverse and diffuse elements in experience, but also in his relationship with his fellow-Americans who were busy discovering Shakespeare, and particularly the national Shakespeare, for themselves. For the needs of the American people for a creative literature were expressed emotionally in the specific desire for a single national poet. They cast longing and envious eyes back at Stratford-on-Avon; they made no bones about their eagerness to emulate it. They were English-speaking, and those who had any culture at all had an English culture; they looked for a national literature after the English kind. This self-consciousness is characteristic of an immature society growing up among the remnants of an older civilisation from which they have broken away, of whose decadence they are suspicious, but of whose cultural achievements they are openly envious. Two nations only in the nineteenth century, America and Russia, were in the ripe condition to feel and express this particular sense of confident aspiration.

The American self-consciousness was at its intensest in New England (whose very name instituted a comparison), where all progressive idealism had its home. Emerson reduced it to logic and in his lecture *The American Scholar*, and elsewhere, gave it all the oracular authority of his nation-wide pulpit; the great Boston literary cliques disseminated it in their writings and their speeches and their conversations; but it was left to the subtle, rather tentative genius of Hawthorne to infuse it delicately into a literary form where it would be neither dogmatic nor obtrusive.

At the time when Melville became aware of him, Hawthorne, who had matured slowly and rather late, was well on in his forties; although he had been writing for twenty years, he was only just entering upon the short productive period of about six years which was to contain all that was most important in his work. A shy, reserved character who lived for much of his life as a virtual recluse at Salem, Hawthorne was fifteen years Melville's senior and arrived at middle age without publishing anything beyond one anonymous and inconsiderable novel and two editions of sketches and stories entitled *Twice-told Tales*, in which curious imaginative fantasies rubbed shoulders with a remarkable series of intense little narratives built round legends of the earliest days of the American colonists, when the first Puritan communities were developing into organised provinces. In 1846, when he was forty-two, and when Melville at twenty-seven was just putting out his first book, *Typee*, Hawthorne published another series of similar sketches, this time entitled *Mosses from an Old Manse*. His next six years were unusually fruitful. In 1850 *The Scarlet Letter* appeared, a most skilful and effective expansion to full novel length of an episode which he might well have used for one of the *Twice-Told Tales*; in 1851 there followed *The Snow Image*, more short stories of the *Mosses* variety, and his next important novel, *The House of the Seven Gables*; and in the next year came the ambitious *Blithedale Romance*. He lived until 1864; but in the last twelve years of his life he published only two more books[1]—one *Our Old Home*, a set of impressions of England gathered while on consular duties at Liverpool, and the other his last completed novel, about contemporary life in the artists' quarter in Rome, *The Marble Faun*.

That is a skeleton outline of Hawthorne's literary career: it is the quality of the imagination inspiring it rather than of the artistic skill expressing it that engages the attention of sensitive minds to-day. And since there was an element in that imagination to which Melville's instantly responded, it is of some interest to pursue it. In the course of years it gave colour to Melville and took in turn some colour back from him. Their association is one of the most tantalising in the history of literature. We know very little of it; yet in tracing what we can we are at work on a far wider field than the bare chronicles of two similar and dissimilar minds. In the persons of these two remarkable solitaries two poles of creative inspiration bend together for a while and then part company. That parting signifies incompatibilities far deeper than the idiosyncrasies of a pair of imperfect artists could warrant alone.

But their first meeting is just as significant. At least Melville's first overt acknowledgment of Hawthorne's importance is. It was the summer of 1850. He had just moved out to Pittsfield. He did not know at the time that Hawthorne was a distant neighbour of his at Lenox and was reading him at the same time as he was reading

[1] Apart from two small volumes designed for children's reading.

Hawthorne. Evert Duyckinck, Melville's friend, editor, and literary patron, seems to have chosen this way of bringing them together, for he sent Hawthorne a set of Melville at the same time as he commissioned from Melville an article on the *Mosses* for the *Literary World*. Hawthorne had earlier reviewed *Typee*, but now he read *Mardi* and *White-Jacket* for the first time. Melville, knowing nothing of this, plunged into the *Mosses* with the enthusiasm of first discovery, and dashed down his essay there and then. It is a curious thing that the *Mosses*, which are only spasmodically remarkable, should have called out from Melville such a valuable statement as this article, which as a piece of writing it would be kind to call indifferent but as evidence of a major imaginative recognition is of cardinal importance. The *Mosses* acted upon Melville's responsive curiosity with catalytic effect.

"A man of a deep and noble nature," he cried, "has seized me in this seclusion. His wild witch-voice rings through me." And again, "I am Posterity, speaking by proxy—and after times will make it more than good, when I declare that the American who up to the present day has evinced in literature, the largest brain with the largest heart, that man is Nathaniel Hawthorne." These are merely adulatory fanfares, not in themselves criticism, though auxiliary to a true critical judgment; and it is characteristic of Melville that he should approach what is actually the most significant passage of his essay by the most daring traverse of all—a comparison, half-apologised for, between Hawthorne and Shakespeare. To be sure he picked on one particular element only; what he called "the infinite obscure of the background" against which Shakespeare contrived his grandest effects; and to this he attached his perceptive approval, to "that undeveloped and sometimes undevelopable yet dimly-discernible greatness," that he recognised in Shakespeare and also in Hawthorne.

There follows his hint of an apology, reinforced by a well-directed thrust at Shakespeare's countrymen for their unconditional adoration of their poet. "This absolute and unconditional adoration of Shakespeare has grown to be a part of our Anglo-Saxon superstitions. The Thirty-Nine Articles are now Forty. Intolerance has come to exist in this matter. You must believe in Shakespeare's unapproachability or quit the country." Well and good, this is a healthy gibe. And here lies its importance: for it will be observed that we are (for the moment) forgetting Hawthorne altogether, and that a sudden note of nationalist asperity is creeping into a voice that was apparently all set to breathe o'er Eden.[1]

"But what sort of belief is this for an American, a man who is bound to carry republican progressiveness into literature as well as into life? Believe me, my friends, that men not very much inferior to Shakespeare are this day being born on the banks of the Ohio. And the day will come when you shall say, Who reads a book by an Englishman that is a modern?"

There is Sydney Smith's answer: it has a defiant brutality in it which is naïve, but stimulating. And Melville went boldly on, urging the American reading public to prize and cherish its native writers—an admirable exhortation—and

"while America has good kith and kin of her own to take to her bosom let her not lavish her embraces upon the household of an alien. For believe it or not, England after all is in many things an alien to us. China has more bonds of real love for us than she":

a still more pointed if perhaps more questionable series of sentiments.

This essay is full of jolts. He goes on to approve the praise of American mediocrity in preference to foreign excellence: and to confess grudgingly that more discriminating praise has been given to Americans by Englishmen than by their own countrymen. This blend of chauvinism and generosity has hardly had time to convince a reader that Melville's true critical faculty has suddenly been commanded by an impulse beyond his control, before he has delivered an attack on those American authors who are content to write within their powers (he meant, primarily, Irving) and stigmatised them as "appendices to Goldsmith". "Let us away with this leaven of literary flunkeyism towards England," he says. "If either must play the flunkey in this thing, let England do it, not us. While we are rapidly preparing," he continues with terrifying prescience, "for that political supremacy among the nations *which prophetically awaits us at the close of the present century*", (italics mine: he strayed a little in his dates, but no matter), "in a literary point of view we are deplorably unprepared for it."

---

[1] Even, apparently, Martin Chuzzlewit's.

He is leading up to Hawthorne again; and in the ensuing passage he hails him, in effect, as the Messianic embodiment of the crowning imaginative consciousness of America, that was to bequeath to that aspiring nation the Stratford-on-Avon myth which their emotion so badly craved. Melville himself had done his best by the adventitious linking of the two great names so early in his essay: he could do no more now than use all his heat and eloquence to set the desired renascence in movement. He began by hailing Hawthorne as a genius, by declaring his own passionate admiration for this man whom he had never met and, he added, "perhaps never shall" (not knowing he was living barely half a dozen miles away) and by drawing his imagined portrait of Hawthorne by a quotation from Hawthorne's own book describing the man who sought for Truth at the Intelligence Office.

Delighted with this sudden and unexpected recognition of a portentous genius, Melville did not wait to finish the *Mosses* before starting on his essay; and he was astonished when next day he turned to the sketches that remained unread and found in some of them—and especially in the two famous pieces *A Select Party* and *Young Goodman Brown*—a conclusive endorsement of his own intuitions. For *A Select Party* dealt fantastically with the very topic on which Melville had the day before spent so much patriotic fervour; with the foreshadowing of the nameless and perhaps yet unborn poet whose destiny it would be to speak for America as Shakespeare spoke for England. Melville felt this as a happier answer to his rhetorical question than he could possible have anticipated. "I cannot but be charmed by the coincidence; especially when it shows such a parity of ideas between a man like Hawthorne and a man like me." And on a development of this note the essay concludes, foretelling the day of the Master Genius of the race, suggesting that his commanding mind might never be individually developed in any one man, and yet contriving to couple in a reader's mind at the end of the essay the two closely inter-related ideas of the unknown national poet and the familiar Nathaniel Hawthorne.

How far Hawthorne deserved these particular attributions is not the present question. Melville's whole essay was rather a plunge, the hit-or-miss gesture of an untidy mind backed, in his case, by unusually astute intuitive powers. When he wrote it he had read Hawthorne, but only sketchily. He had never met him and never expected to. Later they did meet, and became, as nearly as their rugged and recluse natures would allow, close friends. Later still, under some pressure from circumstances but still more, I fancy, from consciousness of the inadequacy of each of them to satisfy the inner idealisms of the other, they parted, desultorily enough. Superficially Melville left so little of an impression on Hawthorne's life that fifteen years after Hawthorne's death Henry James was able to write his biography without mentioning Melville's name. On Melville the association and its decline acted more profoundly.

For Melville, with all his superbly vigorous imagination and his power to convey the immediacy of his experience, was a writer without roots. Education aboard ship is not to be compared with education on land. The impact of a seaman's experience is at once more violent, and more universal, and less cultural in the exact sense than a landsman's. The seaman's ancestors have been drowned, not buried: their bones do not enrich his own tradition. A seaman's authority is elemental, a landsman's local; and to an imaginative writer the *genius loci* with all that it implies is an incalculable reinforcement. The seaman is denied it.

Melville found in Hawthorne the satisfaction of his own unconscious need. A poet, even a great poet, cannot arrogate to himself the spokesmanship of a society, especially a great national and cultural society passionately aware of its tradition, like nineteenth-century America, unless he has succeeded in perfecting for himself a symbolic form appropriate to the inheritance he is assuming. The example of Shakespeare was of course conspicuous to any American likely to try; so, too, was Milton, an even more conclusive test. Shakespeare with the instinct of genius had harnessed a nervous and restive talent to the great symbolic theme of the stabilisation of an English dynasty, and made of his histories at once a poetic discipline and a national revelation; while Milton, embodying in his own voice the accents and angers of that Puritan class and culture which were to dominate English (and indeed American) thought in one way or another for centuries, chose his theme and his treatment of it from the Puritan Bible and invested the middle-class revolution with a dignity that both befitted and belied it. The great Americans had difficulty in doing likewise. Emerson, for example, could preach to America, but could not fairly represent her; his didacticism made it impossible for him to submit his imagination to the necessary hypnotism under which all great creative work is shaped. Edgar Allan Poe, erecting for himself a second-hand symbolism without power to communicate his undoubted individual genius, dissipated a remarkable poetic intensity in pseudo-Gothic sentimentalism; and later in the century the exhaustless energy and humanity of Whitman ran into the sands of an engulfing formlessness, resulting from an inability to construct any symbolism at all to give form and direction to his inspiration.

It was in this creation of a significant myth—significant both by personal and by national standards—that lay the attraction that Melville recognised in Hawthorne. Though he does not and perhaps could not define it, his express preoccupation throughout this unusual essay implies it. In recognising Hawthorne's profound though restricted powers Melville came to realise his own, and found through his appreciation of the origins of Hawthorne's art a substitute for his own rootlessness. Hawthorne "happened" to Melville at a critical moment in his development, when his technical powers were maturing and his multitudinous data were being marshalled for the major exercise of the imagination that could not be avoided for much longer, even though the try-out of *Mardi* had not been altogether a success. When he began in 1850 to consider a successor to *White-Jacket*, he had fortified himself with Shakespeare and he had assimilated his first impressions of Hawthorne. In his then state of creative responsiveness Hawthorne acted upon him, as I said, as a catalyst.[1]

For Hawthorne accentuated, as no other American writer living or dead could do, the mysterious value of the symbol, which hitherto Melville had used involuntarily or imperfectly. That Hawthorne's symbols were utterly different from his only made their effect on him far greater. Hawthorne found his symbolism far from the sea, in local legend and superstition, in provincial history, in domestic architecture, in habit and custom and rule. A family secret, a tribal ritual, a local tradition, were enough to drive him curiously deeper within himself, to turn his subtle mind to a

---

[1] Recently discovered letters have revealed that *Moby Dick* was written twice: first, between February and August 1850, as a straightforward account in the manner of *White-Jacket* of Melville's whaling adventures; then, between September 1850 and October 1851, in its present form. There may therefore be significance in the fact that it was on 5th August 1850 that Melville and Hawthorne met for the first time. (See F. B. Freeman: *Melville's "Billy Budd"*, p. 98.)

dramatisation that should set the custom or the problem in its due relation to right and wrong. There can be no question of the power which these moral preoccupations of Hawthorne's infused into his chosen symbols. It was that power, with its stunning effect, that captured Melville at once. He recognised its authority and his own desire to emulate it. Yet it is at the same time necessary to insist upon the essential differences between them, not only in the symbols which they selected but in the manner of their use. Hawthorne at this impressionable time exercised such a fascination over Melville that the ultimate divergences of character and achievement are even more significant than the likenesses. To appreciate the nature of Hawthorne's imagination is to begin to understand Melville's—more by contrast than by comparison.

Herbert Read has denied that Hawthorne was basically a Puritan. He quotes in support the awesome authority of Henry James, who regarded Hawthorne's Puritanism as an imported rather than an inherited characteristic. It needs temerity to question these authorities; but there can be no gainsaying Hawthorne's inherent obsession (like Graham Greene's to-day) with the idea of the ubiquity of sin; this was an element of his imaginative nature too fundamental to be anything but an essential basic ingredient in the whole man. Sin and its consequences provide the whole scene and action of *The Scarlet Letter*; are themselves the living and pervasive atmosphere of *The House of the Seven Gables*; are repeatedly hinted at and drawn upon for the main tragic undertone in *The Blithedale Romance*, where the voluptuous Zenobia for one is drawn with the relish akin to disgust so characteristic of Puritan denunciation; and hang in a cloud of preoccupation and foreboding over the lives of all the intertwined characters in *The Marble Faun*. Moreover this obsession appears in even more explicit forms in the shorter allegories, like *The Birthmark* and *The Minister's Black Veil*, as well as in the uneasy haunting witchcraft symbolism of such fantasies as *Feathertop* and *Young Goodman Brown* (one of the sketches remarked upon by Melville, and distinguished by terrifying imaginative power and effect). In another sketch, *Ethan Brand*, whose central figure was mistakenly believed to have been based on the character of Melville,[1] the suicidal sense of sin self-induced in the lonely and sensitive man is expressed in that tendentious

[1] It has now been conclusively proved that this would have been impossible. The story was printed before the two men ever met.

and highly characteristic Puritan manner where power and prejudice unite to get the better of imaginative pity.

Whether Hawthorne was a Puritan or not, there can be no doubt
that it was from Puritan ancestry and environment that he derived
this profoundly Puritan obsession. In this context life was resolved
into the struggle between Right and Wrong, with an inevitably
tragic issue attending upon a moment's weakness. It was this
Puritan ancestry that had conditioned Hawthorne's home atmosphere; it thwarted his creative imagination by engendering a
hypertrophic timidity which drove him away from the main
currents of contemporary life. Thus his curious imagination drove
most readily upon the symbolisms of the early colonizers, whose
Province-House and fierce steeple-crowned Governors represented
for him the strictness of an authority which he did not encounter
in his own concrete experience. In the domination of a primitive
society by a dark and uncompromising religion he discovered the
one myth to which he could make his only ready and fruitful
response. The pitiable uncertainty of touch which characterises
the concrete detail of those passages in *The Blithedale Romance* or
The House of the Seven Gables where he has to stray from his central
theme is a conspicuous contrast to the enormous resources of
imaginative strength which he could command when he turned
inwards to his ancestral and spiritual roots. He found in his circumscribed premises an inexhaustibly fertile field of imagination. Within
restrictions which were almost stifling he used his symbol superbly.

He took over ready-made from his forbears a set of oppressive
dogmas of sin and retribution, that his own tentative humanism
would never have conceived for itself. He adapted his symbols
to its over-riding sanctions; out of a system of ethics not of his own
devising he conjured little allegories of disproportionate power.
The rigidity of his limits suited him; he set his tales within the
bounds of a tiny province, a self-contained village, a Brook Farm
community, and into an infinitesimal compass he compressed
an evocative and sympathetic power of imagination that in such
dimensions and in such degree verges often upon the horrific. His
finest work is in these short sketches; finest because best representative of a fascinated imagination that could create art out of the very
contemplation of its own destruction.

Hawthorne's creative nature was diametrically opposed to
Melville's; with Hawthorne it was not the symbol that provided

the initial impetus. Melville's ardour kindled, he hardly knew why, at the sight of the rigging, the whale-boat, the living whale; Hawthorne's imaginative vitality sprang not from the contemplation of a legend of witchcraft but from the irresistible recoil of his total being from contact with mankind. With great skill he harnessed a symbolic imagination as auxiliary to that recoil, and in doing so created great allegory and achieved at times moments of truly tragic austerity. The culmination of the doom on the house of Pyncheon, for example, is not unworthy to be mentioned in the same breath with the doom on the house of Atreus. This alignment of New England tragedy with Greek may be of value in accentuating one aspect of Greek drama sometimes overlooked, namely the highly *moral* and restrictive nature of much of the Greek tragic convention—one which might have lain heavy on modern drama had not Shakespeare's creative charity liberated it. Its bitter implications are everywhere in Hawthorne's finished work; his characters have a ghoulishness reminiscent of the witchcraft lurking in the old legends that fed his fascinated art. All the portents taught his imagination that the reward of sin was to be preyed on in life and death; his delicate fancy obeyed this precept and raised primitive horror out of the common traffic of daily life; and his imagination, the residual independence at the heart of the artist, was powerless to exorcise it.

It must be repeated that it was Hawthorne's power, not his purpose, that captivated Melville, burst upon him at a crucial point in his difficult development and revealed to the responsive artist in him far more than the author (or the excited reader) of the *Mosses* could have guessed at that first moment of recognition. Awareness of Hawthorne came upon a Melville still unsure of his powers, experimental. Almost overnight it matured him. The catalytic action once accomplished, a new substance was created in the imaginative process of the younger writer. Yet it was quite independent of belief or acceptance of belief; Hawthorne's philosophy, which rejected more than it accepted, could never have been entertained by Melville. His art had no place for the implicit censoriousness that restricts Hawthorne's charity. He recoiled from the confined parochialism; like the sea itself, Melville's imagination always accepted more than it rejected. It followed that the sense of sin did not bother him; he saw the oppression of the universe less personally and less restrictively. Right and wrong were not issues that ever interested Melville deeply; what exercised him was the far more primitive, far more elemental conflict of good and evil.

To point the comparison it will be necessary to anticipate a little. Melville's concentration upon good and evil exempted him from the oppressive confinement into which Hawthorne's obsession with right and wrong had driven him. The expansion, both in scope and profundity, of Melville's creative imagination more than compensated for technical crudities and failures of restraint which the older artist would never have allowed. Consequently his tragedy bites deeper than Hawthorne's, unearths more ruthlessly the springs of pity that only instinctive wisdom and great poetic insight can trace. Consider the contrast implicit in their two greatest tragic figures, Hester Prynne and Captain Ahab. They are both destroyed, and destroyed inevitably, by the tragedies inseparable from their creators' philosophies of life; but whereas Hester is driven by her sense of guilt into a negative acquiescence in the restrictions society has set for her, Ahab is forced by single-minded defiance of the evil principle into the inevitable nihilism attendant upon monomania. Hester is the "good" character victimised by submission to a convention in which she hardly recognises the evil; Ahab, not only recognising the evil but fighting it to the death with his bare hands, suffers the terribly ironic fate of absorption in the very evil he is seeking to destroy. His is the profounder tragedy, and its relevance increases with the passage of history.

Temperamentally, the two men were only spasmodically compatible. The adventurous independence of the one struck the timidity of the other as an irritating irresponsibility. The enthusiasm seems to have been all on Melville's side; he dedicated *Moby Dick* to Hawthorne "in token of my admiration for his genius," and Hawthorne, while genuinely admiring the younger man's work, kept clear of any trace of its influence. Perhaps by that time his tenuous talent was too deeply settled in its ways to change; he was nearly fifty, and much of his best work was done. Melville drew from the association a not altogether happy strain of warm parochialism unbecoming to Ishmael. Much of *Pierre* shows strong evidence of this, and so do some of the later sketches of American life and custom in semi-jocular, semi-allegorical form—*I and My Chimney, The Apple-Tree Table, Jimmy Rose. The Confidence-Man*, too, is an unmistakable by-product of the friendship. Yet none of these surface resemblances can be worthily commensurate with the initial revelation, the flash of intuitive vision that descended upon Melville when, at the end of his apprentice period, casting about in his mind for an adequate vehicle for expression of the dynamic matter that was harrying him to let it out if he could only find a way, he read the *Mosses* and was given what he most lacked; a tradition, a purpose for the symbol. Nothing that Melville wrote after he encountered Hawthorne could resemble in essence anything that he had written before. He acquired depth, purpose, shape. Hawthorne's numinous sense of family, of village community, of national idiosyncrasy, of an all-embracing and universal law governing all, provided the homeless disinherited rover with just that sense of security, physical, imaginative and technical, that his vigorous art had lacked. It pinned his dynamic energy into a controlled significant shape. It taught him to create from his familiar symbol a myth adequate to sustain the violence of his imagination. Hawthorne liberated in Melville hitherto unsuspected powers; and the first and finest result was *Moby Dick*.

It was not long before they parted, Hawthorne to become American Consul at Liverpool, Melville to pursue an erratic career of feverish creativeness and deep disappointment before he settled down in a minor Custom-House post. They met once more in Liverpool a few years before Hawthorne's death, when Melville was on his way back from the East. They went for a melancholy walk along the sands at Southport as the light faded; and next day they took of each other a rather spiritless farewell. That was the last; when Hawthorne died in 1864 Melville had seen him only once in eleven years. Yet the sorrow touched him deeply enough for him to write:

> " *To have known him, to have loved him*
> *After loneness long;*
> *And then to be estranged in life*
> *And neither in the wrong;*
> *And now for death to set his seal—*
> *Ease me, a little ease, my song!*"

With the natures they bore it is difficult to see how otherwise their friendship could have ended. Each was the other's complement. Between them, they answered that national call which each of them had made; they can be seen to-day, jointly, as the authentic representation in great art of a great national consciousness.

How that consciousness dawned upon Melville, how the total revelation brought him to complete maturity, must now be traced. It gave him a new confidence, that swelled, at times when he was to need it most, into an admirable courage. Hawthorne's brilliant exposition of the problem of evil awakened a fierce curiosity in Melville himself; holding to the comforts of no settled creed, he was to stand at the mercy of the ambiguous perplexities with which the terrifying immanence of evil was constantly confronting him; yet by facing it desperately and creatively he used that perplexity well. Ironically enough, a phrase that might most fittingly be Melville's epitaph was one of Hawthorne's own—"A man's bewilderment is the measure of his wisdom." If Hawthorne's poetic intuition taught him to utter it, it failed to teach him to live it; he ended his life weary and frustrated, tinkering with four novels and making headway with none; but Melville exemplified it more conspicuously than any American, with a consistent and admirable integrity. Even in those of his books that are patent failures there is never a sign of a failure in intellectual or spiritual courage. Rather than abide in a harbour he distrusted, he would scuttle himself or put to open sea. His philosopher Plotinus Plinimmon in *Pierre* stopped preaching for good, for he saw the futility of fixed principles. "In landlessness alone resides the highest truth," cried Melville in *Moby Dick*, approving passionately "the intrepid effort of the soul to keep the open independence of her sea." Fixed principles smacked to Melville of escapism, of ready-made second-hand makeshift substitutes for right action. When a man had faced the open jaws of Moby Dick from a matchboard boat he knew the value of precepts clearly enough to see through them. Take no thought for the morrow, then; judge not, that ye be not judged; make your mind a thoroughfare for all thoughts, not a select party; a man's bewilderment is the measure of his wisdom; the readiness is all; call me Ishmael.

CHAPTER IX

Moby Dick: the Prelude

ALL ME Ishmael. The solitary is a visionary too, alone in his distress, but alone in his clarity. The loneliness is not a surprise; it had been hinted at more than once in the two books that preceded *Moby Dick.* The persecution of Jackson had set many of young Redburn's shipmates against him, and at last he found himself (the choice of name is revealing) "a sort of Ishmael in the ship"; and the apparent arbitrariness of the prejudice conceived by the sailors in the *Neversink* against the white jacket was an accentuation of the same imperceptible outlawry—an element in Melville's matured attitude to experience that is bound into every book after *Omoo.* The Eumenidean pursuit of Taji was being, in one form or another, prolonged into the lives and fortunes of all his other incarnations; he arrives at the threshold of his culminating experience a dispossessed solitary. From his own travels and adventures Melville had absorbed a patience and a wisdom that combined with his native imagination to give his response both relevance and power; from his national tradition, accepted almost solely through Hawthorne, he had derived an inestimable insight into the value and manipulation of the symbol and the myth. These lent to his solitude vision, poignancy, purpose; but no relief. *Moby Dick* begins and ends in loneliness; for all the crowded, dramatic hurly-burly of its absorbing human action it can be summed up without distortion as the hypnotised progress of the naked soul from the soured loneliness of misanthropy to the scared loneliness of death. Ishmael is discovered alone on land; he is left at the conclusion of the tragedy alone upon the sea.

This would be an unwarrantable simplification of Melville's most complex and subtle narrative were it allowed to stand unqualified. In fact Ishmael's private tragedy is not even the centre of the tale he himself tells; it is but lightly suggestive and symbolic of the profounder agonies at issue. The implications of this enormous myth appear at times almost illimitable, and to seize upon one to the exclusion or distortion of another is a temptation to which it is far too easy to yield. Yet Melville's choice of name and mood to open the story cannot be other than deliberate; and although we should do well to remember that the mood of spiritual exclusion in which Ishmael enters the story (paralleled by the very significant physical exclusion in which, as sole survivor of the *Pequod's* ship's company, he leaves it) is subordinate to the primary conflicts and purposes of the book, we nevertheless do right to remark it, for it establishes the universal tragedy in a personal setting of peculiar poignancy.

> "Whenever I find myself growing grim about the mouth," says Ishmael-Melville on the first page, "whenever it is damp, drizzly November in my soul; whenever I find myself involuntarily pausing before coffin-warehouses, and bringing up the rear of every funeral I meet; and especially whenever my hypos get such an upper hand of me, that it requires a strong moral principle to prevent me from deliberately stepping into the street and methodically knocking people's hats off—then I account it high time to get to sea as soon as I can."

The sentiment is true and understandable; only the expression of it is a little forced, the assumed jocularity a little strident. The Irving-Hawthorne tradition of essayists' whimsy was never an easy fit on Melville's less manageable genius; and the fanciful high spirits with which the first hundred pages of *Moby Dick* are sputteringly and spasmodically jerked into motion seem artificial and inappropriate once the main action of the story is comprehended and the tragic purpose is made clear. Superficially they produce in *Moby Dick* a curious dichotomy reminiscent of that more violent and damaging transition from realism to allegory in *Mardi*; and the unwary reader may be bewildered at the discordant conversion, in the later and greater novel, of the bantering picaresque of the early shore episodes into the oppressive prose drama of the whaling voyage. Essentially I believe the dichotomy to be an illusion[1]; once Ishmael's initial misanthropy can be assumed, the forced high spirits of the preliminary chapters can be readily accepted as a natural emotional reaction to his confessed state of careless cynicism —a temporary relief to a fretted nervous system that will only be stabilised when confronted by a spiritual problem worthy to engage it. The process was as involuntary and imperceptible to Melville as it was to Ishmael himself; yet because the spiritual identity of Melville with Ishmael at the outset of *Moby Dick* seems to have been a compact and fruitful one, the incongruity and the subsequent transition are as organic to the narrative as they are to the narrator, and the unity of the book is preserved rather than disturbed by it. There is a consistency in *Moby Dick* that *Mardi*, with that suggestion about it of having grown under the author's hand into something quite alien to its original plan, completely lacked; from the laconic first sentence, whose three charged words tell more than many novelists' whole introductory chapters, the sardonic levity conducts the reader, without his being aware of it, into the presence of the central symbol over which the life-and-death struggle of the spirit, that was the crisis of this book and of this part of Melville's life, is to be waged.

"Chief among these motives for undertaking a whaling voyage was the overwhelming idea of the great whale himself. Such a portentous and mysterious monster roused all my curiosity. Then the wild and distant seas where he rolled his island bulk; the undeliverable, nameless perils of the whale; these . . . helped to sway me to my wish. I am tormented with an everlasting itch for things remote. I love to sail forbidden seas, and land on barbarous coasts. Not ignoring what is good, I am quick to perceive a horror, and could still be social with it—would they let me—since it is but well to be on friendly terms with all the inmates of the place one lodges in.

"By reason of these things, then, the whaling voyage was welcome; the great floodgates of the wonder-world swung open, and in the wild conceits that swayed me to my purpose, two

---

[1] It is no doubt partly due to imperfections in the conversion of *Moby Dick* from straight narrative to its present form. (See p. 104 n.)

H

and two there floated into my inmost soul, endless processions of the whale; and midmost of them all, one grand hooded phantom, like a snow hill in the air.''

The portent of the White Whale is set in the head of his narrative; and though Melville-Ishmael may seem to digress among excited irrelevancies for the next hundred pages, expounding like Smollett or Marryat the crowded shore-passages at New Bedford or Nantucket with a brilliance of descriptive detail recalling the Liverpool section of *Redburn*, the first chapter remains as a warning in the memory. And Melville this time is assured of his own powers. He has found his symbol, feels and knows his control of it, restrains for the present a too liberal use of it until the acceleration of the action shall make it necessary. For the moment he hints at the whale, hints at unimaginable significances enshrouding it, and returns to the immediacy of his task—to prepare for the voyage.

Characteristically, he provides the lonely Ishmael with an unusual companion. Ishmael moves alone in his surly bravado through the crowded taverns and narrow alleyways of New Bedford and Nantucket—these realised with a Dickensian vividness that Melville at his intensest shares with no other American novelist—and finds in the squabble and squalor of these historic fishing-ports one man only to whom his soul goes out as to a brother—the South Sea Island cannibal Queequeg. Ishmael's meeting with Queequeg in the bedroom of the Spouter-Inn at New Bedford, their fast friendship, their shared meals and tobacco and night-watches and worship (for the savage attends the Whaleman's Chapel, and Ishmael in a scene of moving simplicity joins Queequeg in his obeisance before his little wooden idol) are all presented with a vigorous charm and humour which take the edge off the acerbity with which Ishmael had begun his adventure. By sweetening his mood these scenes render him receptive where before he had been resentful and suspicious; they correct his inadequacies, measure him up to the tragedy. Queequeg is a timely restatement of the ubiquity of that innocence with which Melville's life-work is preoccupied. The continuity of the theme through *Typee* and *Omoo* had been developed in *Mardi* and accentuated in *Redburn*; the sophistication of experience and human society, incidentally symbolised in *White-Jacket*, had blended in Melville's imagination with a deepening sense of tragedy for which his deep study of Shakespeare and Hawthorne was partly responsible, and under the oppression of which the primal innocence of Fayaway and Yillah had become necessarily remote. By the time he came to write *Moby Dick* he was compelled to recognise complexities of experience in face of which the original innocence as he had once realised it seemed inadequate and irrelevant; as the golden world of the Forest of Arden would seem inadequate and irrelevant on Lear's heath. Yet Melville knew, as Shakespeare knew, that without essential innocence tragedy cannot be faced and fought; and, I believe instinctively, he provided for Ishmael at the outset, for comparison, this personification of the old unsullied innocence of the Typees—Melville himself sensing the spiritual struggle ahead and taking with him into the battle the most precious element in his youthful experience.

Much is made in the first hundred pages of the blood-brother-hood of Ishmael and Queequeg; yet although Queequeg ships aboard the *Pequod* along with Ishmael and is prominent enough throughout the story in the various incidents of the voyage, the close relationship between the two is never again referred to. There may be an oblique irony in the fact that it is Queequeg's coffin, prematurely built for him in the extremity of his fever, that chances to save Ishmael alone from the wreck; but apart from this solitary hint, the central theme of the great prose-poem obliterates the earlier relationship for ever as soon as the *Pequod* starts upon her voyage. No deep significance need be read into this, not the only loose end in a book which by its very compendiousness could hardly hope to avoid them. The reason lies no further off than the unusual compulsiveness of the main theme, which allowed little room for subsidiary developments once its obsession had gripped the author as the obsession with the White Whale gripped Ahab.

The description of this quaint and endearing companionship establishes more appropriately the mood of personal readiness with which Ishmael shall dare the voyage; and Melville next sets about the preparation of the physical setting for the departure. Looming at the back of his mind, as *Mardi* and *White-Jacket* attested, and as his essay on Hawthorne's *Mosses* confirmed, was the enduring though hardly explicit desire to speak symbolically for his nation as he knew Shakespeare to have done and believed Hawthorne had the power to do. Leaving Hawthorne to extract from the rooted communities of New England the numinous significances that the old legends suggested, Melville fastened with sure instinct upon the sea and its borders from which to erect a parallel symbolism whose effect should be no less national. Where Hawthorne saw America (and the world) as a community of Puritanical and severely-disciplined pioneers, Melville's less circumscribed vision created the complementary image of a cosmopolitan seaboard redolent of the sea and the business and traffic of the sea. That Melville's national epic had of its nature to be worked out in the open sea far off from any continent imposed on him the increased necessity to establish an unmistakably native character to the point of departure—an individual magnetic quality which would inform the ship itself and never fail of its attraction in retrospect or prospect throughout the long voyage; so that wherever the ship might be upon the oceans of the world, it should yet effectively recall and suggest America.

He achieves this by accumulating his detailed and suggestive realism, as well as a superb short passage of lyrical meditation, upon the little port of Nantucket. The chapter on Nantucket is very short; but it is a beautifully-controlled piece of evocative prose. In less than a thousand words it suggests the curious terraqueous nature of the place; its identification with the sea on its doorstep, its virtual divorce from the remote and alien mainland. Its strange traditional investiture by Indian settlers; its centuries' old history of fishery and exploration, circumnavigation and (Melville of course retains this activity for the climax) whaling; its conquest by travel and commerce of the whole known globe, make Nantucket in Melville's eyes an intense representation of that America for which he speaks, a sandy spit of land far out from the shore yet harbouring in its few acres all the races and activities of the known world. Here the great continent is closest to the greater sea; is closest, then, in Melville's view, to the reality which is the chief matter of his life and his book.

"The Nantucketer, he alone resides and riots on the sea; he alone, in Bible language, goes down to it in ships; to and fro ploughing it as his own special plantation. *There* is his home; *there* lies his business, which a Noah's flood would not interrupt, though it overwhelmed all the millions in China. He lives on the sea, as prairie cocks in the prairie; he hides among the waves, he climbs them as chamois hunters climb the Alps. For years he knows not the land; so that when he comes to it at last, it smells like another world, more strangely than the moon would to an Earthsman. With the landless gull, that at sunset folds her wings and is rocked to sleep between billows; so at nightfall, the Nantucketer, out of sight of land, furls his sails and lays him to his rest, while under his very pillow rush herds of walruses and whales.''

He pins the imagination for the moment to the great American fishing-port, but in the last phrase he lets it go, as it had gone at the end of the first wry-mouthed chapter, to pursue the overpowering image of the whale. The obsession is inescapable; and a few pages earlier he had launched his narrative in the most sustained lyrical passage that he had yet dared in this book or in any other, down the monster's very throat. The skill of these preparatory passages can be too readily overlooked, either in irritation at their superficial incongruity or in impatience at the continued delay of the start of the whaling-voyage proper; but unless it is remarked and re-membered how the vision of the great central symbol of the book is first hinted at, then reiterated in countless small details (like the pictures on the inn-walls, the implements of the chase, and the very names of the taverns themselves,) as well as in constant oblique references to the whale itself, and finally expanded and elaborated in the great set piece of rhetoric in Chapter IX, the unusually subtle and effective marshalling of the two principal contestants for the conflict that begins with the sailing of the *Pequod* will not be fully appreciated. Man and the whale are to come to battle together; by his very familiarity man needs less of a build-up than the unusual symbol of the whale, and the detailed introduction of the central tragic hero can afford to wait. He will at most be representing the uncounted millions of humanity, for whom during the first chapters of the book Ishmael and Queequeg and their vociferous but anonymous fellow-guests and potential shipmates can stand. Meanwhile his adversary must attract from the reader—and this is Melville's chief purpose and completest achievement in those first important hundred pages—sufficient emotional wonder to elevate his image into a bulk and stature worthy to match up to an elemental strife such as Melville had undertaken. All that the careful insinuation of detail had left un-performed of this purpose is triumphantly achieved by the arresting oratory of Father Mapple's sermon.

This extended purple patch is very skilfully contrived to equate in the reader's imagination the image of the whale and the deeper emotions of religion. It was a stroke of genius on Melville's part to achieve his purpose by the adroit use of the classic scriptural apotheosis of the whale, the story of Jonah, and so to transmit to the reader an image heavily charged with the dramatic emotion with which the old hot-gospeller had electrified the familiar legend. But this is by no means all of the sermon's purpose. Read once superficially, it sweeps the receptive mind into ready acquiescence in the near-divinity of the whale itself, into acceptance of Leviathan as God's instrument and of Leviathan's receptive jaws as a kind of universal fate. This is truly enough one of its purposes; but it condenses as well as exalts. Father Mapple's sermon is more than a spontaneous lyric; it is an intricately compact statement of the theme of *Moby Dick* and the present preoccupations of Melville's creative mind. In Jonah there is traceable another Ishmael, with the timorousness of Redburn and the reckless defiance of Taji; more subtly and prophetically still, in Jonah there is predicted another Ahab who pits his will fatally against God's. "As with all sinners among men, the sin of this son of Amittai was in his wilful disobedience of the command of God, which he found a hard command." This deviation from the ordained purpose produces, in Jonah as in Ahab, a distortion in the soul; brilliantly conveyed by Melville in the truly Shakespearian conceit of the cabin-lamp—a passage new in its metaphysical quality in the progression of Melville's development and rich in fulfilled promise of similar triumphs of dramatic observation to follow close upon it.

"Screwed at its axis against the side, a swinging lamp slightly oscillates in Jonah's room; and the ship, heeling over towards the wharf with the weight of the last bales received, the lamp, flame and all, though in slight motion, still maintains a permanent obliquity with reference to the room; though, in truth, infallibly straight itself, it but made obvious the false, lying levels among which it hung. The lamp alarms and frightens Jonah; as lying in his berth his tormented eyes roll around the place, and this thus far successful fugitive finds no refuge for his restless glance. But that contradiction in the lamp more and more appals him. 'Oh! So my conscience hangs in me!' he groans, 'straight upward, so it burns; but the chambers of my soul are all in crookedness!' "

The preacher finds in the whale both a doom and a salvation.
The distorted soul of Jonah is condemned to the sea. "He goes
down in the whirling heart of such a masterless commotion that
he scarce heeds the moment when he drops seething into the
yawning jaws awaiting him, and the whale shoots to all his ivory
teeth, like so many white bolts, upon his prison." Yet even in that
deepest of all imprisonments as the whale sounds down to the
ocean-depths, there is salvation in repentance and in acknowledgment of the will of God.

"Then God spake unto the fish: and from the shuddering
cold and blackness of the sea, the whale came breeching up
towards the warm and pleasant sun, and all the delights of air
and earth, and vomited out Jonah upon the dry land; when the
word of the Lord came a second time; and . . . Jonah did the
Almighty's bidding."

In the surging peroration Melville poses the Christian alternative
to the still untried conflict that was to overwhelm Ahab and his
crew. The repentance of Jonah is the answer to the destructive
monomania of Ahab, had Ahab ever heeded its implications. As
it is, the sermon seems incidental merely, a time-waster before the
voyage starts, a conventional piece of pietistic eloquence that
moves but momentarily; yet there are lights and shadows in its
peroration that glance forward upon the main tragedy with deadly
ironic significance.

"Delight is to him who against the proud gods and commo-
dores of this earth, ever stands forth his own inexorable self . . .
Delight is to him who gives no quarter in the truth, and kills,
burns, and destroys all sin though he pluck it out from under the
robes of Senators and Judges. Delight, top-gallant delight is
to him, who acknowledges no law or lord, but the Lord his
God, and is only a patriot to heaven. . . . And eternal delight
and deliciousness will be his, who coming to lay him down, can
say with his final breath—O Father!—chiefly known to me by
Thy rod—mortal or immortal, here I die. I have striven to be
Thine, more than to be this world's, or mine own."

Set against this enunciation of the true doctrines of Christianity,
the fate of Ahab, "the ungodly, godlike man", is a sombre contrast,
and Father Mapple's sermon is a cogent comment upon it. For

Ahab's tragedy will be not to fall short of courage or inflexibility but to exceed in the pride and strength of his possession of them. He will stand forth his own inexorable and single-minded self, it is true; but he will not own any patriotic duty to heaven. Melville leaves this comment where it lies, embedded in Father Mapple's rhetoric and discarded in the high heats of the later tragedy. As Ishmael's fate and Ahab's fate came to their culmination, entwined inevitably for the present with Melville's own, the great peroration failed to find any response; it still fell upon their ears, if indeed it was remembered at all, as mechanical doctrine inadequate to the situation. Nevertheless, once propounded it remained unanswered through the book. Melville may have intended it so; that does not affect the power and relevance of this extraordinary passage, as organic to the masterpiece in whose head it is set as the fable of the Grand Inquisitor is to *The Brothers Karamazov* or as the great Catholic sermon is to *The Portrait of the Artist*. Read carefully before and after *Moby Dick*, as apologue and epilogue, Father Mapple's sermon never fails to provide new and unsuspected illumination.

The dimensions of the conflict are becoming clearer, as Melville assembles the chosen characters and their chosen characteristics with which he intends to venture into the main action of the book. The rootlessness of Ishmael is flanked by the steady innocence of Queequeg; the apparent carelessness of the one and singlemindedness of the other are in reality designed to converge upon the common object that is the core of the book, the pursuit of the whale. With the descriptions of New Bedford and Nantucket, particularly Nantucket, the theme is enriched by the two-fold image of place and nation, the ship's company lent continental dimensions to match the oceanic context of the enormous adversary they go out to combat. Lastly the discourse of Father Mapple hints at religious and philosophical implications that will be elaborated as the intensity of the drama grows; and throughout each and every one of these correlated elements in the preliminary chapters is interspersed with untiring cunning the detailed and variegated images of the whale.

Add to these elements the inescapable sense of mystery in which the chosen ship and its captain is enshrouded from the beginning, and we have all preparatory details that Melville considered necessary before the voyage proper could begin. Ahab at this crucial moment is a warning rather than a presence; hints of strange powers and stranger misfortunes, and of almost supernatural qualities of temperament and leadership, trickle through to the new men as they sign on board the *Pequod* for the long whaling voyage round the globe. The comic owners Bildad and Peleg, and their kindly sister Charity the Quakeress, relieve with admirable individuality the tension that resides in the very name and reputation of this unseen captain; but for all the comic vigour of the scenes of preparation, there is a sense of mysterious foreboding, heightened in one place by the warnings of the old crazed sailor Elijah and in another by the unexplained half-caught glimpse of flitting figures on the quayside at dawn. And this pervading presage is as dynamic a part of the essential atmosphere from which the voyage and its tragic action spring as any of the other elements that Melville had so carefully and skilfully assembled over the previous twenty chapters or so.

But before losing sight irrevocably of the land, Melville adds one profound touch; a six-inch chapter, as he calls it, stamping the context once and for all with his own personality, his own steady and courageous philosophy. The mysterious figure of Bulkington, a tall, quiet, reserved Southerner whom Ishmael had marked at New Bedford among a party of sailors new-landed from a prolonged whaling-voyage, is encountered again at the helm of the *Pequod* as the whaler pushes off finally from the shore. In three short paragraphs Melville loses his identity with Ishmael, his tragic sympathy with Ahab, his objective task as narrator of their joint fortunes; in this sudden lyrical glimpse of a character only momentarily observed before and (curiously enough) never to be mentioned again, Melville infuses into the seethe of the potential tragedy his own unmistakeable personality.

"The land seemed scorching to his feet. . . . Let me only say that it fared with him as with the storm-tossed ship, that miserably drives along the leeward land. The port would fain give succour; the port is pitiful; in the port is safety, comfort, hearthstone, supper, warm blankets, all that's kind to our mortalities. But in that gale, the port, the land, is that ship's direst jeopardy. She must fly all hospitality; one touch of land, though it but graze the keel, would make her shudder through and through. With all her might she crowds all sail off shore; in so doing, fights against the very winds that fain would blow her homeward; seeks all the lashed sea's landlessness again; for refuge's sake forlornly rushing into peril; her only friend her bitterest foe.

"Know ye, now, Bulkington?" (cries Melville in the exaltation of this penetrating sympathetic vision), "Glimpses do ye seem to see of that mortally intolerable truth; that all deep, earnest thinking is but the intrepid effort of the soul to keep the open independence of her sea; while the wildest winds of heaven and earth conspire to cast her on the treacherous, slavish shore?"

The lyricism is intensified. Melville begins to betray, for the first time in the book, signs of that fierce knotted Elizabethan eloquence which would seize him and his narrative at key points of the dramatic action. Like the summarizing soliloquy which frequently ends the act of a Shakespearian or Websterian drama, his exalted prose wrestles unequally with the inexpressible; compensating here, as in later and perhaps more striking passages, for its undoubted difficulty by its supercharged emotional force. At this strategic point of the action, the culmination of this passage is of challenging importance.

"But as in landlessness alone resides the highest truth, shoreless, indefinite as God—so better is it to perish in that howling infinite than be ingloriously dashed upon the lee, even if that were safety! For worm-like, then, oh! who would craven crawl to land? Terrors of the terrible! is all this agony so vain? Take heart, take heart, O Bulkington! Bear thee grimly, demigod! Up from the spray of thy ocean-perishing—straight up, leaps thy apotheosis!"

In that pregnant chapter, the "stoneless grave of Bulkington", Melville reiterates his renunciation of fixed principles, and emphasizes once more his open denial of the restrictive Puritan canons among which his ancestors, his own nation, and his own contemporaries were muscle-bound. By renouncing the safety of the land, by daring the independence of the ocean, he proclaims at the start of his story his reliance upon the integrity of the imagination alone; his creed to be his own pulses, on which each experience must be proved before he accepts or rejects it. Here, in the most courageous of his utterances, he parts company for ever with the allegorists who work to stated truths, with the moralists whose beliefs and actions are controlled by superimposed systems of thought, with all the restrictions upon the imagination which prejudices and preconceptions, however comforting or convincing, may imply. Here he splits off from Hawthorne even before he joins on to him. Here he prescribes for Innocence the only possible approach to Experience; which is not merely the courage never to submit or yield, but the far profounder courage to meet the unforeseen in the knowledge that there is no guide to it save the response of the individual imagination.

Translated into terms of art, this resolve is equivalent to a choice of the symbolic rather than the allegorical method. Melville declares his abandonment of restrictive preconceptions and feels his way into the future bereft of everything but his senses and his courage, embracing in Keats' phrase a life of Sensations rather than of Thoughts. Upon whatever his senses will encounter, his creative imagination will be allowed free play; for this is the essence of symbolism, that the concrete object shall first present itself to the receptive mind which in its creative exercise upon it shall contrive to penetrate the actuality to the universal significances beyond. The stoneless grave of Bulkington marks also the point at which Melville's ready imagination was finally possessed by the great symbol of the whale.

CHAPTER X

Moby Dick: the Symbol

THE SYMBOL of the whale is the living centre of this book, the living centre in fact of Melville's imaginative life. It marks the equation of his endeavour with his capacity, the successful matching of his adventurousness and his powers. It was appropriate enough that, concerned with the vastest problems to which human imagination can extend itself—man's fate, and his power to resist or fulfil it—he should have chosen the symbol of the vastest living creature known to man. The fascination of the whale had been on Melville ever since his whaling voyage in 1841. None of his earlier books is without a reference here and there either to the creature itself or to the practice of the fishery; they ran in his mind, he could not avoid the reminder, but for the present harvested up the detail for a longer book, in which the whaling voyage should have the principal place. Knowing when he came to write *Moby Dick* that his task was not so much to tell a story clearly as to erect a set of realistic facts to serve as a context for the exercise of his symbolic imagination, he knew that he was faced with the job of realising for his readers that very substantiality of the whale of which he, but not they, had had first-hand experience. Until its hundred-ton actuality could be faintly comprehended, no reader could be expected to see, with Melville, beyond it to the dimmer but profounder significances that it implied to him. The imagination of the genuine symbolic artist, as I have already suggested, works from the familiar object outwards. Melville's was no exception; but first he had to ensure at least the illusion, and at best the fact, of this necessary familiarity. A whale is for obvious reasons an object familiar to comparatively few people. If Melville sought to make of his whale a universal symbol, he had to submit it to a detailed dissection and description whereby his most casual reader would be as carelessly and intimately acquainted with the creature as he himself was; and into this somewhat clinical process he would be bound in addition to infuse at least some measure of the imaginative fascination which the object had always possessed for him. It was therefore his formidable task to communicate, by analysis and suggestion, to readers unfamiliar with the context, the profound imaginative significance to him of an unusual biological phenomenon and a highly specialised trade.

It is necessary to enter this apologia at some length because it has been, and still is, one of the readiest complaints about *Moby Dick* that the action is interspersed with tedious passages of technical and encyclopaedic matter about whales and whaling. It is difficult to understand how such complaints can be made in all seriousness. The prompt answer would be to have the passages cut out altogether; the book would be much shortened, and, to a reader coming to it for the first time, would be barely comprehensible, so essential to a vivid realisation of the action is an accurate understanding of the technical detail. It is only by tireless and insistent construction of his vast theme from its minutest particulars that the actuality of the picture acquires weight as well as the length and breadth which a relatively airy and easy description might at best have given it. And in all effective symbolic art— in Kafka's intricate law-processes as in Dostoevsky's elaborately-fashioned police investigations—communication of the ultimate imaginative vision is achieved in proportion to the degree of familiarity and palpability which the central symbol has been enabled to achieve. Compared with these, and with Maeterlinck and his blind travellers, or Rex Warner and his airmen, Melville was handicapped by having to manufacture his familiarity for himself. In the result he accomplished this with honour; and established his book in the process as a handbook of whaling that most vividly perpetuates for its readers a largely-superseded stage in the history of the great industry. In the loving care with which Melville assembles and lingers upon every recorded fact and detail of his topic is the secret of his success in redeeming the accumulation from tedium; it was indeed the most closely cherished enthusiasm of his maturity, and taking from it the material and inspiration of his greatest work, he seemed yet aware that he owed it more than he had ever put into it either by the sweat of his body or the agony of his brain; at the end of the chapter called "The Advocate", the earliest encyclopaedic disposition in *Moby Dick* of the factual headings of his theme, he breaks into the simple and touching apologia which nails this book even more conclusively to the centre of his imaginative life.

> "And, as for me, if by any possibility there be any as yet undiscovered prime thing in me; if I shall ever deserve any real repute in that small but high hushed world which I might be unreasonably ambitious of; if hereafter I shall do anything that, upon the whole, a man might rather have done than to have left undone; if, at my death, my executors, or more properly my creditors, find any precious MSS. in my desk, then here I prospectively ascribe all the honour and the glory to whaling; for a whale ship was my Yale College and my Harvard."

In this temper he set out with great skill to anatomize Leviathan. He is careful not to pack his factual exposition too closely in the opening of his narrative, for that would have made the presentation at once indigestible and top-heavy; and the early part of the tale, while shot through and through with hints and presages of the fascination and importance that the whale and the whale-fishery are to have in the life of Ishmael and his book, is free of any suggestion of academic aridity. The idea of the whale is infused, as in the little descriptive suggestions of the topic in the pictures in the Spouter Inn and the Twy-Pots, pictorially; or as in Father Mapple's discourse, dramatically. It is not until the *Pequod* is at sea and the tragic narrative is irrevocably launched that Melville interrupts it to lecture on the whale. In Chapter XXIV, "The Advocate", he defends the dignity of the whaling profession by an assertion, prolonged through three or four pages, of its historical importance, concluding with the noble and vigorous peroration that I quoted in the last paragraph; then leaves the whale and the principles of the chase once more to look after themselves while he carefully and artfully introduces the leading human characters who are to be

pitted, in this dramatic conflict, against the might of Moby Dick—
the three subtly-differentiated mates, Starbuck, Stubb and Flask,
and finally the great Ahab himself, held back by Melville for a
dramatic delayed entrance. Not until these four characters have
been introduced, deployed, set for a moment into a preliminary
action or two which shall reveal them in essence, and then with-
drawn into the greater unanimity of the ship, does Melville return
to a more comprehensive passage of exposition upon the monster
itself.

"Already we are boldly launched upon the deep," he says,
"but soon we shall be lost in its unshored, harbourless immensities. Ere that come to pass; ere the Pequod's weedy hull rolls
side by side with the barnacled hulls of the Leviathan; at the
outset it is but well to attend to a matter almost indispensable
to a thorough appreciative understanding of the more special
Leviathanic revelations and allusions of all sorts which are to
follow. It is some systematised exhibition of the whale in his
broad genera, that I would now fain put before you. Yet it is no
easy task. The classification of the constituents of a chaos,
nothing less is here essayed."

This is the opening of the formidable chapter on "Cetology"
which comes as near to encyclopaedic fact-feeding as ever Melville
was to come. Relieved in his own view by a touch of jocularity and
in ours by the absorbed enthusiasm with which his facts are classi-
fied, the catalogue unrolls through a dozen packed pages until the
whole compendious fleet of sea-beasts is brought slowly into review,
from the Sperm Whale and the Right Whale at the head of the
classification, through the Narwhal and the Killer down to the
Mealy-mouthed Porpoise. It is perhaps impossible to expect a
reader to carry all this information in his head, or even, in the heats
of the chases and conflicts which are to follow, to turn back and
refer to the classifications. This is ostensibly a novel, not a natural
history; and many receptive imaginations prefer an image to be
vaguely suggested to them rather than to be stated with unmistakeable clarity. Nevertheless the chapter on "Cetology" has done its
work: not so much by enabling a wide-awake reader to distinguish
a sperm whale from a right whale at sight, in narrative or actuality,
but by impregnating the mind a little more with that infectious
fascination with his subject which is Melville's incalculable

asset. It has imparted a little more necessary body to the inevitably nebulous idea of whales and whaling in the mind of the average reader; and Melville wisely leaves it at that once more. "I now leave my cetological system standing thus unfinished," he says at the end of this chapter, "even as the great Cathedral of Cologne was left, with the crane still standing upon the top of the uncompleted tower. . . . Heaven keep me from ever completing anything. This whole book is but draught—nay, but the draught of a draught."

He was wise in his instinct, to leave it incomplete, the artist's duty being to select and suggest, not to present the exhaustive facts. He transferred his speculative attention back to the ship. It was time for him to announce the particular, rather than the general, tragic theme. He therefore followed up his factual elaboration of his main topic with a careful concentration upon Ahab, and by way of variation, the ship's routine—a set of habits and customs some of which bore closely on the actual business of whaling and some of which did not, but which were as essential in their detailed accumulation to Melville's ultimate purpose as the biological particulars of the whale itself were to be. Through successive descriptions of meal-time routine in the cabin and the long watches at the mast-heads, Melville focuses down once more upon Ahab on his quarter-deck at the moment of his first proclamation to his crew of the real purpose and obsession of his voyage—to hunt down to death Moby Dick, the White Whale, the legendary killer who on Ahab's last voyage had robbed him of a leg and upon whom Ahab's vengeful hatred accumulates throughout the narrative with obsessional violence. Just as Ahab had been cunningly withheld from the centre of the stage until on his eventual appearance he seemed to take on an aspect and a stature larger than life, so the superhuman mystery of the White Whale itself is subtly suggested to the waiting reader partly by the intense elaboration of the scientific particulars about whales and whaling and partly by the increasing fervour of the action aboard the *Pequod*.

Therefore when the general image of the whale is crystallised into the particular image of Moby Dick, Melville has already advanced more than half way towards the achievement of his object. He had built up the generic idea of the whale until it had achieved a necessary familiarity in his readers' minds; he had introduced to confront it a working sketch—soon to be filled in with great vigour and minute detail—of a common whaling voyage. The two generalities thus established, he was to erect out of each a particular element destined under the hand of his creative imagination to attain levels of universality; on the one hand the godlike man in his wilful pride, on the other the godlike beast in its instinctive and hateful strength. By the end of the first volume of *Moby Dick* Melville had most admirably achieved the preliminary equation; and the effective final touches were administered in Chapters XL and XLI, superbly rounding off the conclusion of the first part of his task. Looking back upon the first volume from the supreme satisfaction of the end of the great book itself, the (perhaps unconscious) mastery of Melville's early preparation of his theme is even more apparent than it is in the course of experiencing it for the first time. The central theme of the novel can be arbitrarily summarized as a blend of the three main strands, Ishmael, Ahab, the whale. The first volume culminates in the successful fusion of these three; for while the thirty-nine preceding chapters have all in their random and fragmentary fashion been adding to our small accumulations of knowledge about all three of them (Ishmael being the centre of most of the first part, Ahab of the second, and the whale delicately pervading both), the fortieth chapter 'Moby Dick' is a close examination of the whale in its relationship to Ahab, and the forty-first 'The Whiteness of the Whale' is a most remarkable attempt to convey the extreme individuality of the whale's relationship to Ishmael. And coming as the last chapter of the first volume, this chapter on the Whiteness has every appearance of bearing not so much Ishmael's countersign as Melville's; it is worth close examination as evidence of the cast of mind in which Melville hunted his whale, which is the cast of mind in which his readers must approach him if his symbolism is to carry its full significance.

"There was another thought," says Ishmael-Melville, "a rather vague, nameless horror concerning Moby Dick, which at times by its intensity completely overpowered all the rest . . . it was the whiteness of the whale that above all things appalled me."

He proceeds to elaborate with great fertility and force his conception of the very idea of whiteness; allowing its quality of refining and enhancing beauty in ornament, jewel, or decoration, as well

I

as its suggestion of royal pre-eminence, of joy, of the innocence of virginity or the benignity of old age, of honour and justice and even of the holiest and sublimest divinity; yet reserving his innermost wariness for the essential idea of this hue, which "strikes more of panic to the soul than that redness which affrights in blood."

In this inevitable association of terror, the chapter strikes the most compulsive note that the book has yet sounded. In the grip of his fascinated horror, Melville's quicksilver imagination darts hither and thither from one terrible implication of whiteness to another; from the "intolerable hideousness" of the white bear of the Poles to the "white gliding ghostliness" of the white shark of the tropics.[1] He glances in a passage of airy vigour at the White Steed of the prairies, and in another of hushed awesomeness at the "white phantom" the albatross, both of which he declares to be invested with a mystical divinity harbouring a certain nameless terror. Yet divest whiteness of that strange glory, and pure horror arises again. Albino man, the deadly White Squall of the South seas, the pallor and shroud of the dead, Death on a Pale Horse in the Apocalypse, the eerie whiteness of legendary towers and seas, of distant snowclad mountains, or of far too proximate midnight breakers on rocky shores; all of them persist in the frightened imagination as the embodiments of a mysterious and distorted malevolence, as signs that the universe, underneath its variegations of captivating beauty, is implacable and soulless. At the centre of its warm and breathing loveliness is a cold heart of ice. Melville confesses that this is a presage, an unsupportable conjecture

---

[1] An image that beset Melville's imagination all his life. Years later, his volume of verses on the American Civil War contained a pointed and profound comment *On a Naval Victory*, in which his stoical sadness is reinforced in the last line by a bitter memory of this very symbol.

> *But seldom the laurel wreath is seen*
> *Unmixed with pensive pansies dark;*
> *There's a light and a shadow on every man*
> *Who at last attains his lifted mark—*
> *Nursing through night the ethereal spark.*
> *Elate he never can be;*
> *He feels that spirits which glad had hailed his worth*
> *Sleep in oblivion: the shark*
> *Glides white through the phosphorous sea.*

D. H. Lawrence, that neo-Melvillean visionary, wrote to a friend after a visit to Bognor in the early months of the 1914 war: "It seems to me anything might come out of that white, silent, opalescent sea; and the great icy shocks of foam were strange. I felt as if legions were marching in the mist . . . I am afraid of the ghosts of the dead." And in a postscript he adds, abruptly, "It is the whiteness of the ghost legions that is so awful."

merely—"this white-lead chapter about whiteness is but a white
flag hung out from a craven soul; thou surrenderest to a hypo,
Ishmael"—his intellect cries out to him that his instinct may be
wrong. Nevertheless his superbly vital instinct parries his intellect
with an analogy—of the domestic colt in the peaceful homeland
valleys who will snort and paw the ground in fright if a fresh buffalo
robe be shaken near him, though in fact he can know nothing in
New England of the ferocities of the Western prairies. "Here thou
beholdest even in a dumb brute", he cries, "the instinct of the
knowledge of the demonism in the world . . . and thus, the
muffled rollings of a milky sea; the bleak rustlings of the festooned
frosts of mountains; the desolate shiftings of the windrowed snows
of prairies; all these, to Ishmael, are as the shaking of that buffalo
robe to the frightened colt. Though neither knows where lie the
nameless things of which the mystic sign gives forth such hints;
yet with me, as with the colt, somewhere those things must exist.
Though in many of its aspects this visible world seems formed in
love, the invisible spheres were formed in fright."

At the height of this great chapter Melville's eloquence is guided
by his recent reading and chosen predilections into channels
familiar to the seventeenth-century metaphysicals whose poetry,
and particularly whose prose, he had so eagerly absorbed and in
whom he found most fertile imaginative affinities. Donne and Sir
Thomas Browne, Fuller and Jeremy Taylor, had been among the
rich and rapid reading of his early maturity; and the ornate model
of their prose was always for Melville a fascination and a pitfall.
At those times when his speculations and his eloquence accorded,
the memory of Browne's cadences gave him the key to unravelling
intricacies of conjecture which might even have baffled Browne,
and the result was a splendidly harmonious rhetoric in which the
intolerable wrestle was rewarded with illumination. Here in the
exaltation of his intuitive glimpse into the malevolence of the
unknown, Melville's prose attempts in a peroration a solution of
the tormenting paradox of the attraction and repulsion of the
whiteness—why it should so captivate, and yet so appal.

"Is it that by its indefiniteness it shadows forth the heartless
voids and immensities of the universe . . .?" he says. "Or is it
that . . . whiteness is not so much a colour as the visible absence
of colour, and at the same time the concrete of all colours; is it

for these reasons that there is such a dumb blankness, full of meaning, in a wide landscape of snows—a colourless, all-colour of atheism from which we shrink? And when we consider that other theory . . . that all other earthly hues [he puts names to them, skies, woods, paintings, butterfly-wings, girls' cheeks] are but subtile deceits, not actually inherent in substances, but only laid on from without . . . and that . . . the great principle of light for ever remains white or colourless in itself, and if operating without medium upon matter would touch all objects, even tulips and roses, with its own blank tinge—pondering all this, the palsied universe lies before us a leper; and like wilful travellers in Lapland, who refuse to wear coloured and colouring glasses upon their eyes, so the wretched infidel gazes himself blind at the monumental white shroud that wraps all the prospect round him. And of all these things the Albino whale was the symbol."

In this magnificent exposition and what has preceded it is summed up for those who care to examine it the spiritual situation from which the tragedy of Moby Dick, and perhaps of Melville, stems. The relation of the pervasive temper of the whole of the early part of the book, with its insistence upon misanthropy offset by jocularity, to the conclusion of the chapter on Whiteness in its reiteration of the predicament of the "wretched infidel gazing himself blind at the monumental white shroud that wraps all the prospect round him" is important for this reason; that both in the dramatic mood of the early episodes, and the speculative mood of the concluding chapter, the central philosophy is one of at least a temporary despair. It is dangerous to argue back from the universality of a piece of imaginative literature to the particularity of the personal development of its author; but with every reservation duly noted there is still an inescapable sense remaining that the first part of *Moby Dick* is the oblique record of a state of spiritual dereliction experienced by Melville himself. It is perhaps an undue simplification to call it loss of faith; but that is a convenient label denominating a hundred variations of mental and spiritual experience, and for many of these Melville's penetrating imagery answers truly and authentically. Whatever may have been the primary cause and nature of his disillusionment, the horrific metaphysical process by which colour is stripped from every aspect of life, real or imaginative, and the response of the human soul to the whole variegated universe falls uniform and dead is a familiar psychological experience that has rarely been so faithfully reproduced. If the integrity of art has any meaning at all, then it cannot fairly be questioned that *Moby Dick* was begun under the stress of a mood in which the palsied universe lay before Melville like a leper. He had looked into the brilliant variety of life—Fayaway in the garb of Eden, the glittering coral reefs of Mardi, Liverpool in its squalor and hubbub and cluster, the mastheads in the middle watch or the Horn in half a gale—and seen its beguiling surfaces dislimn into a common colourless whiteness, signifying nothing. Ishmael and Melville had lost faith in positive purpose; except that Melville, intuitively seeing Nothing replacing whatever God he had previously worshipped as Lord and Creator of his universe, saw Nothing as a positive and baleful destroyer menacing with death whatever of life remained in the residue of humanity. This was the logical conclusion to the landless quest of Bulkington.

This was his imaginative mood; it would have sterilised many men at the start of their work. Melville's activity it intensified, gave his imagination a new potency of response. His horror at his vision operated, fortunately, to create, not to recoil from creation. His vision of Nothing had been coupled simultaneously with a vision of the impersonal malevolence of this same universe which had been formed in fright. With unerring adroitness and power he built both these mysterious conceptions into his great central mysterious symbol; and on the forehead of the whale, his vision of the destructive force loose in the universe, he clamped the dreadful whiteness that was the token of his vision of nihilism and death. The White Whale was created as image of the primitive terror that opposes itself to the life and purpose of even the most enlightened and sophisticated man. Its ghostly whiteness reflects the terrifying pallor of the breakers outside the circumvallating reef of Mardi, into which Taji had turned his desperate suicidal prow; reflects at a further remove the sense of separation with which the whiteness of his jacket had endowed the innocent sailor on board the *Neversink*—the menace of nihilism, the destroying loneliness banded with the malevolent terror to create this monstrous myth.

Melville personified his intuitive sense of evil in the figure of the White Whale; but this alone did not carry his book to greatness. A philosophic statement of a truth even when given symbolic form, is one thing; a dramatic treatment of the same truth is quite another. The one is static, the other dynamic; the one expresses a vision, the other enlarges it. Melville chose the dramatic way. He felt the need for a treatment for his subject which could show the elemental conflict in panoramic action—"the running battle of the star and clod", as he was to name an equivalent combat in his long poem written many years later; accordingly he prepared against the ever-present background of his obsessed awareness of evil a subtle duplication of protagonists. The crude statement of the problem "Melville against the Evil Spirit of the Universe" was given a more complex and more effective form; Moby Dick as the Adversary was confronted by the passive, receptive Melville in the guise of Ishmael, and by the proud inexorable, authoritative Melville (who had Puritan ancestors) in the guise of the great and crazy Ahab. Melville, withdrawing from the contest the better to be able to visualise it objectively, found himself deeply engaged in the hunt in two separate identities. By projecting, say, his own loneliness into Ishmael and his own obsessed bitterness into Ahab, Melville gave his drama a double authenticity of experience as well as a high dramatic quality quite beyond the powers of his previous works. Against the ferocious malignity of the whale he opposed both the good-humour and essential innocence of Ishmael and the implacable hatred of Ahab; again, one static, the other dynamic. Ahab especially is cunningly contrived as an inevitable contrast to the system against which he wars; for whereas Moby Dick has, not without pains, been established as a creature of ice, Ahab is deliberately presented in a hundred apparently casual touches as a man of Fire. Even before he appears, his fame runs before him in the bated breath of Captain Peleg, part owner of the *Pequod* and Ahab's own employer, "He's a grand ungodly, godlike man, Captain Ahab . . . been used to deeper wonders than the waves; fixed his fiery lance in mightier, stranger foes than whales." The fire-epithet is rhetorical enough, but appropriate; Ishmael himself, when Ahab first stands upon his quarter-deck when the *Pequod* is some days out of Nantucket, chooses an immediate and spon-taneous simile from the same symbolic source. "He looked like a man cut away from the stake, when the fire has overrunningly wasted all the limbs without consuming them, or taking away one particle from their compacted aged robustness." And the scar reinforces the choice of symbol—the scar, continuing "right down one side of his tawny *scorched* face and neck", that is rumoured among the sailors to have come upon him "not in the fury of any mortal fray, but in an elemental strife at sea". Scorched by the elements and branded by the lightning, the essence of Ahab has perhaps an oversulphurous reek; yet the realistic details accumulate; the steward tells Stubb that of a morning he "finds the old man's hammock-clothes all rumpled and tumbled . . . and the pillow a sort of frightful hot, as though a baked brick had been on it."[1] In the scene where he binds the crew to the deadly chase of the White Whale, the fatal oath is pledged in "fiery" liquid, the spirits being simultaneously quaffed down "with a hiss"; and in the short soliloquy which follows, Ahab, sitting alone at the stern-windows of his cabin, concentrates his intense purpose into a few lines of triumph and resolve and makes the "dry heat upon my brow" stand for the implacability with which he now turns upon every aspect of living nature. Much later in the book, in the highly-charged chapter entitled "The Candles", Ahab casts back at the electric elements a dramatic defiance, grasping at the height of the thunderstorm the steel-headed harpoon from which the crackling sparks are leaping, and defying the challenge of the corposants burning at the mastheads. "Oh thou clear spirit of clear fire!" he cries to the storm, "whom on these seas I as Persian once did worship, till in the sacramental act so burned by thee that to this hour I bear the scar; I now know thee, thou clear spirit, and I now know that thy right worship is defiance. . . . Oh thou clear spirit, of thy fire thou madest me, and like a true child of fire, I breathe it back to thee."

The whole turbulent speech of Ahab in this chapter is stiff with compact significance; it is the emphasis on fire alone that suffices at this stage to confirm the nature of Ahab's part in the tragedy. Melville has set his scene for the deadly war between ice and fire; the whiteness of the whale and the redness of the unconsecrated will; the negative evil of the void against the positive evil of destructive purpose.[2]

---

[1] "Bless my soul!" cries the doctor of the *Samuel Enderby* which Ahab has boarded in a friendly "gam"; "this man's blood—it's at the boiling-point! His pulse makes these planks beat!"

[2] This lurid association intrudes even upon scenes of quiet fulfilment. In Chapter CXV Ahab comments upon the strange behaviour of the sperm whale as it dies, turning its head to the sun, "He turns and turns him to it—how slowly, but how steadfastly his homage-rendering and invoking brow. . . . *He too worships fire.*" Here Ahab expresses for the only time, and through this particular imagery, his masonic comradeship with the creature he hunts.

The strands of this complex work are tangled enough, but they are not inextricable. In this same chapter the fiery quality of active defiance is allied to another essential characteristic in Ahab which has been noted before in Ishmael and Bulkington and which accordingly signs itself unmistakably as authentic Melville—the temper of unshackled independence. "I own thy speechless, placeless power", Ahab cries to the clear spirit of clear fire, "but to the last gasp of my earthquake life will dispute its unconditional unintegral mastery in me. In the midst of the personified impersonal, a personality stands here. Though but a point at best; whencesoe'er I came, wheresoe'er I go; yet while I earthly live, the queenly personality lives in me, and feels her royal rights. . . . Come as mere supernal power, and though thou launchest navies of full-freighted worlds, there's that in here that still remains indifferent."

The dramatic picture and the dramatic setting are plain. Melville has deliberately rid his central characters of confusing complexity, has set them to counterbalance each other in a hard and clear-cut pattern of tragic action. As Ishmael represents innocence, and the Whale the destructive forces in the universe, so Ahab is the self-contained energy of the independent will. As Melville manœuvres his characters and their purposes into position, he strips them of the artificial concomitants of civilisation, of all distracting tradition or companionship; Ishmael is imperceptibly sundered from his new-found comrade Queequeg, Ahab from the ties of the old deep Quaker-Puritan stock from which he had remotely sprung, Moby Dick himself from the company of all the other shoals and schools of whales that the *Pequod* encounters in her wide and meandering circumnavigation. Together the three go naked to the conflict, each in his own way as elemental as the others. Melville has built his symbols with care and prevision; the whale in the centre, shrouded in a mystery of whiteness and horror, but elaborated with great care and skill into a palpably realistic image by the constant addition throughout the book, and to within a hundred pages of the end, of significant factual detail; Ahab its chief adversary, the embodiment of fanatical purpose detached from morality or convention and sworn to self-fulfilment or self-destruction; and Ishmael the footloose ranger, carefree, sardonic, but receptive to all impressions, the ideally creative and interpretative observer of the tragedy implicit in the contiguity of the two principals.

The conversion of these symbolic images into a creative myth, embodying a significant reflection of the profoundest human pre-occupations, was Melville's achievement in *Moby Dick*. Whether it was his purpose, instinctive or deliberate, is not relevant; it seems likelier that his symbolic imagination fastened greedily upon his chosen image and expanded it to impressive dimensions beyond his original intent. The main fact to be noted is that that conversion succeeded. Had it failed, through distortion of balance or deficiency of tragic intensity, through concentration upon factual detail òr inadequate control of character and action, the novel would have stood a gigantic and barely readable ruin, an agglomeration of undigested fact and misconceived melodrama. That it succeeded is a commonplace; the manipulation of the detail and the infusion of the dramatic intensity are both conducted with a massive and steady control that is new even in Melville. It remains to examine in greater detail this process by which symbol became myth and the flash and drive of an unusual imagination were converted into a novel of great genius.

CHAPTER XI

Moby Dick: the Myth

HAVING ESTABLISHED his symbol and his protagonists, Melville had next to contrive a living setting for the action—and action itself, too, that should spring naturally and organically from the setting he designed for it. His answer to the challenge of this formidable task was the creation of the *Pequod*—not the vessel itself merely, but its character and the characters of those on board, singly and collectively. He created it a miscellany, a World's Fair of nationality and habit, a deliberate representation of racial accord and divergence. Nantucketers mix with Danes and Dutchmen, a Manxman and an Alabama negro jostle Maltese, Icelanders, Chinese and English sailors with Spaniards, Sicilians, Shetlanders and Tahitians on the common ground of the fo'c'sle—" an Anacharsis Clootz deputation[1] from all the isles of the sea, and all the ends of the earth, accompanying old Ahab in the Pequod to lay the world's grievances before that bar from which not many of them ever come back." Chief among the common sailors, and

---

[1] This reference will not perhaps be readily understood without a word of explanation. Anacharsis Clootz was a German who in 1790 appeared at the bar of the French assembly at the head of a deputation of thirty-six foreigners, and in the name of this "embassy of the human race" declared that the world adhered to the Declaration of the Rights of Man. The incident made a lasting impression on Melville, who made similar references to Anacharsis Clootz in *The Confidence Man* and (nearly forty years later) in *Billy Budd.*—See Matthiessen's *American Renaissance*, X, 3, p. 410.

occupying positions of distinction and authority among them, are
the three pagan harpooners, Ishmael's cannibal friend Queequeg,
the towering coal-black negro Daggoo from the African coast, and
the lithe mercurial Red Indian Tashtego from Gay Head, the
remote promontory close to Nantucket where the last remnants
of an Indian settlement still survived when *Moby Dick* was written
—these three exercise an unobtrusive domination over the sailors
both by character and by right of custom. and accentuate still
more the great breadth of representation that the multitude of the
ship's company achieves, as well as injecting into the random
cosmopolitanism of the crew a common savour of primitive superstition in high places.

This element of incalculable power was encouraged by Ahab
in so far as it assisted his monomaniac purpose; against it the
more sophisticated rationalism of his officers, the mates, was
helpless. Indeed the mates, who operate broadly as the forces of
reason in the ship, seeking to control the crew by seamanship and
common sense rather than by the inspiration of a maniac vengeance,
are tragically ill-equipped for any role which could have balanced
them effectively against the overpowering personality of Ahab.
The second and third mates, Stubb and Flask, are in the scales
of this particular tragedy barely make-weights; Stubb the good-
humoured, easy-going, materialistic man without fear and without
imagination, who could "hum over his old rigadig tunes while
flank and flank with the most exasperated monster"; and Flask,
who followed fish "for the fun of it", whose "ignorant unconscious
fearlessness" made him "a little waggish in the matter of whales",
an admirable fisherman but of a light and unchangeable frivolity
at even the gravest crises. Only Starbuck, the chief mate, regards
his destiny and Ahab's with the eye of a conscience commensurate
with the problems besetting it; a Quaker from Nantucket, he is a
staid, steadfast man, with a deep natural reverence which the wild
loneliness of his life tended to incline to superstition; "but to
that sort of superstition", (Melville most pertinently adds, having
the pagan harpooners and their primitive emotionalism very much
in mind) "which in some organisations seems rather to spring from
intelligence than from ignorance". He is wise and prudent, will
have no one in his boat who is not afraid of a whale, regarding
the most reliable courage to be that which arises from a careful
estimation of the danger; a man of temperate and reliable quality,

perhaps in a barely noticeable way the most attractive character in the novel, for his strength is unassuming and beautiful and his weakness is movingly convincing. Melville is right to insist on Starbuck's weakness, since it contributes, by his failure to check or defy Ahab's monomania, to the catastrophe of the story; "his was that sort of bravery, which while generally abiding firm in the conflict with seas, or winds, or whales, or any of the ordinary irrational horrors of the world, yet cannot withstand those more terrific, because more spiritual terrors, which sometimes menace you from the concentrating brow of an enraged and mighty man." This failure of Starbuck's is failure only in the context to which destiny has ironically called him; in his conflict, on behalf of reason and judgment, with his captain who is invoking the most primitive bloodlusts in aid of his mesmeric captivation of the crew of the *Pequod* for concerted vengeance, Starbuck is able to move and even melt Ahab momentarily, but never to shake or divert his purpose. In Starbuck a pitiful unresolved struggle between his divided loyalties to his God and his captain undermines still further the native irresolution not uncommon in a man of serious and idealistic purpose. It is Melville's incidental lesson, through Starbuck and his tragedy, that the passionate intensity of an evil will is inevitably more than a match for the best of idealistic intentions, if left without the reinforcement of a purpose as bold as its foe's.

The setting against which the main action is to be played is taking shape, the levels of the personnel are being slowly determined; Ahab and his cloud of loneliness and mystery dominating the three ineffective mates by the power of his personality and the three dangerous harpooners by the magnetism inherent in his latent barbarism. Under them hums and bustles the life of the ship—dramatically personified in the quaint and vigorous set-piece of the chapter entitled "Midnight, Forecastle", in which the cosmopolitan variegation of the crew stirs and sparkles in an impressionistic play-like cameo of sensual and quarrelsome vitality. In this active little conversation-piece, animated like a Peacock novel or the Night-town scene in *Ulysses* by its transmutation into dialogue designed to spotlight the outstanding characteristic of each individual interlocutor, the variety, the incipient quarrels, the potential conflicts, of the diverse members of the crew are passed before the reader in specific detail—the phlegmatic booziness of the Dutch sailor, the amorous irrepressibility of the Maltese and the Sicilian, the businesslike devotion of the Nantucketer to his trade, the fiery suspicion of the Spaniard and the grim quarrelsomeness of the giant Negro boiling up to a fight hailed with transports of joy by the Irishman and with the eager cry for ordered fair play from the English sailor. Here is Melville's rapid and cinematographic sketch of his representative community, that should serve as background and foil to the deadly tragedy of Ahab; at one and the same time as representative of America and of the common mass of mankind as the chorus in a Greek tragedy was representative of Athens and of the common people of the known world. In face of the tragedy of Agamemnon Aeschylus gave his chorus comment only, a helpless detachment without action; but Melville added a touch of organic drama to this lightning picture, drawing their common impatience and passion to the very brink of a murderous quarrel and dispersing it at the last crucial moment by the mate's shouted order to stand by to reef topsails at the approach of a sudden squall. Demonstrating truly enough the solidity, in face of a common danger, of a community uncompromisingly individualistic, Melville contrives at the same time to bring the scene into accord with the main progress of his action by making it, as well as a microcosm of his nation and his world, a tiny prevision of the tragic drama into which it was being built. He effects this through the individual agency of the little black cabin-boy Pip, whose pitiful fate thereafter is to lose his reason, and accompany the climax of the tragedy with pertinent babble worthy of a Cassandra or a Shakespearian Fool, and whose anguished superstitious mutterings as the storm breaks will be echoed in the concluding chapters with a terrible poignancy.

The *Pequod*, declared D. H. Lawrence, is the ship of the white American soul. "What do you think of the *Pequod*, the ship of the soul of an American?" he cries in his excitable, spasmodic, penetrating essay on *Moby Dick*. "Many races, many peoples, many nations, under the Stars and Stripes. Beaten with many stripes. Seeing stars sometimes. And in a mad ship, under a mad captain, in a mad, fanatic's hunt. But splendidly handled. Three splendid mates. The whole thing practical, eminently practical in its working. American industry!

"And all this practicability in the service of a mad, mad chase."

Lawrence as usual tends to arrogate Melville's universal problem to more rigidly-specialised terms of his own, but in those few quoted remarks he has expressed enough to point the way that the tragedy will move. It is possible that the *Pequod*, to Melville, meant America—certainly his crew and its hierarchies are most faithfully representative of the great nation, from the cream of Nantucket seamanship on the quarter-deck to the subject-race harpooners at the mastheads and the negro slave in the cabin. It is more probable still that the Pequod, to Melville, meant the civilised world, upon out a deadly conflict with all the terror and malevolence that civilisation has tried, but is unable, to destroy. Most probable of all—and here we are once more at the centre of the imagination of the great symbolic artist—the *Pequod*, to Melville, meant the *Pequod*, in unsleeping chase after the White Whale. And what the White Whale might ultimately mean, or the *Pequod*, could rest for Melville in dormant abeyance until the tragedy could play itself out and the myth, which is the symbol in creative action, could point its own way to its ulterior significance.

The elaborate preparations which were necessary to put the reader in possession of sufficient store of fact and tradition to carry the weight of the subsequent spiritual tragedy must have been massy and laborious work for Melville. It does not read so. His constructional skill had learned much from his failure in *Mardi* and from the necessary discipline ordained upon him in *White-Jacket*, where huge masses of technical detail had to be given shape and meaning and life. He used it with matured cunning in *Moby Dick*, alternating his passages of bare cetology with sudden incidents of intense action or unusual suggestiveness. Once launched upon his tale, his superb gift of nervous and palpable narrative took sole charge of his intractable material and controlled it with a mastery less apparent for the rapid and absorbing readability of the result. The second volume opens with a re-insistence on mystery; dramatically, with the crew's muted gossip about unexplained coughs and creaks below hatches; more discursively, with a lengthy discussion of a whale's voyaging habits and the secret impulses that control them, the legendary fame of a handful of the more illustrious monsters, and the near ubiquity and near-invincibility of the greatest. This is all part of the one insidious design, to make the name of Moby Dick at once a mystery and a terror. To these tantalising hints of mystery and veiled power Melville adds the picture of a crazed Ahab consumed with an unholy desire for vengeance upon the centre of mystery itself, until "the spiritual throes in him heaved his being up from its base . . . and Ahab would burst from his state-room as though escaping from a bed that was on fire"; and by his cumulative art the hunt is fairly pictured in all the insensate energy with which it is to be pursued to the end. The main narrative sequences of the book, which are yet to follow, are thus assured of a magnificent momentum.

Immediately the book flowers into action; the first lowering and chase, though of course after poor mortal whales merely and not Moby Dick, are described in a brilliant medley of seethe and suspense, with quick flashed glimpses of the action and the danger that are a whaleman's unthinking routine. This particular chase ends in failure, with Starbuck's boat capsizing as he backs it up to his whale in a squall; and the boat's crew spend the night in the waterlogged wreckage and are not picked up until morning. But Melville is not content to have intensified in straightforward corroborative action those senses of urgency and half-seen terror that had been hinted and insinuated before: though on this chapter as it stands he would have pulled it off. He adds yet another dramatic element to the tragedy: the disclosure, at this the first lowering of the voyage, of the presence of the strange Parsee Fedallah and his Indian followers, as rowers in Ahab's boat. If we did not believe before in Melville's repeated asseverations that Ahab was possessed of an evil spirit, we are offered less equivocal evidence here. The Parsee is Ahab's evil spirit. The appropriateness of the particular manifestation in which Melville has chosen to embody it may perhaps be questioned; for at no time do Fedallah and his dusky companions impart to the atmosphere any intensity that was not present in Ahab himself set against the variety of his living crew. Admittedly Fedallah is an apt enough incarnation of the demoniac forces in league with Ahab's purpose, and his haunting prophecies to Ahab about the manner of his eventual death (a curiously distorted reminiscence of *Macbeth*, and we can push the analogy to equate Fedallah's influence over Ahab with the power of the Three Witches in that play) give an effective but somewhat theatrical twist to the closing passages of the book. There is also an especial pertinence, recalling Ahab's symbolic affinities, in the fact that Fedallah is a fire-worshipper. Nevertheless he is the nearest to pinchbeck melodrama that Melville comes in this great story. It is difficult to escape the suspicion that

Melville took him ready-made from stock, as he took nothing else in the novel; trading perhaps involuntarily upon the fashionable vogue (traceable in many forms in nineteenth-century romantic fiction, poetry and prose) of importing the mysterious East for good measure of *diablerie* into familiar Western settings, frequently for no better purpose than to make the flesh creep. Hawthorne's clumsy handling of a similar element in *The Blithedale Romance* is one of the chief reasons for the disappointing failure of that novel; and not even its organic connection with the central symbols of the stories or conduct of the plots can prevent it from introducing an alien crudity into such admirable pieces of construction as *The Moonstone* and *The Master of Ballantrae*.[1] All the subtlety of Fedallah's macabre demonism, admittedly used by Melville as a deliberate intensifier of genuine dramatic effects inherent in the tragedy of Ahab, is inadequate to compensate, even in isolated moments like the discovery of his body lashed by tangled harpoon-ropes to the living whale, for the artificial solecism of the original invention.

Yet his carefully timed introduction into the story contributes to the pace and punch of the narrative, now well under way; adds to the element of fatal compulsion, that is beginning to obtrude itself upon the reader's consciousness, a further quality of destructiveness to equate it very soon with that memorable racing tide which seized on Taji's prow " like a hand omnipotent " and bore him beyond the world. And as if instinctively aware of the makeshift qualities of Fedallah and his Indians, Melville compensates a bare chapter later by substituting as a symbol of the growing compulsion of the quest the beautiful image of the spirit-spout, the silvery jet descried by night moving tantalisingly over the sea far ahead of the *Pequod's* bows. Ever and again in the ·silent serene weather, this solitary spout would be seen at night by the whole crew, only to disappear completely when the ship made sail to overtake it. The episode, or rather the series of recurring episodes, is related with great restraint and beauty; and explicitly as he states his conclusion in the paragragh I now quote, it was as clearly implied in the intensity of the scene he had described in its cunning relationship to the preceding passage of narrative.

---

[1] Dickens avoided it almost entirely; but at the end there is an intrusion of the breath of the Orient in the opium fumes of *Edwin Drood*, where the Thugs were only prevented by Dickens' death from a dramatic invasion of the English novel.

"Nor with the immemorial superstition of their race," says Melville, underlining what he had already compelled the reader to surmise, "and in accordance with the preter-naturalness, as it seemed, which in many things invested the *Pequod*, were there wanting some of the seamen who swore that whenever and wherever descried; at however remote times, or in however far apart latitudes and longitudes, that unnearable spout was cast by one self-same whale; and that whale, Moby Dick. For a time, there reigned, too, a sense of peculiar dread at this flitting apparition, as if it were treacherously beckoning us on and on, in order that the monster might turn round upon us, and rend us at last in the remotest and most savage seas."

With this chapter Melville seemed to sense that he had for the moment pushed the relevant dramatic action as far forward as his material would allow. For virtually the whole of the remainder of the volume (Volume II of the three-volume book, occupying roughly one-third of the total length) he concentrates upon factual aspects of the fishery, and on incidental rather than dramatic action. He spreads himself upon the pictures of whales, on the legends and the glories surrounding the business of whaling; this we have already sampled, and he cunningly recurs to it to counteract any possible failure of the suspension of disbelief which may mar our ever more necessary receptiveness as he rounds to his climax. When he relates an incident it is to illustrate in fuller detail something of which we knew already (the murderousness of Moby Dick is again elaborated in the *Town-Ho's* story, and the encounter with the *Jeroboam*, with its crazed and prophetic seaman, is no more than a reiteration of the incident of Ishmael's and Queequeg's meeting with Elijah on the dockside at Nantucket before the ship sailed). Melville at this stage of his narrative-drama is coolly and designedly marking time; consolidating and intensifying his formidable store of factual material, which at the crucial moment of the tragedy is to be flung with all its cumulative authority into the final conflict. Yet this is not to suggest that Melville never permitted himself an imaginative excursion, even in the toils of an over-riding purpose like this one on which his best faculties were constantly engaged; and there are moments in this section of the story, (long after he had propounded in "The Spirit-Spout" the pace of his drama and then left the suggestion to simmer while he went back to build up the detail), when the immersion of his poetic

K

imagination in his theme resulted in elaborate and staggering fancies, united to his drama at a profound level but superficially the product of momentary observation and brilliant sympathetic conjectures.

There is the haunting chapter entitled "The Funeral", in which the peeled white body of the flayed and plundered whale is slipped from the tackles at the ship's side and floats off upon the water. The description is complete in a paragraph or two, but the image is indelible; the calm untroubled sea and sky, the rippling passage of the ship, and the great humped bulk of the corpse abandoned far off on the sea, with the sharks and vultures active about it in shoals and flocks. ''For hours and hours from the almost stationary ship that hideous sight is seen. Beneath the unclouded and mild azure sky, upon the fair face of the pleasant sea, wafted by the joyous breezes, that great mass of death floats on and on, till lost in infinite perspectives.'' And he goes on, in his black mood of bitterness induced by this funereal vision of the symbol of death obtruding without stint upon serenity, to remark, first with savagery on the predatoriness of the sharks and vultures that prey on even the mightiest of creatures, and second, with a sardonic return to a characteristic obsession, on the consequences of mistaking such a far-off corpse for a rock surrounded with white breakers, whereby many a non-existent hazard has been charted into the traditions of navigation; and ''for years afterwards, ships shun the place; leaping over it as silly sheep leap over a vacuum, because their leader originally leaped there when a stick was held. There's your law of precedents,'' cries Melville in the full transport of his mood as Bulkington. ''There's your utility of traditions; there's the story of your obstinate survival of old beliefs never bottomed on the earth, and now not even hovering in the air!'' A chapter of Death in life; vividly contrasted some while later by the less metaphysical but even more dramatically memorable chapter of Life in death, where the wild Gay-Header Tashtego slips and falls into the sperm-laden head of a captured partly-stripped whale lying alongside, and instantly the whole head tears sheer away from the overstrained tackles and plunges into the sea; the thrilling rescue of the imprisoned Indian by Queequeg, who slashes his way through the sinking head with a boarding-sword and hauls Tashtego out by the hair, is followed by a lightly-handled dissertation upon the felicity of such a death—''to be smothered in the very whitest and daintiest of fragrant spermaceti; coffined, hearsed and tombed in the secret inner chamber and sanctum sanctorum of the whale." With these curious twin insistences upon the pervasiveness of death, the one delicate and humourous, the other contemplative and sombre, Melville increases the atmospheric pressure of his tale in preparation for the approach to the climax.

This Melville enters upon at the outset of Volume III, with a memorable flourish. Having by a process of loving accumulation of detail achieved the apotheosis of the whale, he multiplies the effect by the introduction of his symbol, not so much in might as in multitudes. In the celebrated chapter "The Grand Armada", the overwhelming numbers as well as the overwhelming size of the monster are deployed before the reader's eyes; the whale is seen as a harmonious part of the world of whales, not as hitherto, merely as a hostile part of the world of men. This is curiously impressive. Because the whaleboats stumble on a vast shoal of whales and are dragged into the calm centre of a tumultuous circle, to emerge unscathed at last, the strange distorted image that Melville had fostered throughout the book, of a malevolent, solitary monster at war with a fanatical revenger, is replaced by the far more impressive one of a human civilisation confronted by a whale civilisation in a battle to the death. The glimpses which Starbuck's boat was enabled to catch of the coupling and courting whales, the pregnant and nursing whales, the evidences of the homeliest and commonest processes of life, illuminate and fortify beyond measure the power of the whale as Melville's chosen image. They lend the whale a familiarity, a commonplace routine that makes his generic destructiveness all the more terrible. Ahab has a wife and child; so, maybe, has Moby Dick. The banality of this observation is far offset by the nature of its implications. Good and evil are alike born of commonplace loyalties, that make the issues at all points less capable of simplification. Behind Moby Dick, as behind Ahab, is a powerful and weighty tradition; that both Ahab and Moby Dick have in their own way chosen independence weakens neither their individual contribution to the drama nor the unconscious operation within them of the tradition they have (in Ahab's case consciously) discarded. This strange insight into a powerful society is Melville's manner of accentuating the enormous access of energy (and dramatic cogency) enjoyed by the individual who for one reason or another contracts out of it.

This chapter is no ostensible part of Ahab's tragedy or Moby Dick's campaign; it is an incident merely in the development of Ishmael's receptive imagination, a further stage in his transit from innocence to experience. "Even so", Ishmael remarks as the whales in the inmost ring of the turbulent shoal couple and dally in an unhurried freedom, "amid the tornadoed Atlantic of my being, do I myself still forever centrally disport in mute calm; and while ponderous planets of unwaning woe revolve round me, deep down and deep inland there I still bathe me in eternal mildness of joy."

This is an important statement. Melville has discovered the stillness at the centre of tumult, the profound and vivid illumination of meaning at the centre of chaos, that, once experienced, is the end of primal innocence and the ultimate acceptance of conflict as a creative element in nature. Yet it is also important to remember—and Melville goes on later to show that he never deceived himself in this—that such a poetic detachment never implies spiritual detachment from the contradictory condition of men. Ishmael remains calm in the tempest that stronger and perhaps less responsible forces have let loose about him; he is none the less fatally implicated in them. The chapter on "The Try-Works", bathed in a fierce unnatural glare, is remarkable evidence of the concern which Ishmael knows he has for a tragedy, which can involve the universe and yet fail to disturb his schooled serenity.

The try-works is the great kiln-like edifice built into the timber of the whaling-vessel for the purpose of boiling the oil out of the sperm and the blubber. The huge furnace is fed principally by fritters and scraps of the whale itself; the heat is intense and the smoke thick and horrible to inhale. By midnight, after a successful chase, the try-works is in full blast; the flames lividly curling and darting below the great pots, the thick smoke piling off the furnace in heaps as the harpooners stoke the fire. The gesticulating pagans outlined against the dim reeking flame, the pitch blackness of the night, the evil swirl of the filthy smoke give Ishmael first a dramatic insight into the action and next a conviction of his identification with the cosmic horror; for at first "the rushing *Pequod*, freighted with savages, and laden with fire, and burning a corpse, and plunging into that blackness of darkness, seemed the material counterpart of her monomaniac commander's soul". That is a penetrating and arresting image, expressing with telling exactitude the organic relation between the symbol and the myth; Ishmael the spectator deeply aware of the significance of the drama and so convincingly accentuating it; but the next step in his imaginative adventure is more impressive still, for as he stands at the tiller he falls into a momentary standing sleep, from which he awakes to find no compass before him, nothing but "a jet gloom, now and then made ghastly by flashes of redness." The horror of the instant is profound; the sense of direction almost of recognisable identity or existence, departs; "a stark, bewildered feeling, as of death, came over me". The horror is luckily transitory; in his instant of sleep he had turned himself about and was fronting the ship's stern; and the realisation comes back to him just in time to prevent the vessel flying up into the wind and probably capsizing. Nevertheless the momentary impression is ineffaceable and hideously apposite. "Uppermost was the impression that whatever swift, rushing thing I stood on was not so much bound to any haven ahead as rushing from all havens astern." Ishmael's involuntary insight identifies his vision with Melville's own; it is his first unencumbered vision of evil, and by accepting it imaginatively he is no longer the detached misanthropic innocent but attains tragic stature; comes alongside Ahab in the primal struggle with universal destiny.

For he elaborates the fact that he was mesmerised into this nearly fatal sleep by looking too long upon the fire. Ahab, he implies again and again, has worshipped fire so long that he is a part of the element and the fire is a part of him. "Give not thyself up to fire", says Ishmael in comment upon the try-works, "lest it invert thee, deaden thee, as for the time it did me." Ahab, with the Parsee aiding, worshipped fire and thereby achieved a vision of the world's evil; which Ishmael here partially endorses, but with a reservation born of an imaginative vision that Ahab put from him. "There is a wisdom that is woe; but there is a woe that is madness," says Ishmael. Ishmael retains the consciousness of sanity transcending madness; Ahab does not. And Ahab, not Ishmael, perishes. Even so Ishmael-Melville is quick to insist, at the end of this very same chapter, that the depths of a tragedy like Ahab's are infinitely higher than the heights of commonplace humanity; for like a Catskill eagle that forever flies within the gorge, he flies always among mountains; "so that even in his lowest swoop the mountain eagle is still higher than other birds upon the plain, even though they soar." Ahab's failure, here as always patently foreshadowed, is not of the common kind; and Ishmael's passive innocence, by enlarging to active acceptance, makes him from now until the end of the book one with Ahab in quality if not in energy.

It is the energy of Ahab which now takes charge. The dynamic acceleration of the tragedy towards its fulfilment is embodied, to the exclusion of all but a few insignificant figures and incidents designed to put the finishing touches on the completed picture of the great whale-symbol, in the intensification of Ahab's private monomania. Ishmael, his vision achieved, unobtrusively retires; and every important incident recorded thereafter is built deliberately into the pattern which must most vividly present itself at the instant of climax—the conflict of the insensate human being with the malevolent and destructive beast.

The emotional presentation of the whale is achieved, as it had to be, indirectly. Moby Dick until the very last moment must necessarily be a rumour only, though the rumour needed also to be as palpable as the gnarled and pulsing flesh and blood of the man confronting it; and episode after episode in the last third of the story adds its own individual contribution to the impressive accumulation. Nearly every one of the lone cruising vessels that Ahab speaks has its peculiar reminiscence of the White Whale. Comparatively early in the book the *Town-Ho* had given vivid news of its destructiveness; next the *Jeroboam* combined with its crazy sailor, with his haunting prophecies, the violent loss of its chief mate in conflict with Moby Dick, who from that moment had become "a nameless terror" to the ship; and after encounters, both humorous and satirical rather than indicative of tragedy, with the *Virgin* and the *Rosebud*, Ahab meets the captain of the British ship *Samuel Enderby*, whose desperate struggle with the famous whale had robbed him, like Ahab, of a limb. Cheerful and unmalicious, the English captain with his ivory arm confronts the sour and haunted Ahab with his ivory leg. "No more White Whales for me; I've lowered for him once, and that satisfied me. There would be great glory in killing him . . . but hark ye, he's best let alone." The English captain, serene, un-worried, honest, is amazed at Ahab's obsession. He is inadequate matter for tragedy, and Ahab leaves him. The subsequent encounter with the gay *Bachelor*, full to the hatches with good oil and triumphantly bound for home, is subtly contrasted with Ahab's mood and the incidents to follow; for the commander of the *Bachelor* (Melville, four years married and with a growing family, has perhaps added a deliberately sardonic touch

here) has only heard of Moby Dick and does not believe he exists
at all; and the next vessel described is the ominously-named *Rachel*,
casting desperately about the sea in search of her lost boat with
the captain's son aboard, too certainly a prey to Moby Dick himself.
In a scene of great tension Ahab, bent on the chase, refuses to aid
the *Rachel* in her search; and the ships part in mournful silence, the
Rachel still tacking and beating this way and that, "her masts and
yards thickly clustered with men, as three tall cherry trees when the
boys are cherrying among the boughs". Last of these foreboding
meetings comes that with the "most miserably misnamed"
Delight[1], carrying the shattered remains of her whaleboat and the
body of one of five of her crew whom the White Whale only the day
before had attacked and destroyed. The unrelieved grimness of this
short episode, coupled with the poignancy of the *Rachel's* plight,
provides the culmination of Melville's efforts to present the whale
as a convincing and dangerous protagonist in his universal tragedy
before his actual introduction of the monster itself. Each of these
ships acts, obliquely or directly, like a messenger in a Greek drama
bringing news of an action off-stage which is to play a vital part in
the action before the audience. With the departure of the *Delight*
the scene is cleared for the final struggle; the symbol has been
presented in the round—factually, satirically, poignantly, tragically,
and with, latterly, a powerful reinforcement of emotion. Moby
Dick is now a pervasive force of great potency. Just as, to a lesser
extent, Ahab's arrival in the flesh had been cleverly delayed while
rumour built him up to heroic stature, so Moby Dick has been invested long before he appears with a premonitory aura of terror
commensurate with the personal hypnotism of Ahab's presence.

And for the last third of the story Ahab is Energy directing the
process of events. So far as it is possible, in Melville's fatalist
cosmos, for a protagonist in his drama to be in control of any force
or action whatever, Ahab has that power and that control. Only
Melville knows, and hints as much to his reader through the
muttered forebodings of Starbuck, that this control is illusory; that
Ahab is compelled not by the positive will to do, but by the fascination
of his own destruction, presenting itself to him in the insensate guise
of his cherished vengeance. Long since he has thrown reason overboard, and in the closing stages he symbolises this renouncement

---

[1] One critic sees in the ironic naming of this vessel a dramatic backward reference
to the lyrical invocation to "delight" in Father Mapple's sermon in Chapter IX.

by the frenzied destruction of the quadrant. In a fearful thunder-storm the compass needle is turned; and the log-line, rotten with disuse, parts in a heavy sea. "I crush the quadrant," cries Ahab in exultation, "the thunder turns the needles, and now the mad sea parts the log-line. But Ahab can mend all." The mood is on him in which defiance and self-will, lashed into demoniac intensity by the fervours and delays of the voyage and the certainty of its impending culmination, take complete control of his conscious purpose. "Good is the Passive that obeys Reason," says Blake. "Evil is the Active springing from Energy." The character and fate of Captain Ahab are sufficient comment and corroboration of that profound and subtle remark.

Ahab has abdicated from reason; and though in complete physical and mental control of his actions, is as good as insane, possessed of a devil whose power overrides his own. Blinded by his egocentric obsession with vengeance, he is deprived of the full sweep of reason and intelligence which a tragic hero needs. Pride and insensate will are fit substance for tragedy; madness is not; and madness, unless carefully handled, can break down the potential structure of tragedy into tasteless melodrama. The lesser Elizabethans fell again and again into this dangerous trap; Shakespeare, incorporating a perilous tradition into an organic poetic form of tragedy that demanded more care and integrity of control than ever before in the history of literary craftsmanship, avoided by an instinctive tact and resourcefulness the failure into which even Webster stumbled. To make his tragic hero mad is to overset the dignity and value of tragedy; tragedy is without subjective significance if the central figure is denied a straight vision of the forces that overcome him. Hamlet is only mad nor' nor' west; and Hamlet mad is more perceptive than the rest of the Court of Elsinore sane; while Ophelia's distraction is (dramatically) Hamlet's tragedy and not her own, an objective incident merely. Lear is, of course, the *locus classicus* of the mad hero; and Shakespeare has saved his tragedy from melodrama by the simple and brilliant device of the Fool. The juxtaposition of the zany whose wits were never certain speaking obscure and gnomic truth to the masterful intellect whose passion has overthrown its reason is the masterstroke which preserves the equilibrium at the centre of this catastrophic drama. *Timon of Athens*, its contemporary and companion, fails of that balance and remains on that account a ruined monolith. The wisdom of Lear's fool fills up with enduring

truth the cracks in Lear's own intellect; Lear's patent but disintegrating strength buoys up the wavering fool to this duty. They
complement each other; and Melville, whose reading during the
past two years had been deep and who had discovered and absorbed
Shakespeare with an altogether unusual enthusiasm and sensibility,
found his own greatest tragedy at its crisis deriving directly from
the heart of Shakespeare's drama. The very novel bursts into
dramatic soliloquy, which in turn develops into a dialogue approximating much more closely in rhythm and idiom to an Elizabethan
play than to a naturalistic nineteenth-century conversation; stage-
directions sprout from the text; and the nervous and decorative
prose becomes perceptibly more rhetorical. There is too much in
Ahab of the passionate intensity which hounded Lear to his madness to make it anything but certain that the Lear-motive and the
Lear-imagery were uppermost in Melville's mind as he created
his greatest character; and, insensibly or not, he provided Ahab
with his complementary Fool, who like Lear's should unwittingly
correct the hubris and restore the tragic equilibrium. The little negro
Pip, whose wits had been scared out of him for ever when Stubb's
boat unthinkingly abandoned him upon the sea, babbles a curious incoherent jargon into Ahab's ear so strangely apposite and suggestive
that even mad Ahab is calmed and stabilised by his presence.

Shakespeare had presented the Fool as he stood, and left his
audience to rationalise his utterances, and his significance, for
themselves; Melville is more specific. He implies a sharp differentiation between the craziness of master and fool (as of course Shakespeare, without the benefit of the novelist's licence for exposition and
explanation, had done in far smaller compass in *Lear*); and he
suggests it by a vivid description of the revelatory riches of Pip's
hallucinations, as against the implicitly dark and fuliginous terror of
Ahab's. "The sea had jeeringly kept his finite body up, but drowned
the infinite of his soul. Not drowned entirely, though. Rather
carried down alive to wondrous depths, where strange shapes of the
unwarped primal world glided to and fro before his passive eyes;
and the miser-merman, Wisdom, revealed his hoarded heaps . . .
[Pip] saw God's foot upon the treadle of the loom, and spoke it; and
therefore his shipmates called him mad. So man's insanity is
heaven's sense; and wandering from all mortal reason, man comes
at last to that celestial thought, which to reason is absurd and
frantic; and weal or woe, feels then uncompromised."

This is to give mad Pip an almost divine insight; which Ahab is denied, and Ishmael, although he may recognise its presence. Ahab follows the baleful element fire, and is consumed; Pip is overwhelmed with the kinder element water, where Melville himself always felt at home, in which the "grand god" (they are Ishmael's words) Moby Dick swam; and he achieved that reason which is beyond sanity. The complex paradox gives pith to the strange relationship of Ahab and Pip; and knots up the strands still more tautly for the climax. Ahab, by disclosing for Pip a residual tenderness that the common observer would have thought had been sealed irrevocably behind that adamantine purpose, retains for himself, in the midst of his mania, sufficient humanity to preserve him within the bounds of tragedy[1]; while Pip, for his part, unconsciously provides the divine antiseptic comments that keep Ahab's intransigence in check.

One last supreme moment of calm is granted the ship before the action breaks out into the great three-day chase; a moment which Melville handles with a double skill, contriving to infuse into the one short chapter ("The Symphony") the nearly incompatible elements of serenity and tension. The serenity is in the "transparently pure and soft air" of the clear steel-blue calm; the tension in the quiet confrontation—the last—of the inflexible Ahab by the desperate yet dignified pleas of Starbuck that he call off the doomed chase of Moby Dick and turn for home. Starbuck calls up his most passionate reserves of reason and emotion, with talk of his own and Ahab's wife and child, and the sweet summer mornings of far-away Nantucket. Ahab is still too human to remain unmoved; but a force which he feels to be outside himself averts his eyes from the allurements. Fate it is who commands, not he; in a final lyrical outburst of resigned despair he rejects Starbuck and resigns himself to fate. Battered and broken by a lifetime of unyielding struggle and spiritual torment, Ahab is still giving fleeting glimpses (like the restored Lear this time) of an idyllic beauty he yearns after but cannot realise; and the melting loveliness of his last image is the more poignant for the inflexibility of the haggard determination that rejects it. "It is a mild, mild wind, and a mild-looking sky; and the air smells now, as if it blew from a far-away meadow; they have

---

[1] Compare the remarkably similar situation in *Lear*:

> "*Poor fool and knave, I have one part in my heart*
> *That's sorry yet for thee.*"

been making hay somewhere under the slopes of the Andes, Starbuck, and the mowers are sleeping among the new-mown hay.
Sleeping? Aye, toil how we may, we all sleep at last on the field.
Sleep? Aye, and rust amid greenness; as last years' scythes flung
down, and left in the half-cut swathes.''

The dawn of the next day sees the raising of Moby Dick; and the
narrative flowers with a lordly ease into the magnificent description
of the chase. It is doing the novel no service to paraphrase these last
great chapters; they have their undisputed place in romantic
literature, and for economy of control as well as vividness of detail
they are without flaw. In them the conversion of the complex symbol
into the simplicity of the enduring myth is fulfilled with no sense of
strain or bathos. Nervous instancy is in every action, electrifying
every image, crackling in every line of bow-taut narrative; this
writer, whose concepts had so often struggled (and were to struggle
again) among unruly metaphysic or jostling importunate imagery,
here compels at the height of his art every fully-charged word to
his immediate service. The preparation for this climax was the
devastating conflict, and it is that preparation which my analysis
has sought at least partially to unravel; the climax itself, which
such an unravelling cannot improve but may perhaps hope to clarify
and reinforce, is as inevitable and as final as death. When the whale
drives on at the ship, and annihilation comes, in the half of a printed
page, upon every tittle and scrap of the whole universe of clenched
sinewy activity of which life and this book are compounded, the
finality and loss are deadly but they are not unexpected. For
Ishmael the world has narrowed to the dimension of the *Pequod*;
but the *Pequod*, in Melville's abounding imagination, had expanded
to the dimensions of the world. And now in an instant the *Pequod*
is destroyed, and Ishmael is left alone upon the sea.

The prelude has led to the realisation of the symbol; the pursuit
of the symbol has blended into the natural creation of the myth.
Cogent and convincing and painfully memorable, the myth has
spelt inevitable destruction. *Moby Dick*, begun perhaps in spiritual
distress and bewilderment and continued in a tingle of curiosity and
perplexity, answer itself without compromise, in the blank annihilation of its end. Its end is as nihilistic as Timon's; nothing has
availed humanity in its misguided traffic with its livelihood and its
destiny. The courage of the whole crew, the energy of Ahab,
the conscience of Starbuck, the innocence of Queequeg, the

independence of Bulkington, the gaiety of Stubb and Flask, the paganismof the harpooners, the poignant natural insight of the heroic crazed Pip, and the fruits of all their life and labour, are all swept in an instant into a state of utter meaninglessness and negation. Moby Dick alone remains, malevolent and purposeless, an eternal menace to civilised order. Ishmael by chance is preserved, a man now doubly lost, for the *Pequod* had been the saving world to which his misanthropic soul had clung and which had redeemed him from misanthropy. Now he is alone again.

Melville's diagnosis of the eternal tragedy of man—a penetrating one in the perfectionist American century, when the native air about him was loud with complacent nationalist optimism from Emerson on the one hand to Hannibal Chollop and Elijah Pogram on the other—pointed to the fatal destructiveness of his unrestricted will. In his most admirable qualities of courage and independence and adventurousness, American man (and Melville clearly indicates, every other race of man as well), is betrayed by this deadly wilfulness, which enlarges those qualities at once into a *hubris* potent to destroy not merely the proud man but the humble he carries with him. D. H. Lawrence saw this evil very clearly, and recognised Melville's capacity to understand it too. He regarded Moby Dick as the "deepest blood-nature of the white race", hunted down "by the maniacal fanaticism of our white mental consciousness", which naturally destroyed itself in the hunt. For him the novel spelt "the doom of our white day". It reinforced his belief in the power of the dark gods to resist all attempts to civilise them. This was directly apposite to Lawrence's own philosophy; it is no wonder that the book made a lasting impression on him. It is not possible, perhaps, to read Melville's symbolism so glibly without believing so strongly in Lawrence's own individual reading of human evolution; but it is possible to find in the book a meaning which may have as convincing an application to a less esoteric philosophy. Melville wrote it out of an inner vision which corresponds to no man's theory but Melville's, and no other man can interpret that vision as exactly as he has, in concrete symbol, expressed it himself. This is a truth common to all great symbolic art, and it should not, though it does, need repeating. It seems presumptuous to rationalise too closely upon the compulsive expression of the emotional imagination. All that is admissible is to analyse, select, appreciate, reset in what seems the most significant order the salient characteristics of this masterpiece of literature; and to extract from that difficult exercise the essential elements which appear to have made it such an organic, such a significant work of genius. From this there emerges unobscured the bitterness of the lesson that Blake had seen so clearly; that uninformed by humility, by passiveness, and by love, the will kills. "Evil is the Active springing from Energy." All the glory and the ingenuity of man are vitiated by the injudicious will; it is a commonplace of history. And the will, by violating man's constructive instincts, arouses those which are more destructive and more dangerous; which like Moby Dick fascinate and challenge and destroy him.

This may have been Melville's general observation, and his symbols answer it in their development into the colossal myth embodying it. But his great book was born of more than this. It was born of physical ardour and experience, of years of drudging travel, of hours and hours of reading and conversation and conjecture, of an altogether unusual though but partly tutored eloquence and inventiveness; and, combining with the natural but phenomenal maturity of all these, a personal philosophic despair whose origin can neither be traced nor diagnosed but only guessed at through the outward form it took in his writings. Its effect upon his work was profound and lasting; it is here in his masterpiece that it is felt most impressively, since here alone he was able to co-ordinate it with the fullest power of his art. It informs this book totally; so that while it can be, and has continued to be, enjoyed as epic and encyclopedia, tract and tragedy, handbook and heroic romance, the finest novel America has yet given to the world, it proclaims unmistakably Melville's spiritual desolation. The deepest tragedy of Ahab is not his own violent destruction; but the survival and the loneliness of Ishmael.

CHAPTER XII

Pierre and the Defeat of Innocence

*M*OBY DICK for all its bulk and length is tautly controlled; at no time has the shaping slipped beyond the author's intent or capacity. *Pierre* was not so fortunate. Melodrama and metaphysics are dangerous companions, and for reasons we must examine closely Melville mixed them with an injudicious hand until verbosity and portentousness flowed all over the central conception and plunged the urgency of his theme fathoms deep below the flaccid surface of an unconvincing story. In *Moby Dick* an equilibrium was achieved which for all its passionate endeavour *Pierre* misses; yet it is a grave mistake to dismiss the later novel into oblivion on that account. It is on the one hand an artistic failure, a naïve and clumsy romance for the perfection of which Melville had neither the experience nor the taste; but on the other it is a careful continuation of the search prosecuted in *Moby Dick*—not this time for an enemy, but rather for an ideal. That the result is the same is a corroboration of all Melville's tragic intuitions.

"Doubts of all things earthly, and intuitions of some things heavenly," remarked Melville in a late chapter of *Moby Dick*. "This combination makes neither believer nor infidel, but makes a man who regards them both with equal eye." Ishmael, alone upon the waters after the shipwreck of the *Pequod*, had his doubts and intuitions most uncompromisingly confirmed, yet in the telling of his tragedy retained that admirable objective balance that is one of the prime elements in the book's greatness. Ishmael-Melville suffers and accepts, the Passive that obeys reason, riding the spiritual catastrophe that overwhelmed Ahab; Pierre-Melville suffers and rebels, the objective equilibrium distorted, the creative values implicit in the doubts and the intuitions rendered sterile. Yet the book is not a repudiation of the values that *Moby Dick* proclaimed. It reaffirms and elaborates them. Nothing in *Moby Dick* is so expressive or explicit as the remarkable pages in *Pierre* in which Melville condenses into a dozen paragraphs his considered statement of the conflicting elements which alike inspire and frustrate humanity; and it is convenient to begin consideration of *Pierre* with these for text, since they serve *Pierre* even more closely and appropriately for apologue than Father Mapple's discourse serves *Moby Dick* or the Grand Inquisitor fable serves *The Brothers Karamazov*. In his acutely conceived antithesis those same balanced "doubts and intuitions" of the earlier book find a more elaborate, more closely examined parallel. The chapter stamps the book with the spiritual authority which its predecessor revealed on all levels of expression but which, for reasons to be examined in a moment, is hampered and obscured in *Pierre*. Only in such chapters as these does the essential quality of the work make itself plain, thrusting the crudities of the melodramatic presentation into a perspective in which they seem somehow less damaging.

The key chapter is in the form of a pamphlet discovered by Pierre among the cushions of the coach taking him and his protégées from the security of Saddle Meadows to the uncertainties of the city. It is the book's half-way house; all that has preceded it is the preparation for tragic action; while all that is to follow is held to stem inevitably from the fatal disharmony in human nature which frustrates every action that Pierre attempts and which this pamphlet obliquely but subtly anatomises. The book's sub-title (*Pierre: or the Ambiguities*) has been as generally ignored as most sub-titles, and as unwarrantably, for it is a deliberate pointer to the growing intensification of Melville's obsession with the paradoxes by which man exists indeed, but by which he is compelled through ignorance and wilfulness to his own destruction. Here as the centre-piece of his book of the ambiguities he has set his chapter on the two kinds of truth; the elemental discrepancy at the roots of all human tragedy.

He begins on the safe and familiar ground that it had perhaps been better if he had never left—the analogy from navigation by chronometer.

> "It seems to me, in my visions" (says Plotinus Plinlimmon, the author of the pamphlet) "that there is a certain most rare order of human souls, which if carefully carried in the body will almost always and everywhere give Heaven's own Truth, with some small grains of variance. For peculiarly coming from God, the sole source of that heavenly truth, and the great Greenwich hill and tower from which the universal meridians are far out into infinity reckoned; such souls seem as London sea-chronometers, which as the London ship floats past Greenwich down the Thames, are accurately adjusted by Greenwich time, and if heedfully kept, will still give that same time, even though carried to the Azores."

This is stated with an economy of phrase which is a pleasure and a relief after Melville's 200-page long flounder among romantic and metaphysical cliché that had preceded it.

> "Now in an artificial world like ours," he resumes after some elaborations, "man is further removed from its God and the Heavenly Truth, than the chronometer carried to China is from Greenwich. And, as that chronometer, if at all accurate, will pronounce it to be twelve o'clock high noon, when the China local watches say perhaps it is twelve o'clock midnight; so the chronometric soul, if in this world true to its great Greenwich in the other, will always, in its so-called intuitions of right and wrong, be contradicting the mere local standards and watch-maker's brains of this earth.
> "Bacon's brains were mere watchmaker's brains; but Christ was a chronometer."

There can be nothing but acquiescence in the truth and effectiveness of this passage; and as we study it further, Melville's purpose in *Pierre* becomes clearer. For he goes on to insist, not upon the absolute value of the chronometrical soul as against the restricted watchmaker's brains of common humanity, but (characteristically) upon the positive though limited value of the common order of human souls. "As the China watches are right as to China, so the Greenwich chronometers must be wrong as to China . . . and thus, though the earthly wisdom of man be heavenly folly to God; so also, conversely, is the heavenly wisdom of God an earthly folly to man. Nor does the God at the heavenly Greenwich expect common men to keep Greenwich wisdom in this remote Chinese world of ours; because such a thing were unprofitable for them here, and indeed a falsification of Himself, inasmuch as in that case China time would be identical with Greenwich time, which would make Greenwich time wrong."

Melville proceeds to discuss with great earnestness the un-doubted practicability, in the world's context, of conduct regulated by chronometrical standards. The dilemma of the man who per-ceives their beauty and yet knows it to spell suicide to a practical scheme of existence, who knows his heavenly intuition to conflict fundamentally with his earthly code or creed, is examined and, though not resolved, illuminated by the clarity of logic. The answer to the problem can only be found in compromise—a pro-cedure of which the imagination fired by the "chronometrical" vision is inevitably suspicious, but which will have to be resorted to if the necessary equilibrium is to be found and sustained. The horological man (Melville's term for the ordinary man regulated by terrestrial ideas) must learn to absorb into his familiar values a dilution of the chronometrical ideals which he has faintly per-ceived; the chronometrical soul must regulate his intensity of purpose to accord with local horological limitations. "A virtuous expediency", concludes Melville, "seems the highest desirable or attainable earthly excellence for the mass of men, and is the only earthly excellence that their Creator intended for them." He hints at the danger of the doctrine that man must aim at heaven, and attain it, in all his earthly acts, in pain of eternal wrath; seeing that man too often realises the complete impossibility of success and in consequence turns desperately to reckless extremes of evil— the fatal despair, he calls it, "that has too often proved the vice-producing result of the undiluted chronometrical doctrines hitherto taught to mankind." In his advocacy of a wise discrimina-tion between the counsels of perfection and the counsels of utilitarian expediency, he claims that he is giving practicable virtue to the vicious and consolation to the earnest. And with this stoic conclusion the pamphlet comes to an abrupt end.

L

This much can be deduced at first sight; that *Pierre* is adventuring further than any of Melville's previous books into problems involving human conduct and the exercise of free will; *Pierre* develops the destructiveness but the will here is explicitly unfettered. The central figure of *Moby Dick* had elemental opponents only; Pierre has all of these, and his own capacity for judgment and selection too. To continue the tale of the progressive disintegration of Innocence embodied in the sequence of Melville's novels as they were written and published, the tragedy of Ishmael can be said to be the tragedy of Innocence overwhelmed by Experience, while the tragedy of Pierre is rather the far more piteous tragedy of Innocence in rebellion against Experience. The more vigorous the resistance he puts up, the more ruthlessly his moves are countered; on to the absolute questions of good and evil, with which *Moby Dick* had trafficked, are superadded the Hawthornian elements of right and wrong. Pierre is called upon to satisfy the Puritans and the Stoics at one and the same time; and the effort is too much for him. The subtleties of the Plinlimmon pamphlet reveal their relevancies to him too late; his attempt to impose a "chronometrical" pattern upon events barely within his own intellectual and moral comprehension is as disastrous as his reading of that pamphlet should have shown him it would be. (The irony of the discrepancies between his conduct and the pamphlet's precepts is pointed by the device of making him mislay the pamphlet when he feels he has most need to refresh his first imperfect impressions of its pertinence; and by the subsequent disclosure that it had merely slipped into the lining of his coat and was therefore close to him all the time had he but known it; an example of Melville's over-sedulous care in pointing an allegorical image, which in a context of greater immediacy he would have struck off with a spontaneous ease concealing art rather than drawing attention to it.)

The story of *Pierre* has in itself the elements of impressive drama, and there are no essential absurdities in either the central plot or in the broad manipulative treatment that Melville gives to it. A brief summary reveals not only its symmetry and compactness, but also its undoubted potentialities, as a fertile tragic theme. Pierre, a sensitive and intelligent youth of nineteen, is the adored and adoring son of a youthful and attractive widow living in feudal comfort on an ancestral country estate. He is heir to a fortune, his betrothal is suitably idyllic, his hopes are golden and his contact

with experience both actually and prospectively negligible. The
only ominous note struck at the outset is the artificial intensity of
his relationship with his mother, a blend of false sentimentality and
jealous possessiveness which contains all the elements of conflict
when their personalities develop beyond the point of equilibrium.
The occasion for such conflict is provided by the arrival in the
neighbourhood of a mysterious young girl, who without warning
reveals herself to Pierre as the illegitimate daughter of his dead
father—the father whom he has idolised in the past until his
memory is as sacred to him as his present love for his mother or
his Lucy. She throws herself upon his mercy; her miserable history
and the strange mesmeric quality of her character compel him to
recognise her claim; but knowing both by intuition and experience
the implacability of his mother which in the present case would
unite with a more personal jealousy to lead her to hatred and
rejection of Isabel, Pierre after a desperate and pitiful self-commu-
nion determines to sacrifice himself for Isabel's sake by taking the
only course which will preserve his father's memory intact in his
mother's mind and save Isabel from the results of her bitterness.
He therefore tells his mother that he is secretly married to Isabel,
and departs from home for ever, taking her and her outcast protégée
Delly to seek their joint fortunes in the city, under the double
humiliation of his mother's furious anger and his own necessary
rejection of the girl he really loves. On arrival in the city he is
cold-shouldered by his cousin, once his bosom friend, from whom
he had expected welcome and assistance; he hears soon that his
mother, after disinheriting him, has died insane; and he is forced
to support his melancholy household in conditions of unwonted
and pinching poverty by trading for the present on an inflated
occasional reputation as a writer, achieved in the past year or two
through trifles in the more precious literary magazines. Faithfully
attended by Isabel and Delly, he sets to work on a book that shall
at least do something to restore their fortunes; and he is reinforced
by the arrival, against her family's strong opposition, of his rejected
sweetheart Lucy who, divining more behind his dereliction than
he could ever have disclosed to her, begs to be received as one of
his household. Ironically, the very experiences which have so
catastrophically matured his imagination have simultaneously
rendered his writings, so eagerly sought after before, unacceptable
and unsaleable in the eyes of his commercial exploiters; and his

book is savagely rejected at the very moment when, his health broken by privation and despair, Pierre is assailed by threats from his cousin and Lucy's brother, who band together to publish him as a common seducer and liar. In his rage and desperation he shoots his cousin dead in the street. The same night he is visited in prison by Isabel and Lucy; the former in the ecstasy of anguish reveals to Lucy her relationship to Pierre, and when the shock kills Lucy on the spot Pierre snatches from Isabel the phial of poison he knows she always carries; and she is in time to drink the dregs that he leaves when he dies.

The theme is redolent of Melville's fascinated reading of the Elizabethan drama; part of its grotesquerie is its violent translation from the gaudy Renaissance courts and cloisters to the naturalistic background of New England and New York. All the familiar trappings of murderous jealousy, incest, poison, bastardy, madness, portraits—concomitants of a dozen plays contemporary with Shakespeare or Webster—are reproduced in a setting in which incongruity is the least of the obstacles to the suspension of disbelief. Even the servants, coachmen, officers of the police-station and the prison, are Elizabethan rather than contemporary; their language is that of Shakespeare's clowns, not of Dickens' ostlers or cabmen. The transition from the brilliant nervous naturalism of the earlier books in which he had successfully controlled large numbers of active characters—particularly *Redburn* and *White-Jacket*—is conspicuous; but it is less abrupt for the intensification in the second part of *Moby Dick*, of the posed dramatic dialogues and declamatory soliloquies. Technically, it must be admitted, there has been preparation for the change; but the imagination is given less assistance in *Pierre*. In the earlier book the intricate realism of the surroundings has helped to impose conviction on the most extravagant action; and acceptance of the heightened tension has left the reader very early on in a mood of ready response. In the later the eloquence seems forced; genuine as the originating emotions are, they are presented against a background which was not, for the most part, native to Melville's imagination. Where in *Moby Dick* the scene and its details tingle continuously at his fingers' ends, experience electrified into evocative atmosphere, in *Pierre* he imposes his emotion from outside on to a scene which he has been obliged to manufacture out of the disjointed reminiscences either of his unassimilated reading or of experience whose quickening power had been less effective. Far too much of his essential scene setting, therefore, is of a sentimental and derivative romanticism whose crude naïveté carries disconcerting hints, not only of such genuine artists as Disraeli and Edgar Allan Poe, but (in unguarded moments) of Amanda Ros and Daisy Ashford. And against the overblown exaggeration of such a setting, the profoundest metaphysical conjecturings would find it hard to carry conviction, even if expressed in more temperate terms than Melville's exalted Jacobean prose can afford them.

This is the serious initial handicap which every earnest estimate of this novel has to surmount at the start; and it has crippled all but the most pertinacious of critics. It has obscured not only the mature constructional skill—the loose amorphous fluidity of *Mardi* had been replaced in *Moby Dick* by a control over dramatic tension which in *Pierre* is elaborated rather than relaxed—but what is more important still, the profound and urgent spiritual speculations to which *Moby Dick* could only provide one symbolic answer and to which *Pierre* was designed to provide another and if possible a more satisfying one. It is not easy to come at the truth in a couple of sentences; but all the signs point to the gradual stifling of Melville's superb imaginative powers by the hypertrophy of his conjectural obsessions. A natural genius in the conversion of direct experience into creative art, he could not balance this faculty with an equal power of control over philosophy and metaphysic; and when in the service of his ever-active spiritual perplexities he had exhausted (as virtually he had by the end of *Moby Dick*) his store of galvanic experience, he had nothing but an untrained intellect, and an amateur technique in the use of it, to carry him further, though every instinct continued to impel him forward. The racing activity of his brain is evidenced by the barely believable energy which plunged him directly into *Pierre* with hardly a moment's respite after the completion of *Moby Dick*, an achievement after which any normal author would surely have been entitled if not forced to a prolonged breathing-space. Such activity can only be regarded as admirably courageous; testifying to his realisation, even as he completed his masterpiece, that it was already out of date in his mind, superseded by an urgency which he could not in honesty deny. His imagination failed, and his book failed too; it was the beginning of the strange rift in Melville's development that cracked his literary achievement in two and all but foundered him at the very peak of his powers. A penetrating critic, Fitzjames O'Brien, commenting a few years later in *Putnam's Magazine* on the decline in popularity of this unusually promising and original writer, spoke the first word—and it may be the last, for there can be little to supersede it—when he referred to Melville indulging himself "in a trick of metaphysical and morbid meditations until he has almost perverted his fine mind from its healthy productive tendencies. A singularly truthful person—as all his sympathies show him to be—he has succeeded in vitiating both his thought and his style with an appearance of the wildest affectation and untruth. His life, as we should judge, has been excessively introverted."[1]

Moreover there were many factors hampering *Pierre* at the outset. The first was Melville's health. It can be gathered from his own direct and oblique accounts of the creative process, both in the grim and realistic later chapters of *Pierre* itself and in the earlier but no less impressive descriptions in *Mardi* of the physical and mental rigours endured by the imagined author Lombardo and the actual narrator of the book, that the period and act of creation for Melville set up a shattering physical strain. At the time when he finished *Moby Dick* and, by compulsion or choice, started at once upon its tough successor, there had hardly been a month, since the remarkable sequence of books had started with *Typee*, when he had been free from the sustained grind. The obvious exaltation in which he completed *Moby Dick* must have driven him to the limits of his physical resources. The White Whale's flurry was a poor dramatisation of the powerful conflicts he endured; the "devouring profundities", the "unfathomable cravings" consume all his vigour. "He is fitting himself," cries Melville of the agonising labours of Pierre, "for the highest Life, by thinning his blood and collapsing his heart. He is learning how to live by rehearsing the part of death . . . this book, like a vast lumbering planet, revolves in his aching head. He cannot command the thing out of its orbit; fain would he behead himself, to gain one night's repose." Mr. Van Wyck Brooks, with his rather too ready propensity to assume autobiography in every phrase of Melville's narratives, assumes that Melville himself suffered the nervous disorders that he made descend upon Pierre, and that the temporary blindness and vertigos that assailed his hero were authentic transcriptions of sicknesses that he had himself suffered in the heats of his

[1] Quoted by Van Wyck Brooks, *The Times of Melville and Whitman*, p. 129.

composition. With all due discount allowed, the probability is evident that the robust sailor who left the sea in 1844 had worked himself sick by 1851, with a sickness that invaded the mind as well as the body; and though mental and bodily illness are not necessarily inimical to the highest expressions of art, they are dangerous elements to accompany a fresh adventure of the imagination.

The second crippling factor is more important. It is, in fact, fundamental. *Moby Dick* had seen him at the peak of his art. There the symbol, given its head by a superb intuitive act of faith, revealed in the sombre yet beautiful close of the tragedy the answer to his conjectural doubts and fears. *Moby Dick* was Melville's supreme symbol but it could not and did not provide him with the supreme answer. His active speculations roved immediately beyond the point to which his artistic faith had led him. The core of the failure of *Pierre* is the failure of Melville to find a symbol adequate to a task even harder than that which had confronted him in *Moby Dick*. It was almost inevitable that in that particular and peculiar context—an exhausted man renewing unsatisfied a search which his highest imaginative flights had only lately failed to satisfy—any attempt of that kind should end in disaster. Nevertheless his efforts, probably for the most part unconscious ones, to seek out symbols to support his new metaphysical curiosities, are most revealing.

Mr. Jack Lindsay has remarked of Dickens that his greatness as a novelist lies in the way in which he can define general tendencies in terms of personal relations.[1] Melville, at least in the bulk of his work, provides a direct contrast to this. His importance can be gauged rather by the way in which, in his work, natural objects of his own experience—a voyage, a ship and its crew, the whale, the sea, the human will—are elevated to a symbolic significance in which they both represent and illuminate the timeless conflicting elements in the universe. The closer personal relations, at least up to the end of *Moby Dick*, left Melville's creative imagination undisturbed. The static friendship of a Toby or a Jack Chase, the cold enmity of a Jackson, the touching but unfruitful blood-brotherhood of Queequeg and Ishmael, are none of them exceptions to this declaration. Fayaway is a pretty picture, Yillah and Hautia are relatively ineffectual allegorical figures representing conceptions as yet unripe for symbolic presentation, all the characters in *Moby Dick* are subordinate to Ahab whose personal relations

[1] *Charles Dickens*, p. 281.

for the most part are of the sketchiest. It is too broad a statement that until Melville embarked upon *Pierre* he had never attempted a study of a personal relationship that was designed, either productively or destructively, to have a decisive effect upon his story. He did not need to; his effective symbols he could find elsewhere. But after *Moby Dick* he found that he had dredged up from his past travels all the quickening memories that had sustained him through his writing life. There were no more left; and yet his cerebral speculations demanded a further symbolic vehicle for what he still needed urgently to express.

Therefore he turned to the commonplaces of romance, the narrative and dramatic conventions which had sufficed the second-rate writer for centuries, and used them as far as he could as substitutes for the genuine experience upon which all his effective imaginative writing had hitherto been based. He turned from the elemental topic of adventurous man at combat with unknown territory or unknown sea, and attempted what was at once the simpler and the harder task—the topic of man in conflict with his own kind. In a way it was right instinct that led him to do so; the subtler elaborations into which his conjectures were developing demanded a more intricate symbolisation than his previously chosen topics could ever afford; but since the spark of his creative intuition was never fired so readily by the contemplation of character as it was by the impact of simple physical action or simple natural phenomena, the new topic of his choice revealed a certain imaginative bankruptcy.

But it revealed at the same time much that is of high value. It threw him back upon the common resource of an inadequate imagination—autobiography; and the more that this detracts from the value of the novel as an organic work of art, the more it re-establishes it as an indispensable document in the unfolding of a great writer's consciousness. *Pierre* is not very important fiction, but it is very important Melville. Mr. Robert S. Forsythe, in his sympathetic introduction to his edition of the book, issued in 1930, has perhaps over-stated his case in his anxiety to acquit Melville of a collapse into a maundering despair—an anxiety natural enough in view of *Pierre's* casual and sometimes contemptuous dismissal at the hands of so many critics. He believes that *Pierre* was an experiment by Melville in the problem novel. That conjecture tells us little of the nature of any such experiment,

what it implied or whether it succeeded or failed. But he goes on to
assert that Pierre is "not a mere confession of its author's despair
and soul-sickness: the book presents an invented situation objectively—the story of Pierre Glendinning, not that of Herman
Melville." In so far as Melville may not have fallen in love with his
half-sister, been disinherited by his mother, or killed his cousin,
the conclusion is superficially true enough; but it is misleading to
regard the book as in any way objective when the author has been
so patently driven, for lack of more potent symbols to hand, back
to his own personal traditions and personal memories to reinforce
the imagery clothing the fable. Here again we have the poverty of
symbol to thank for the revelation of the compulsive egoism that
created *Pierre*. It is as if Ishmael, the last man left alive at the
catastrophe of *Moby Dick*, had spent his day and night upon the
waters in searching himself for an answer, and as if *Pierre* was the
fruit of his contemplation. Ishmael had lost everything; he had
nothing to turn to but Melville. Nor had Melville. Just as *Moby
Dick* is a close examination of universal society in terms of religion,
Pierre is an equally close examination of the individual in terms of
morality. And Melville was the only individual Melville knew. The
situation of *Pierre* may have been, as Mr. Forsythe says, invented
(with considerable aid from the melodramatic convention of several
generations and a very special debt to *Hamlet*); but it was invented
out of Melville's deepest self-awareness, a subjective tragedy and
not an objective narrative.

This is evident from the beginning in the pains Melville took to
invest Pierre in the honours and inspirations of his own personal
family tradition. There is no other valid way to account for the
intricate care with which the background of Saddle Meadows is
built up piece by piece out of the authentic records of Melville's
own ancestors. "Saddle Meadows" itself is a mixture of Melville's
own house "Arrowhead", in Pittsfield, where *Moby Dick* and
Pierre were written, and the manor house near Albany where he
had stayed as a boy at the home of his mother's brother; and later
prose sketches in Melville's Hawthornian vein, such as "I and My
Chimney", and the first of the *Piazza Tales*, confirm the fascination with which his restless mind was always attracted to the serene
landscape of the Berkshires, finding tokens of refreshment and
repose there. Anchoring his story in a setting with which he could
identify himself creatively, he attached to his hero's ancestors all

the attributes of his own forebears which helped to root his tale and his imagination in the most fertile ground possible for his purpose—their connection with the honourable history of their country. Thus the first few sections of the novel are devoted to an assertion of the Glendinning family dignity traced through the martial honours won by Pierre's father and grandfather at crucial phases in the development of modern America. His great-grandfather is stated to have died on the ancestral lands in battle with the Indians, cheering on his men as he sat unhorsed on his saddle on the grass—from which incident the name of "Saddle Meadows" was afterwards given to his home. His grandfather, too, had defended for months a stockaded fort in the Revolutionary War; and surviving the battle to live into an honoured old age, he died in 1812. "Like a hero of old battles, he dies on the eve of another war; ere wheeling to fire on the foe, his platoons fire over their old commander's grave. . . . The drum that beat in brass his funeral march was a British kettle drum that had only helped beat the vainglorious march . . . of that bragging boy Burgoyne."

This is pure family history; for Melville's mother's father, General Peter Gansevoort, had defended Fort Stanwix against the British in 1777, captured colours and drum from St. Leger's expedition, and died in 1812. The saddle episode does not belong to him but to a fellow general who met his death in the march to the relief of Fort Stanwix. That Melville cherished a deep regard for the associations of this name is confirmed by the fact that he gave the name of Stanwix to his second son.

Further identifications are possible, though they should be hinted at rather than insisted upon. That Allan Melville and the elder Pierre Glendinning both died when their sons were twelve, and are both, the one in fact and the other in fiction, commemorated in chair-portraits, make up sufficient evidence for the source rather than the narrative detail, of the character of Pierre's father; that the elder Glendinning died in delirium and the elder Melville is believed by some authorities to have died "deranged", is merely an instance of the lasting quality of a childhood impression. The identification of Isabel with Melville's own pious sister Augusta is unimaginative and unrewarding, being possibly more than half due to an unconscious memory of an earlier Augusta famous in literary history as the object of a more than brotherly love. And whether or not Maria Melville was equated in the novelist's mind with his own creation of Pierre's mother Mary Glendinning, the imaginative use that he made of the relationship is so much more important than its problematical actuality that further conjecture about incidental autobiographical incidents is vain. All that need here be established is the deliberate attempt which Melville has made to identify his problem-hero with his own ancestral past. Pierre is his own, not actual but imaginative, innocent self with his own peculiar family-consciousness, race-consciousness, history-consciousness. The aristocratic demesne at Saddle Meadows emphasises both the virile traditionalism and the secluded innocence of sentient young America. Just as the relation between the *Pequod* and America considerably broaden the application of *Moby Dick*, *Pierre* loses much of its effect if its national significance is ignored. From now on Melville's awareness of contemporary society and its development will colour decisively the selection of his theme and treatment.

Therefore there can be no reasonable doubt that Melville's own consciousness is as much the central preoccupation of Pierre as if the tale had been what it is not, a straight autobiography. But whereas his poetic or religious consciousness had dominated *Moby Dick*, it is his moral and social consciousness that determined the power of *Pierre*. (It did not, unhappily, prove capable of determining its own form as well; that is one of the reasons for the failure of the book as art.) It is on that account that it is perhaps not as necessary as it might superficially seem to read important psychological significances into his account of the relationships between Pierre and his mother, Pierre and his half-sister, and so on. The driving themes that give the book its interest and value are not primarily personal ones. The personal relationships in *Pierre* are chosen by Melville merely as convenient machinery to operate his principal thesis, and not as central dramatic situations out of which his theme inevitably develops. Abstract speculation had impelled him to certain philosophical conclusions; and in his memory and his reading he found second-hand symbols to express them. That is the reason for this set of familiar situations and themes already catalogued; and we need look no further than Melville's reading of Elizabethan drama, and his fascination for the prose styles of both the seventeenth-century prose writers and his own contemporary Carlyle, for an explanation of his choice. It cannot be too often insisted that the inspiration of *Pierre* was not Melville's love for his father or domination by his mother, or any other ambiguous emotional tangle. These may have existed, probably did, but that does not matter; what did exist was his obsession with the ambiguities implicit in the demands both of nature and society; and he chose stock symbols partly out of derivative weakness and partly out of the instinctive sympathy with the great traditional myths of which *Hamlet*, *Pierre's* spiritual original, is the prototype. Hamlet is the perplexed sensitive man appalled by the necessity and the impossibility of right choice; so, at another stage of the myth's development, is Pierre. Hamlet is destroyed because he is incapable of choice and knows it; Pierre, because he is incapable of choice, does not know it and dares to choose. He is less wise than Hamlet and more brave.

Conceiving his perplexed sensitive man, Melville confronts him with his symbolic ambivalences, the fair Lucy and the dark Isabel. But these are not simply equated with good and evil, ideal and sensual, like Yillah and Hautia (although they derive in part from these shadowy forebears), for both Lucy and Isabel are innocent of destructive purpose, being essentially passive with all their discrepancies in passion and history. The compulsion of evil must come from some other source; and Melville locates it in the daemonic possessiveness of Pierre's mother, the pride and sensuality devouring love with an almost perverse delight. The tragedy in the story stems originally not from Pierre's father's sin but from Pierre's mother's jealousy. In her supreme egoism she would be mother, wife and sister to him all at once; and in the culmination of the tragedy her jealousy destroys all three.

Its destructiveness is so complete because Melville at this period was obsessed with the evil attendant upon the misuse of power. He may have borrowed Mary Glendinning partly from Gertrude of Denmark, partly from general Renaissance dramatic traditions, and partly perhaps from certain characteristics in his own mother; but he derived his consciousness of the deadly prerogatives of power from his own poetic imagination, from the same source from which he had dredged up the character and tragedy of Ahab. He understood instinctively the dangers of the too-easy perversion of the mother-son relationship as demonstrated in *Hamlet* (and many times corroborated in fact in the lives of such important imaginative artists as Turgenev, Baudelaire, Ruskin, Proust and D. H. Lawrence) and wove this important psychological strand with admirable skill and effect into the action of his novel. But it is important to remember that this is not the whole of the tragedy. It may be that Pierre's own tragic flaws are to be laid at his mother's door, but if this is good psychology it is not good drama; and the importance of Pierre's tragedy and Melville's book is that Pierre's own weakness contributes to his own destruction.

It is Pierre's tragedy that with all his ancestral tradition behind him he is as helpless before the demands of direct experience as the new-born babe. His traditions are of the kind to protect him from hardship rather than prepare him for it—an implied criticism of the feudal aristocratic way of life which preserves into a changed society the values and standards fitted only for the system which it has superseded. The superficiality of Pierre's intellectual and imaginative equipment is symbolically presented in the bitter satire on literary America of the 'fifties; in which, as Melville knew only too well, a new commercialism was arising to capitalise the genuine imaginative renaissance and so ultimately to destroy it. Melville presents, under the guise of Pierre's derivative little fragments hailed as masterpieces, his mature opinion of his own early and exaggerated popularity; and later, in the complete misunderstanding and misrepresentation of Pierre's first work of any weight or importance, he comments wryly on the failure of his own masterpiece to be accepted even by discriminating critics. In this specialised form Melville underlines the inadequacy, the inevitable and expected inadequacy, of Pierre to confront misfortune with any success; and proceeds from this point to underline the peculiar appositeness of his failure and to show how his very courage and his very innocence are the direct causes of a downfall which, under Melville's stars, was not to be avoided.

For Pierre's actions, from the moment of the revelation to him of his father's sin and his own consequent dilemma, are inspired first by a quixotic idealism born of a romantic immaturity and next by a fatal obstinacy in the face of enlightenment. His action in impetuously befriending Isabel and Delly at the cost of his own security and good name has a youthful nobility that underlines the tragedy of the consequences; but there is an essential irresponsibility, in the very arbitrariness of his decision and abruptness in carrying it into effect, that is rooted more deeply in his character than even the honourable altruism that accompanies it. Therefore it is no surprise to find his flight to the city ending in disaster; courage such as his, based on traditional codes of idealism with no corresponding sanction of experience, is nothing but dangerous delusion. Under the strain of unfamiliar circumstance, his idealism turns to sour egotism. Impelled by the noblest reasons, he converts his conscience into selfhood, wraps his enthusiasm in fanaticism, breaks his health and unbalances his reason, and compasses the ruin of himself, his family, his lovers and his friends.

The second half of the book is an attempt, only partially successful, to suggest how a character, reinforced by noble ideals only, deteriorates morally and imaginatively when those ideals are put to the test of experience and meet opposition for which they are not prepared. Pierre is, psychologically and dramatically, an immature Ahab. If it followed from this that the book *Pierre* merely stated over again in an imperfect form a thesis which had received complete expression in *Moby Dick*, then it would have for the most part to be written off as a retrogression; but since it contains the very important additional element of social morality, it must be regarded at least as proof of Melville's determined attempt to match an intellectual advance with a comparable imaginative expansion. The destructive will of Ahab is matched by the destructive will of Pierre; dramatically for obvious reasons a less effective force, but intellectually one of subtler implications. It is difficult to agree with Professor Matthiessen's opinion that in *Pierre* Melville conceived a tragedy "opposite to" Ahab's. This is of course of a piece with his later remark that the tragedy "has very little to do with political or social values". On the imaginative plane both of these statements seem true; but viewed as an intellectual exercise (and *Pierre* succeeds here, though as an imaginative experiment it does not) *Pierre* seems a natural extension into the field of human society of the earlier book's more primitive religious theories.

Pierre's flaw is not in his integrity; it is in the combination of his innocence and his idealism. "Don't use that foreign word *ideals*", says Dr. Relling to Gregers Werle in *The Wild Duck*; "We've got the excellent native word *lies*." Pierre fiercely renounces the intellect; he destroys at the height of his crisis his copies of Dante and *Hamlet*, for as Melville hints he was too mature for their superficial graces and not mature enough for their profundities; they both give him renewed cause for anger against fate and taunt him for his delay. Therefore he destroys them. "The heart! the heart! 'tis God's anointed; let me pursue the heart!" he cries. Renouncing the intellect, he embraces a passionate impulsiveness. A wiser man would have recognised the danger into which he fell at once; for his innocence, preoccupied with the trammels of the intellect, over-looked the far more dangerous, insidiously puritanical fetters of idealism whose hold on his emotions was more secure than the intellect's and (equated in Relling's words with lies) far more des-tructive. Gregers Werle's idealism involves the death of Hedwig and the dissolution of the Ekdals' illusory happiness, the "livslög-nen", the life-illusion without which existence is impossible; Pierre's leads to the murderer's cell and the sombre tableau of the three dead lovers with which the book closes—reminiscent of the Laocoön statue used as a symbol earlier in the book, the doomed figures entwined with the snakes of a destructive will. Pierre has tried, without possessing the maturity, to act like a chronometrical man in a world of horologicals. The Plinlimmon pamphlet is pro-foundly in point. Melville sets it at the centre of his book because it provides the only answers to the book's problems.

The figure of Plinlimmon himself marks the logical extension of his pamphlet's doctrines, and the only answer that Melville himself feels able to offer. If idealism, a too impetuous identification of the self with perfectionist social theories, results only in the self's humiliation and the distortion of its purposes, then idealism must be avoided even if it means courting the opposite extreme. Plin-limmon's pamphlet has already dropped the hint; "a virtuous ex-pediency is the highest attainable earthly excellence for the mass of men"; and Plinlimmon in person is an emphatic witness to the creed of non-attachment to which Melville's increasing disillusion was guiding him. This mild and elderly philosopher had attained a wide reputation as a sage among the disciples and scholars of the intellectual community among which Pierre sought to carry on his writing when he was finally settled in the city. The treatment of the society is mildly satirical, as Hawthorne's was in the almost exactly contemporary *Blithedale Romance*—both writers making legitimate capital out of the selfconsciousness of the rapidly developing in-tellectual movement in New England, fertile ground for numberless Thelemes as ineffectual as they were laudable—but his references to its mysterious leader are more lingering and enigmatical than would be appropriate to a satire. Here is a detailed account of a character who baffles Melville, it seems, as much as he baffles Pierre. He did no work, read no book, wrote nothing—his published works were imperfect renderings of his conversation, transcribed by his attendant enthusiasts—interfered with nobody save in his entirely passive influence upon those (like Pierre himself) who allowed themselves to become fascinated by his personality. "The whole countenance of this man . . . expressed a cheerful content. Cheerful is the adjective, for it was the contrary of gloom; content— perhaps acquiescence—is the substantive, for it was not Happiness or Delight. But while the personal look and air of this man were thus winning, there was still something latently visible in him which repelled. That something may best be characterised as non-Benevolence. Non-Benevolence seems the best word, for it was neither Malice nor Ill-Will, but something passive."

This passive quality of Plinlimmon is the central antithesis to Pierre's impassioned wilfulness. It is too obscure and too baffling— to Melville as well as to Pierre—to be valid as an antidote; but its presence was noted, and its significance was the foundation for much of Melville's perplexity in the years immediately following the composition of *Pierre*. The "repose" noted by Pierre in the sage's impersonal face, a "repose neither divine nor human, nor anything made up of either or both" is felt, again both by Melville and by Pierre, as a curious and profound challenge to a way of life hitherto too readily accepted. That repose, that mysterious independent indifference, answered with its haunting fascination the nagging energy of common humanity, supplied once more what Melville's intuitions were beginning to respond to as the only possible escape from the crowding preoccupations of civilisation, the negation of action, Keats' negative capability, the passiveness of the flower contrasted with the intolerable busyness of the bee. "Vain! vain! vain! said the face to him. Fool! fool! fool! said the face to him. Quit! quit! quit! said the face to him . . . And now it said to him, Ass! ass! ass!" And to Pierre's mental interrogations the face would not respond; it never broke its iron isolation. Non-benevolent to the end, it refused to be embroiled. It retained its independence.

"The intrepid effort of the soul", declared Melville of Bulkington in *Moby Dick*, was "to keep the open independence of her sea, while the wildest minds of heaven and earth conspire to cast her on the treacherous, slavish shore." Bulkington, aloof and enigmatic, is held in the tail of the narrator's eye at every review of the ship's company of the *Pequod*, unacknowledged but never absent, so potent the mysterious attraction of a man who scorns and repudiates fixed principles. He finds his apotheosis in the "spray of his ocean-perishing", but his resurrection in Plinlimmon; and two years afterwards Melville's most extraordinary short story perpetuates, this time so explicitly that the problem cannot be avoided like a hint but must be squarely tackled as a proposition, the victory of the passive and independent spirit over the engaged energies of social or moral compulsion. In the person of Bartleby the Scrivener Plinlimmon condescends to break his isolation and defy society by death. And this kind of death is the creative sort; Melville makes no mistake about that. Pierre is wasted but Bartleby is not. It is yet another step forward on his lonely imaginative adventure.

Because it is difficult to respond to *Pierre* with the same imaginative and emotional readiness which answers to *Moby Dick*, the book lies under an incurable handicap. In the bold experiment Melville must have understood how the failure to embody his theory in a symbol had resulted in the double failure of symbol and theory alike. There is a story that about the time when he completed *Pierre* Melville's health was in such a depressed condition that he was actually examined for his sanity, and superficial critics might point to the book as strong evidence to justify the suspicion. But surely a little patient study should be enough to disprove it for ever. The book has passages of great poetic insight and eloquence that none but a powerfully controlled imagination could have conceived and designed—notably the two remarkable allegorical insets on the Memnon Stone and the Enceladus rock—where fleetingly the symbols came under the giant control of a great poet and communicated in Titanic imagery conceptions almost too profound for expression. Again, in the Plinlimmon pamphlet the thought is balanced, relevant, persuasive, the work of a visionary whose art has for once proved adequate to his intuition. But these passages are ill co-ordinated, stitched unconvincingly into inferior fabric; their elevance, though genuine, is buried under masses of bewildered and bewildering obscurantism mixed with matter that would disgrace a women's magazine. The great lessons at the heart of *Pierre* are in danger of being left unread. If they only added up to the sum of the lessons of *Moby Dick* it would not be worth while analysing *Pierre* and recommending its careful revaluation. Yet it contains the record of developments in conjecture, in intuition, in poetic imagination and spiritual adventure, to which the triumph of *Moby Dick* was merely a prelude, and which in themselves were only the

M

necessary foundations upon which much of Melville's later and neglected work was built. Ishmael-Melville has escaped alone from the wreck of the *Pequod* to try his innocence in the realm of social morality. Innocence, in the person of Pierre-Melville, meets a deeper destruction than ever Ahab found; but out of the nearly universal ruin Plinlimmon-Melville escapes, chastened and misanthropic, to reconstitute in solitude such innocence as Experience had left him. And just as Ishmael's survival and loneliness form the deepest tragedy of *Moby Dick*, so Plinlimmon's isolation—born this time of experience, as Ishmael's was of innocence—provides the one ray of hope that the remarkable and unfortunate *Pierre* throws forward into the future.

CHAPTER XIII

Tartarus of a Traveller

IT IS A mistake to regard *Pierre* as the beginning of a decline into silence. So much emphasis has been placed by critics on the vigorous promise of the early narratives culminating in the brilliant success of *Moby Dick*, so soon to be dispelled by the ineffectuality of the works and fragments of works that followed, that the downward curve of Melville's attainment has almost tacitly been established and much of the material actually forgotten. Some of what remains is so distasteful as to be practically outlawed, *The Confidence-Man* for its Timonism, *Clarel* for its tedium. For many who take a brisk bird's eye view of Melville, there is nothing significant between *Pierre* and *Billy Budd*. Even such a sympathetic critic as Mr. Middleton Murry has referred to the "long silence" which was "the only appropriate epilogue to Melville's masterpiece." Which was generous, but inaccurate. Melville was never again so furiously productive as during the two or three years of intense activity that threw up *White-Jacket, Moby Dick* and *Pierre* but the five years that followed *Pierre* produced two full-length novels and a remarkable set of short stories, not to mention a considerable collection of prose sketches contributed to *Putnam's Magazine* which were never printed in book form until long after his death. And it is likely that many of the long list of poems which were not published for many years to come were down in first draft at least during the difficult years of the 'fifties. It is quite wrong to think of the machine breaking irreparably in *Pierre*. Nevertheless it is quite common.

It is important, however, to avoid the opposite pitfall. There can be no question that for Melville the 'fifties was a time of peculiar distress, even of despair. There is nothing in his own biographical history that can satisfactorily account for this; and even when conjectures are put forward about the failure of his books, the unfortunate destruction of large stocks of them by a fire at his publisher's, his slow decline in material prosperity, and even the unhappiness of his marriage and mysterious tensions in his family relationships, they yield us no solution of the main problem of the source and nature of the despair that drove an unusually expansive writer into an uneasy, almost suspicious, reticence. It may have been based on bitterness of experience to which we have no clue; or on an advancing disillusionment which his naturally picturesque imagination coloured abnormally high; or on a poetic and intuitive sympathy as impersonal and untraceable as Shakespeare's. Whatever it was we can find it only in his books; and what it was does not matter at all provided that we use those books with a proper sense of their relative value both to Melville and to their readers.

There is a marked change in Melville after *Pierre*, a sufficient reason for much of his later work to be dismissed. But there cannot be much doubt that in fact that change is artistically for the better. Whether he suffered a spiritual shock and, if so, what kind of a shock it was, is neither very clear nor very important; but what is important is that something imposed a discipline upon his writing that had never been able to control it so thoroughly before. Among other accesses of experience may have been the natural (and perhaps profound) disappointment that he had not been able to follow up the supreme symbol of *Moby Dick* with a corresponding and complementary symbolism in *Pierre*. If so the experience was salutary; he instantly retracted the dangerous tendencies of his ambition. He abandoned for the time the more unwieldy symbolisms, and turned to the short prose sketch and the short story.

The reason for this was no doubt partly economic. Professor Raymond Weaver in a detailed analysis of Melville's sales and receipts[1] has shown that although the five years of prolific

---

[1] Introduction to *Shorter Novels of Herman Melville* (Liveright, 1928).

production that ended with *Moby Dick* had brought him about 8,000 dollars all told, his earnings fell away disastrously from that point. *Moby Dick* itself was financially a complete failure; *Pierre* even more so—(Melville's accumulated royalties on this one book for the rest of his life amounted to just about $100.) In the whole year 1853, when seven of his books were in print, the total number of copies sold was 315. He was bound to look elsewhere for sufficient income to keep himself and his family; desultory farming was no more successful than his attempt to find a consular appointment, apparently a favourite resort of American authors at that time. Therefore he set out, with something of desperation in his effort, to write the kind of thing that might appeal more quickly and sell more readily. He found it easy to imitate Hawthorne's sketches and this accounts for the derivative mediocrity of a large proportion of his productions. The surprise and the revelation lie in the excellence of certain of these experiments. In two or three instances, not many more, a happy choice of subject or an almost fortuitous appropriateness of his theme to his mood resulted in a technical masterpiece—the added discipline of space demanding just that economy of treatment that his former exuberance had ignored. In these few instances his penetration and his power lost nothing by the essential limitations; they only gained in an unusual intensity, a power to isolate his mood in a controlled symbolism the more effective because at last uncluttered with metaphysical argument or irrelevant narrative detail. In these pieces the artist in Melville is at last given the chance to come to terms with the traveller, the metaphysician, the amateur poet. He mastered his moods here as only once before he had, on a large scale, successfully mastered his symbol.

Not all of these pieces are worth discussion. Indeed it is not easy to agree that all of them were ever worth printing, so flaccid and tasteless are some of the less inspired sketches. The best, on the whole, are included in the collection published as *The Piazza Tales* in 1856, a remarkable if uneven set of stories reprinted from *Putnam's Magazine* and *Harper's Monthly*. It is important not to overlook *The Piazza Tales*; they mark a stage in their author's progress which has never received adequate critical justice, and they have enriched American literature with at least two of its greatest short stories. The order in which the pieces were composed is uncertain, but neither with these collected sketches nor with those others which were not reprinted until many years after Melville's death does accurate chronological placing matter very much. It is enough if we can isolate the few pieces in which his recognisable genius was in charge, for they form the solitary link that connects his last full-length work with the next important developments in his career. Of the short stories and sketches not more than four need concern us deeply at this stage; they are all in *The Piazza Tales* volume, and they subdivide rather neatly into two groups.

Pierre had been conceived out of an obsession with the duplicity, the "ambiguity" of life. Melville had tried through art to exorcise the demon, but had not succeeded; *Pierre* had raised nearly as many problems as it had sought to answer. And Pierre's failure to come to terms with the metropolitan hustle into which all modern life was rapidly being converted only reflected Melville's own increasing reluctance or disability to come to terms with ordinary human relationships. It is a remarkable fact that *Pierre* was really the last, as it was the first, book in which Melville ever made a square attempt to deal with the common psychological relations between humans at all; which does not mean so much that they baffled him as that they ceased to absorb him. He recoiled from humanity into an unusually austere solitude.

Early in the 1850's he retracted his human contacts as he retracted his artistic adventurousness; his art, like his life, became one-dimensional. His failure to cope with the ambiguities in *Pierre* repeated itself, fascinatingly, in two of the *Piazza Tales*; it made one of them a masterpiece. The subjects and treatment of these two tales may serve later to explain the origin, at least, of the subjects and treatment of the others.

The first is the preliminary sketch—it is hardly substantial enough in theme to be called a story—which introduces *The Piazza Tales*. Appropriately enough it is called *The Piazza*; and presents, with a rather significant epigraph from Fidele's burial in *Cymbeline*, the old-fashioned farmhouse with its pastoral views across to the mountain ranges, to which the narrator comes as to a rural retreat. This farmhouse is clearly Melville's own; he has used it in a number of his other sketches and stories, notably "I and My Chimney", and of course in *Pierre*; and the idyllic view across to the Berkshire mountains, with Greylock conspicuous in the centre, captivated him so that it became part of his imaginative life. The

enormous chimney was enlarged into a potent symbol of his own
egoism; the mountain profited by a mood of Melville's which was
something less than misanthropy and something more than
whimsy, and received the dedication of *Pierre*; the whole wide
landscape which Arrowhead commanded and which had imprinted
itself indelibly upon Melville's preoccupied consciousness as he sat
day after day staring at it and writing *Moby Dick*, ranged itself
round him now as a setting for his new explorations. He comes
back to it as to a retreat; according to the sketch *The Piazza*, he
comes solitary and sick, retired into meditation and recourse to
romantic poets. *The Piazza* for Melville represents a deliberate
retirement; a retirement from which—and this is of great importance to an understanding of his moods at this time—he is coaxed
out, only to meet disappointment.

The tale itself is a common banality, of the kind that leavens a
children's address at a Nonconformist church service. The narrator
in his loneliness looks across to the mountains and sees far in the
distance a golden glitter that interests him strangely. After many
days and weeks of watching and conjecturing he makes it out to be
the reflection of the sun upon the windows of a house. Months of
further romanticizing upon the sort of house it could be lead him
ultimately to travel to see it closer. After a weary journey he
arrives at the house to find it nearly derelict, and tenanted by a
bereaved and sorrowful young girl, whose sole consolation is to
look in her turn across the valley and to romanticise even more
eloquently upon the beauty of the distant homestead which the
narrator had lately left. A neat commonplace tale with a neat
commonplace moral, if Melville had cared to turn aside from his
main preoccupation to draw it; but that he did not press the point
is a sure sign that his story had its origin in the profundity of the
illusion rather than in the facile sententiousness of the popular
interpretation. The comforting conclusion that one's own drab
lodging seems gay and inviting to the watcher across the valley did
not interest Melville at all; the story appealed to him as a corroboration of his increasing belief that the whole of natural beauty
was illusory, and that human devotion and human hope were
illusory too. *The Piazza*, although in itself it is inconsiderable,
forms a quiet and idyllic *coda* to the sound and fury of *Pierre*; its
setting is for much of the time the same, the deep pastoral beauty
of the countryside is lovingly presented in both, the subject of

each (cutting away complications) is the death of illusion, and only the conclusions differ. *Pierre's* climax and catastrophe cut the book off short, leaving no explicit indication of the philosophic response which the tragedy calls out; *The Piazza* restates the tragedy quietly, advising resignation, invoking in Melville and those who are to follow him out to the end an essential stoicism which must from now on be taken for granted. "The scenery is magical", he says in the closing sentences; "the illusion so complete. And Madam Meadow Lark, my prima donna, plays her grand engagement here; and, drinking in her sunrise note, which, Memnon-like, seems struck from the golden window, how far from me the weary face behind it. But every night, when the curtain falls, truth comes in with darkness. No light shows from the mountain. To and fro I walk the piazza deck, haunted by Marianna's face, and many as real a story."

The insistence upon stoicism, the silent acceptance of suffering, is a vein which later *Piazza Tales*, as I shall show, go on to tap at first profusely and later almost to the exclusion of all others. The bereaved girl in *The Piazza* is merely a sketch for the other and more famous bereaved girl in *The Encantadas*. But before the obsession with stoicism superseded the somewhat subtler concern with the ambiguity of truth, he gave the earlier problem wonderful expression in what must be on all counts the greatest of his short stories. In *Benito Cereno* he produced a compact, gripping narrative of the sea in about a hundred pages of prose that packs the emotional content of the best passages of *Moby Dick* into an unfamiliar, disciplined form. Here the theme of ambiguity that had been a prime factor in the conception of *Pierre* (though it was overlaid in the expression by so many other implications of the main tragedy) and was restated clearly but without emphasis in *The Piazza*, received for the first and perhaps the only time in Melville the fully effective symbolic treatment that it deserved. *Benito Cereno* is a great story, with an atmospheric intensity much resembling Joseph Conrad's and a technique of suspense masking most dramatically the controlled physical and psychological realism which gives the narrative its powerful impact; the whole representing, in one of Melville's best sustained allegorical essays, the profoundly disturbing conflicts which he perceived at the heart of human nature. Like so many other of Melville's works, it has been only very spasmodically available in Great Britain of recent years; and even Mr. Ellery Sedgwick's thoughtful treatise on Melville of 1942 failed to take it into account in his general criticism, which had the effect of "thinning out" his study in the middle, as Melville's own work would seem "thinned out" if *Benito Cereno* were for any reason subtracted from it.[1] For myself I have no doubt that it occupies a key position in Melville's imaginative development; that quite apart from its supremacy as one of the finest of his purely artistic achievements, it relates to a mood, and a peculiar emancipation from that mood, which taken in their context illuminate much of a part of his life and work with which criticism up to now has been too little concerned.

Benito Cereno is the story of the New England commander of a large trading vessel, at anchor in the harbour of a small island off the southern extremity of Chile. He is pictured as a man of undistrustful good nature, recognising none of the evils latent in humanity; a man, as it turns out, of honesty and courage, but with something more than his fair share of credulity and benevolent stupidity—an accurate representation of Melville's tolerant but unflattering opinion of the common run of his fellows. Into the bay comes a stranger ship, showing no colours and mysteriously uncertain in her manœuvres. Captain Delano, the New England trader, lowers a boat and sets out to greet the newcomer, who is revealed on closer inspection to be a Spanish merchantman carrying negro slaves. On boarding he finds the blacks heavily predominating over the whites and hears a tale of fever, shipwreck and repeated misadventure that accounts for the derelict appearance of the vessel and for the preponderance of slaves over freemen. There is an air of mysterious suspense about the ship and its personnel which is not allayed by the appearance of the Spanish captain, an aristocratic young man with the debilitated air of an invalid, who is attended on his progress about the deck by a faithful and assiduously affectionate negro servant. There is much in the manner of Benito Cereno, the Spanish captain, to puzzle the honest American trader; for the indiscipline aboard his ship cannot be wholly referred to his own sickly state of health, and his manner harbours an almost contemptuous reserve. The state of his crew and cargo is in all

---

[1] It is only fair to say that Mr. Sedgwick, although according to his widow he had entirely completed his book, died before he could give it final revision. The fact that Mrs. Sedgwick refers in her preface to the absence of *Benito Cereno* from discussion suggests that she and others may have regarded the omission as important.

respects deplorable; even before the captain's eyes uncontrolled rough-and-tumble between blacks and whites appear to go unpunished; Cereno seems to condone them all, as indifferent to the deterioration in behaviour as to the deterioration in condition of all those about him. Even the naturally obtuse sensibility of the trader is not proof against the oppressive uncertainty of the atmosphere; his normal equanimity is disturbed by suspicions for which he can find no convincing justification; and during his stay on board the Spaniard, which is prolonged by the delay of his own boat which he has sent back for a supply of fresh provisions, he alternates distressingly between tremor and reassurance, fidgeting at a hint of the unusual here and calmed once more by a touch of familiar routine there, until at the end of the day it is time for him to return to his ship. To his relief—for the atmosphere of mystery has oppressed him with an ever-increasing weight—he is allowed to enter his boat; and he is congratulating himself upon his release from fears which he now feels to be groundless, when the mysterious Spanish captain suddenly hurls himself into the boat alongside him, followed instantly by his faithful negro slave. And it is only when the negro's dagger is seen to be aimed not at the American, but at the Spaniard, that "a flash of revelation swept across the long-benighted mind of Captain Delano"; and he realised the truth whose ambiguous horror had been presented at his unseeing vision all day long; that the Spanish vessel was in the command of the revolted slaves, and that the sinister Benito Cereno was no potential dastard, but a meek prisoner on board his own ship. The paradox once explained, all the perplexing anomalies fall at once into place. The whole day's adventures are instantly explicable. Terror departs, and action, symbolised in the brisk routing of the negro pirates and the rescue of Cereno and his Spaniards, resolves the mystery.

This story is told superbly. No summary can give more than a hint of its architectural mastery, its marshalling of detail and incident something after the manner of Defoe and his intricate realism, its dramatic power and poise, its astonishing after-effects which seem to reverberate in the mind long after the story is concluded. Melville himself must have felt great satisfaction in this long-unrecognised masterpiece; for throughout the story he remained (as so rarely he did) tautly in control, communicating (as, again, so rarely he did) a sensation of hard and hammered writing without the tell-tale relaxation of verbiage in which he so often indulged; and moreover he must have known that, with or without intent, he succeeded within rigid limits in realising his central vision of the illusory nature of experience—which he had attempted to do in *Pierre* on a far more ambitious scale with much less success. *Benito Cereno* bristles with suggestion and analogy; it symbolises of course the broad conflict between the primitive and the civilised in mortal nature, and particularly the dread uncertainty in which the man of good will can find himself when he sets out to determine which is in control: the cunning ruses resorted to by the baser element to gain ascendancy over the finer so that the illusion of the predominance of the latter is convincingly preserved, are realised with a perspicacity that stamps Melville as a brilliantly acute psychologist whose intuitions (like those of Blake, that other perceptive recorder of subconscious conflicts) have anticipated by many years the findings of more systematic and more laborious students. Whether or not *Benito Cereno* can be closely related by analogy to Melville's own personal circumstances, physical or spiritual,[1] does not, I believe, affect the very wide validity of its application. It is fundamental to the nature of the development of his views on humanity, and clarifies much that is obscure in the earlier, more tentative suggestions in *Pierre* that human actions have double impulses and that human behaviour is the result of an often unanswerable dilemma. It was this deadly duplicity, fundamental to experience, that obsessed Melville at this stage to the exclusion of all other philosophical considerations. *Pierre*, with all its wider implications, found time to suggest it; *The Piazza* simply stated it; *Benito Cereno* elaborated it and lent it compact dramatic force. Squarely and unmistakably it stood at the centre of Melville's imaginative vision, colouring all his future. Innocence, exploring experience, found the way hopelessly divided. It was a more desperate plight than Ishmael's, or Taji's, or even Pierre's. Their answer was nihilism, which meant that no answer was needed, an answer being provided by Destiny. *Benito Cereno* raised, without

---

[1] I make this observation because I am aware that there are some critics who believe that Melville's imaginative development in the 'fifties reflects unusually distressing personal circumstances, and believe that it is possible to trace them. Mr. E. L. Grant Watson, a very perceptive student of Melville, once remarked to me in conversation that he believed *Benito Cereno* to be about marriage. In giving me authority to quote this, he asked me to make it clear that he interprets the story as "symbolising those phases of the married state where conscious motives and apprehensions are dominated by the chthonic and unsuspected, or only dimly suspected, motives of the Unconscious."

satisfying, the question that the earlier works had implied without raising. Melville was journeying even deeper into despair; but at least he was further upon the road.

As I have already hinted, he sought for a solution at once, and his search is best embodied in the other two principal stories in the group. Again, the answers he found were not new answers; they were hinted in *Pierre* and earlier, just as the questions had been. But these stories gave shape and cogency to moods which the very careful narrative art proves not to have been transitory, which can be traced indeed back to his earliest work and forward to his latest, until his whole life's work is illuminated by an unusual consistency of purpose.

The longer of these two remarkable stories is *The Encantadas*, a work which has received high praise from most of Melville's critics. I feel that such praise is directed more to the highly effective presentation of the prevailing atmosphere and the vivid poignancy of the central episode than to the artistic completeness of the whole, which I have never felt to be satisfactory. It is in the rather unusual form of nine short sketches, constructed less as fictional narrative than as guidebook fact, around the uninhabited Galapagos islands, a desolate archipelago in the Pacific which furnished for Melville's predominating mood a telling symbolism of dereliction. Regarded as a whole the piece has little construction, and though it has an impressive beginning it shreds away aimlessly into a disjointed series of factual or legendary scraps. It saves itself by a fierce generation of mood so pointedly significant as to make *The Encantadas* a key, not only to Melville's middle period as a whole, but to the peculiar course which his imagination chose as a way out of the dilemma postulated in *Pierre* and *Benito Cereno*.[1]

These, the bleakest of his traveller's tales, are a melancholy commentary upon the spirited adventurousness of the early South Sea books. Especially they relate back to the kindred fantasy of *Mardi*, whose glittering chain of islands, stretching out before the travellers into the shimmering distance, is bitterly contrasted now with the "five and twenty heaps of cinders dumped here and there . . . looking much as the world at large might, after a penal

---

[1] I do not mean to suggest dogmatically that *The Encantadas* was a deliberate attempt to answer a problem propounded earlier. I do not even know for certain that it was a later composition. All that is clear is that at this time two moods predominated in Melville, one suggesting a dilemma and the other a solution. The order in which they presented themselves to him does not matter.

conflagration;" a group conspicuous for solitariness, desolation, everlasting drought, wiry and distorted vegetation, clinker-bound rocks, treacherous undertows, giant tortoises, and physical and spiritual aridity. *The Encantadas* ushered in Melville's desert-phase; in which the potency of sea-symbolism deserted him and gave place to the cracked parched imageries of waste and desolation that were with him in strong force until *Clarel* helped him to exorcise them. Melville was retreating from dilemmas that at least represented life, to solitudes which smacked pervasively of death.[1]

The sketches are uneven; many of them readily paralleled in any casual volume of travel that treats of uninhabited or out-of-the-way places, some few of them imprinted with the tragic power that of all travellers Melville had commanded best. The curious episode of the captured tortoises, with their "dateless, indefinite endurance . . . that seemed newly crawled forth from beneath the foundations of the world" strikes a note of impersonal stoicism that was to sound throughout the stories. The dead desert rock of Rodondo, the great sea-crag visible thirty miles off and invariably mistaken for a sail, takes on a mysterious quality of indifference and time-lessness under Melville's hand as he describes the dense flocks of sea-birds hovering in dissonant flights about it, accentuating rather than relieving its loneliness. The episodes of buccaneering treachery associated with one or another of the islands merely intensify the natural conviction that these are the islands of the damned. But the life of the series is concentrated in the story of Hunilla, and it is this story that has won for it its reputation and infused into the adjoining sketches so much of its own tragic and concentrated beauty.

It is a long episode with little incident in it save the bare facts: of the young half-breed Indian girl put ashore at the Encantadas by a French whaler with her newly wedded husband and her only brother, with the intention of collecting a store of tortoise-oil; of the sudden drowning of the two men before her eyes, distantly and in silence; of the slow miserable months that followed, leading to the certainty that the whaler had abandoned her; of the ultimate slender chance that revealed her to the ship that was to save her

---

[1] For publication he cloaked himself in the curious pseudonym of Salvator R. Tarnmoor, which suggests all the pinchbeck ghoulishness of Poe—a hint which is mercifully not communicated to the body of the work itself.

life. There is poignancy enough in the incidents themselves, but since Melville has bent upon the aloof figure of Hunilla all the pitiful conjectures with which the contemplation of humanity was now racking him, the tenderness and the tact of the narrative lift this episode to a level of hardly bearable emotion. In Hunilla Melville sees humanity's grief personified, humanity assailed by misfortune as undeserved as hers, as powerless as she to withstand it, but (and this is the saving reservation), with a potential courage as stoical as hers to endure it. If there is any virtue in meek endurance, Melville publishes it in Hunilla; he does not comment upon it, value it, judge it, but records it as dispassionately as he can. It is clear that he saw no reason for comfort, and he gives none; the old Christian emollients were for the present of no value to him, for there are phrases in *The Encantadas*, and it is implicit in much of what he wrote at this time, suggesting that the loss of faith originally limited in Ishmael had persisted and intensified; but at the very end of the tale he makes that passing, pointed reference to the archetype of passive endurance that drove James Russell Lowell to declare that it was the finest touch of genius that he had ever seen in prose. "The last seen of lone Hunilla she was passing into Payta town, riding upon a small grey ass; and before her on the ass's shoulders, she eyed the jointed workings of the beast's armorial cross."

It would be a mistake to read comfort into the Christian reference; it is barely more than a hard-won tribute to the stoicism of the man of sorrows. Yet at least it has the effect of elevating Hunilla into a universal symbol, in whom suffering and dignity combine to ennoble humanity, which without her detached stoicism would be degraded as well as destroyed. And in the other remarkable tale in the *Piazza* collection Melville lays unusual emphasis on another kind of dignity, where passiveness is advanced into a positive quality, and Hunilla's refusal to submit is expanded into a disturbing and potent refusal to engage. Hunilla withdraws into her stoicism; Bartleby the Scrivener into non-attachment. Thus Hunilla, a religious emblem, is converted into Bartleby, a social emblem; which is a significant projection, indicating Melville's new preoccupations with contemporary social values.

Bartleby the Scrivener is a deeply disquieting story; the more so for being drawn from outside Melville's common selection of settings. Indeed the lawyer's office, with its clerks and its office-boy, might have been transplanted from *Pickwick*, and the florid good-nature of the narrator of the story would have seemed very comfortably in place in Dickens. But this of course is deceptive. The unimaginative but friendly protagonist is not new to these stories of Melville's middle period; Captain Delano was one, and the narrator of *The Piazza* was in some sort another. The mediocrity, to whom the incalculable symbol of tragedy is revealed, is equivalent in Melville's mind to the common popular conscience whose duty it is to make terms with the common suffering; and the recurrence of this figure in so many of his contemporary themes is an interesting sidelight on Melville's essentially social approach to the questions which his own distresses suggested. In the present case the easy goodwill of the master is visited with nightmare; the humble scrivener who for his own private and unstated reasons refuses either to obey his orders or to leave his employment. There is no question of indiscipline and no question of intransigence—merely an impregnable denial of co-operation. To every request however kindly or persuasively proffered, the mysterious Bartleby answers politely with the same unwavering formula, "I would prefer not to".

The narrative, conducted throughout on a level of sober and even severe realism, masks a symbolism as fantastic as any in Melville. The deadly evocation of an endless routine, the strange solitary figure of the clerk whose protest is his final and fatal defence of the remnants of his individuality, the subtly-engendered atmosphere of baffled bewilderment which his attitude creates—all have their important part in a highly original creation which had to wait until Kafka for a comparable parallel. The plain figure of Bartleby, considered dispassionately, is absurd enough; but in his context he is so disruptive of all normally-accepted conventions that the emotional power and sanction of such a steady refusal as his must be regarded as one of Melville's most original discoveries. The insidious webs that the complexity of Society was spinning round the individual were being steadily multiplied in the 'fifties of the last century. Melville, in common with a very few of his contemporaries, had never closed his eyes to the danger. His early voyages to the South Seas had been in effect a kind of protest; quite as vigorous, though perhaps not so explicit, as Thoreau's Walden experiment bred of the feeling that "the mass of men lead lives of quiet desperation", while the last part of *Pierre* had contained vivid descriptions of the ugly discipline imposed by modern urban civilisation upon the lives of individuals. In *Bartleby* the stoic conclusion was faced, in a compressed and haunting prose piece containing as much of pity as of horror: that the courageous way out of the fatal dilemmas was independence, and that independence led to death. Bartleby the scrivener finds peace only in the grave—with the attendant consolation that he rests with kings and counsellors. Yet somehow Bartleby emerges from his own tragedy as the victor; he creates, but does not participate in, the spiritual disturbance which has quickened the imagination of the mediocrities he encounters. He becomes the still point about which their unstable world turns. The paradox of Bartleby is that although his principles destroy him, it is the preservation of those principles alone which can save the world that rejects him. Just as Hunilla by her meekness has recalled the man of sorrows, so Bartleby by his fate has recalled the despised and rejected. The Christian overtones were never far from Melville's mind; and as we shall see much later, their insistency increased.

Not that *Bartleby* is Christian. The figure of Bartleby is paralleled inside Melville's works rather than outside them, by the obscurer but still potent figure of Plinlimmon, whom we have already met in *Pierre*. Hunilla, instinctively, and Bartleby, deliberately, are extensions of Plinlimmon's withdrawal. Bartleby, in fact, is the bleakly logical conclusion of all the nobility and independence implicit in Plinlimmon; a criticism of society which distrusts those attributes as well as of their individual possessor who will attempt no compromise with it. It is in fact the most devastating criticism of society that could conceivably be made. Bartleby's death damns society, not himself.

Bartleby represents perhaps the profoundest conjectural depths which Melville plumbed in the years that followed *Moby Dick*. He had set up for himself in that masterpiece such a formidable cohort of virtually insoluble metaphysical problems that it is not to be wondered at that his answers to them were erratic and uncertain, and attained their greatest cogency only in fragmentary form. The uncertainties in which he wavered were so intrinsically a part of his imaginative development that no sustained attempt to embody them in fiction could be anything but tentative and amorphous, like the conclusions he strove towards but could not reach. The artistic failures of *Pierre* and *The Confidence-Man* were natural, and we have to take them calmly for granted and search for their value and importance beyond art; and his only other long novel of the 'fifties has been so handicapped by the juxtaposition of fictions that failed to be appreciated (sometimes justly, sometimes not), that in the general criticism of Melville it has been ignored or stigmatized as often as its fellows. Even Matthiessen has slight praise for it; and he is merely the leader among a set of critics who speak with one voice. Yet there is a refreshing directness about *Israel Potter* that should be especially remarked in this phase of tantalising experiment and obscurity; and, apart from the sufferings that overshadowed this decade, it contains a broader symbolism that has never been sufficiently marked, linking it closely to the important nationalist element in Melville's earlier work.

Israel Potter is in plain fact the easiest to read of any of Melville's books, being on the surface a lively picaresque account of the true adventures of a Bunker Hill veteran whose travels brought him into exciting contact with many of the leading spirits of the Revolutionary and post-Revolutionary period. The failure remarked by Matthiessen and others is born of the fatal uncertainty which prevented Melville from being satisfied with the book as either an adventure story or a spiritual parable, and the inadequacy of his attempt to present it as both at once. Nevertheless it is a failure that need not hamper enjoyment; the adventures are for the most part related with a clear and nervous precision that improved on such previous masters as Smollett or Marryat, and the parable, though clumsily enough introduced, is as pertinent as Hunilla's if less suggestive than Plinlimmon's or Bartleby's. The story is in large part fact; being founded on a tattered copy of an old book, rescued, as Melville says, "by the merest chance, from the rag-pickers", and rearranged and improved much as Browning was later to rearrange and improve the old yellow book picked up on a stall in Florence.

Melville's eternal delight in sea-voyages, in the chance and vicissitude of travel, in the courage and resource of the individual human being, has studded this novel with a series of memorable characters and episodes. Most of these he relishes objectively, and this provides the springy readability of the tale. There is a brilliant, unforgettable description of the sea-fight between Paul Jones' flagship the *Richard* and the English man-of-war *Serapis* by the dim light of the rising harvest moon, that equals the finest descriptive action passages that even Melville achieved. There is the tense

N

episode of Israel's vigil in the secret chamber at the house of the English squire who abets the Revolutionary cause—a vigil horribly prolonged through the sudden death by apoplexy of the squire himself, the only mortal who knew of Israel's presence there. There are the Marryat-like struggles for the mastery of enemy vessels, dramatic exchanges from one ship to another in mid-ocean, and all the ruses and subterfuges incidental to the passage of a Yankee spy between France and England. There is the clear vigorous sketch of the battle of Bunker Hill itself; there is the lively and humorous encounter with George III in the gardens at Kew. In all these episodes the shadow of the old preoccupations is for the time removed, and Melville emerges with cheerful eye and squared elbows as a masterly story-teller, observant, witty, uninhibited. Perhaps the most impressive of his objective achievements in this book is the slily satirical portrait of Benjamin Franklin, with his methodical cheese-paring efficiency, his meanness and his morality, who can be admired for his disinterestedness but distrusted for his arid utilitarianism—the virtual opposite of every quality that appealed to Melville most.[1]

Those are the parts of the tale that Melville treats with most vigour and clarity, precisely because they do not engage him at the most significant levels. The remainder is no less powerful; and although it must be admitted that it has helped to capsize the book, it must be regarded in the light of the fuller consideration of Melville's work as more important. The subjective elements in *Israel Potter* answer to all those qualities in humanity and its attitude to destiny that acquaintance with Melville would lead anyone to recognise as his favourites at once; the "ungodly, godlike" attributes that had flourished in Long Ghost, in Taji, in Jack Chase, in Ahab, and had fused into the proud and deliberate aloofness that by now was Melville's own and his specific for all spiritual uncertainties. Hence the extravagantly sympathetic portrayal of the pirate Paul Jones, a conventional "lone wolf" figure whose swashbuckling manner detracts a little from the tragic dignity with which Melville tries to present him, a romanticized version of Ahab crossed with Bulkington. Hence too the very

---

[1] D. H. Lawrence's essay on Franklin is illuminating in this context. His passionate antipathy to Franklin's "Perfectibility" contrasts with his instinctive sympathy with Melville's creative attitude to life. Lawrence's remarks on the two writers do all that is necessary to explain Melville's rather equivocal treatment of Franklin.

remarkable episode of Ethan Allen, whom Melville has marked beyond possibility of doubt as his favourite character in the book. This man, a rebel officer of the Revolutionary War, had been captured by the British at Montreal and treated with inexcusable cruelty and ignominy; and Melville describes the shameful manner in which he was exhibited in fetters, like a baited bear, to the stares and jeers of the fashionable and unfashionable at Falmouth. But his dignity was never troubled and his defiant courage answered every insult in its own kind; and the unconquerable spirit and fearless independence of this captive brought him ultimate liberation.

Most characteristic of its author, however, and therefore most significant, is the personal theme of the unfortunate Israel Potter himself. John Freeman has spoken of the book as being untypical, for in it Melville "is exiled from the native world of his imagination". This is not wholly true. His imagination fastened upon the wanderer's story and drew from it a wry, comfortless irony appropriate even more to Melville than to Potter. The bitter identification is unmistakable, for the hills and woods of Israel's pastoral childhood are the same as Melville himself had watched from Arrowhead at the time of his greatest imaginative adventures, and that he had dwelt on again and again in *Pierre* and *The Piazza* as the idyllic setting for potential tragedy. Still more is it fitting, in Melville's contemporary mood, that the few thrilling months of high adventure should be followed by forty years of drab destitution in the hideous poverty of early nineteenth-century London—an experience which Melville faltered at describing; intended as the central tragedy of the book and cunningly hinted at throughout, it horrified him into perfunctory dumbness when the time came for its presentation. Even so, he allowed himself his *coda* of disillusioned comment; for the old man, journeying back at the end of his life to visit the scenes of his boyhood, finds his name forgotten and the plough driven over the family hearthstone, while he himself is rudely hustled aside in the crowds assembling for a Fourth of July procession complete with its banners glorifying the memory of the heroes of Bunker Hill. And the book's sardonic dedication to the Bunker Hill Monument speaks of those anonymous soldiers "who may never have received other requital than the solid reward of your granite". The personal parable, while not obtrusive, is never absent from these stories of the 'fifties; and it cannot have been accidental, though on the other hand it can hardly have been deliberate, that the servitude of Bartleby and the long destitution of Israel Potter both foreshadowed the long penance and obscurity to which Melville was so soon to be committed.

Potter is inescapably Melville; just as in the broader symbolism at which I hinted earlier, Potter is perceptibly America, a figure of national significance. In the *Pequod* and the *Neversink* he had embodied the variety, the potentiality of those conglomerate tribes to whom union was a mighty possibility rather than a fact; in the person of Israel Potter he gave indications of the courage, resource, independence, and dire attendant misfortunes which were characteristic of the ambitious nationalist spirit. Israel Potter running away from home symbolises the young America of the Revolution; Franklin and Potter's impatience with him, Paul Jones and Potter's sense of kinship with him, Ethan Allen and Potter's indignation for him, are all representative of stages in the emergence of a national character in which Melville felt a deep patriotic pride and which he sensed to be threatened by an obscure but deadly danger. He was to explore one of the main manifestations of that danger in *The Confidence-Man*; another and more violent one was to overwhelm the country in the impending Civil War. The signs of the times spelt little to Melville but materialism and destruction, the youthful vigour of Israel Potter dispelled in misfortune, the promise of the Revolution betrayed in a lethal self-interest and indifference.

As Melville's personal fortunes declined, this sense of freezing indifference assailed all his imaginative endeavours. Travel was no longer an escape or an adventure, but a voyage through desert symbols to inevitable death. The Encantadas are a heap of dead rocks, Bartleby lies cold as a stone in the prison yard, Israel Potter is submerged in the fogs of London. Even the saving independence of spirit has little answer to Melville's "three Armageddons, London, adversity and the sea, which at one and the same time, slay and secrete their victims". The end of travel held no comfort but death, whose prevailing symbols were not, like Ahab's, fiery and companionable, but like the traveller's in *The Tartarus of Maids*, a bitter little descriptive essay on the indignity of mass labour, icy and indifferent. "Pale with work, and blue with cold," says Melville of the girl operative in the paper-mill; "with an eye supernatural with unrelated misery." The freezing solitude of this moving little piece can stand as an apt symbol of his spiritual country at this time; a Tartarus that afforded the traveller no rest and little hope, and left him barely courage and energy enough for further speculations that he felt would only be futile. Yet his loneliness never deprived him of pity, that seemed for a time his only available warmth. The mute courage of Hunilla wrung a moving testimony from a heart that disillusion had come near to cracking: "Humanity, thou strong thing, I worship thee, not in the laurelled victor, but in this vanquished one." And it is from the episode of Hunilla too that the most appropriate epigraph for this bitter little chain of stories comes, for in it the detached non-benevolence of Plinlimmon, the self-sufficient independence of Bulkington, the protracted sufferings of Israel Potter, are ennobled to a stoical purity that once more recalls the height of the Christian ideal. "To Hunilla, pain seemed so necessary, that pain in other beings, though by love and sympathy made her own, was unre-piningly to be borne. A heart of yearning in a frame of steel. A heart of earthly yearning, frozen by the frost which falleth from the sky."

CHAPTER XIV

The Confidence-Man: the Embittered Masquerade

EVERY work of art has a double validity, and we judge it imperfectly if we do not take that into account. Many works are able to satisfy at once by the perfection or universality of their expression; they become themselves critical standards, they lose objectivity, a too constant regard for them tends to distort the perspective of critical judgment. Their success as pure art has temporarily obscured their relative value as an organic expression of a living mind. It is just the opposite with those minor works which owing to some defect have failed to please. They are condemned for their artistic shortcomings without reference to their integral importance in the development of the author conceiving them. The fact that a creative mind at a unique stage of its growth found its only satisfaction in such expression argues the presence of certain values that must not be overlooked.

This is not intended as a justification of bad art. It does not apply to it, if by bad art we can agree to mean a superficial imitation of good art. We can contrast this, and take great care not to confuse it with that kind of imperfect art which is a genuine but incomplete work of self-expression. The difference between them may often be recognised in the unmistakable sense of power and personality that lies, often obscurely, behind an example of imperfect art. I have already referred in a similar context to Blake's *Prophetic*

Books. Many of D. H. Lawrence's novels and poems labour under this handicap; so does *The Winter's Tale.* All these abound in defects serious enough to sink beyond recall any similar production by an artist with less conviction and quality; and this has often led to their critical condemnation. The reason for this is frequently the refusal of the critics to search out in these works that double validity, artistic and personal, which is stamped upon all art and literature worthy of survival or consideration.

The Confidence-Man is a conspicuous example of this critical failure. First of all it quite naturally suffered, as *Pierre* and others had suffered, by being a minor work by the hand that constructed *Moby Dick.* Moreover it suffered twice over with Melville, who during his lifetime had won a fair if temporary popularity as the man who had lived among cannibals and after his death won a universal reverence as the creator of the Whale; *The Confidence-Man* escaped both categories of esteem and missed with both barrels. It was readily forgotten; aesthetically that is no surprise. The public who never took to it, the critics who never attempted to come to terms with it, the literary historians who ignored it, can all shelter behind their glaring justifications—its eccentricity and obscurity, its overbalance into petulance, its crude generalisations upon a society to which it did not pretend to do justice. Obscure it was and obscure it stayed.[1] Satisfying neither of Melville's publics, neither traveller nor transcendentalist, fulfilling no artistic standards which any traditionally-minded critic could accept, it remained, and still remains, a mysterious hiatus in the works of an author now being slowly haled back to popularity. It is an unsympathetic book, but then at the time when he wrote it Melville was an unsympathetic man. It has never had many readers, and probably never will have. (Mr. Roy Fuller's suggestion, in his introduction to the Chiltern Library edition, that those who find Melville's rhapsodic style a deterrent may well be led to Melville through this book, has the virtue of hopefulness if not of probability.) Yet it exists as a part of Melville, and imaginative students of his genius cannot afford to bestow a casual dismissal on one of his key works simply because it does not fit a formula. *The Confidence-Man* is as organic a part of the Melville formula as *Moby Dick.*

---

[1] The recent reprint in the Chiltern Library (1948) seems to have been the first since the Collected, which in its turn was only the second. A year or two ago copies were so rare that it was impossible to obtain one from America.

The sensitive American critic Yvor Winters regards it, after *Moby Dick*, as bracketed with *Pierre* as his completest statement of his subject; and this is a tenable theory.

The scene of this extraordinary novel is a Mississippi steamboat, the *Fidele*, plying between St. Louis and New Orleans. On its decks swarms a jostling crowd of voyagers, for the most part anonymous, faceless and voiceless, a conglomeration merely with a corporate vitality that gives the book its mainspring. And here Melville is once more at pains to emphasize the nationalist implications of his chosen symbol. In the second chapter he describes the variety of the company on board with a comprehensive relish recalling his delight in the cosmopolitanism of the ship's company of the *Pequod*. "Natives of all sorts, and foreigners; men of business, and men of pleasure; parlour men and backwoodsmen; farm-hunters and fame-hunters; heiress-hunters, gold-hunters, buffalo-hunters, bee-hunters, happiness-hunters, truth-hunters, and still keener hunters after all these hunters. Fine ladies in slippers, and moccasined squaws; Northern speculators and Eastern philosophers; English, Irish, German, Scotch, Danes; Santa Fé traders in striped blankets, and Broadway bucks in cravats of cloth of gold; fine-looking Kentucky boatmen, and Japanese-looking Mississippi cotton-planters; Quakers in full drab, and United States soldiers in full regimentals; slaves, black, mulatto, quadroon; modish young Spanish Creoles, and old-fashioned French Jews; Mormons and Papists; Dives and Lazarus; jesters and mourners, teetotallers and convivialists, deacons and black-legs; hard-shell Baptists and clay-eaters; grinning negroes, and Sioux chiefs solemn as high-priests. In short, a piebald parliament, an Anacharsis Cloots congress of all kinds of that multiform pilgrim species, man."

The richness of the material, its range and vitality, are left in no doubt; and in the next paragraph Melville adds a comment on the direction and circumspection of that vitality which gives the key both to the nature of the world he envisaged and his attitude to it. "A Tartar-like picturesqueness; a sort of pagan abandonment and assurance. Here reigned the dashing and all-fusing spirit of the West, whose type is the Mississippi itself, which uniting the streams of the most distant and opposite zones, pours them along, helter-skelter, in one cosmopolitan and confident tide." The key-word is "confident"; the task of the book is to examine the idea of confidence, and to try the strength of a community based upon the conception, or illusion, of its validity.

Out of the cosmopolitan confusion emerges a curious succession of individuals focusing the interest in turn. Each plays his part in his short scene, and duly disappears in the milling crowd as the point of fascination shifts to the next episode. This chain-sequence is the only pattern the novel has. It starts at St. Louis, but it never reaches New Orleans; it peters out arbitrarily at the end of one of the subsidiary episodes, and the reader, who has been hypnotised by the very urgency of Melville's mood into focusing eagerly upon the little spotlit scenes, is left stranded on the last page with a strong impression of feverish activity dispersed upon air. The book at times promises so much; an imaginative conception of real value hovers dimly behind the truncated expression. It remains the unfinished ruin of an ambitious enterprise that never had a fair chance to succeed.

The individual episodes are conducted with originality and a kind of savage humour. Out of the buzz and hum appear grotesque impossible creations who startle at the same time as they mystify. A flaxen-haired deaf-mute writes Biblical texts on a slate; they are all taken from I *Corinthians* 13, the famous passages on Charity, and induce in the bystanders nothing but sceptical jeers. Next follows an uproar over the questioned genuineness of a negro cripple who shuffles round on his stumps begging for coppers. Soon he is swallowed up in the crowd and we are swung over to a grave respectable citizen in mourning who strikes up acquaintance with a merchant, pitches him a hard-luck story, and accepts, reluctantly but finally, a banknote. Later the scenes shift cinematically all over the boat. There is a fierce and effective picture of a miser, whose savage suspicions do not save him from being duped into investing in a bogus company; there is cross-talk between a rich cosmopolitan and a shaggy Missouri trapper inclined to misanthropy; a mystical philosopher moves blandly among the company; a herb-doctor dispenses quack medicine to anyone who will accept it. These are not all; but they are representative of it all.

One difficulty must be cleared away at once, for it is fundamental to a right understanding of the book. Melville's presentation of these characters is, though lively and urgent, not altogether successful. They are clearly meant to represent in their individual actions the surging variegated life of the vast community of the

West which he sketched in the paragraphs I have just quoted. Those paragraphs pack a tremendous suggestiveness, which is not adequately realised in the individual exemplars of the following chapters. Professor Matthiessen has suggested that Melville lacked the intimate experience of Mississippi traffic that could have informed his ambitious attempt with the cogency of creative understanding. Whatever the reason for the inadequacy, there is a vividness in what he said he was going to describe that is unhappily absent from the body of the description itself. The life of the book is in the conception and not in the expression. It is pervasive, but it is not organic. Thus the characters Melville created to personify his bitter theme are not individual enough to claim the attention either as living persons or as units in a larger society. They are by-products of a central emotional urgency which was admittedly enormous; it multiplied and invigorated these active little grotesques like the details in a drawing by Bosch or Breughel. They are, in fact, figures of personal fantasy and not of co-ordinated satire; Dickensian dramatisations of an artist's prevailing mood.

Superficially *The Confidence-Man* is unacceptable. It offends against all the canons of fiction. The story it tells is hardly a story at all, and the subsidiary episodes remain episodic. But inevitably we are thrown back upon the consideration of the double validity of a work of art. From the first page to the last the book is urgently, inescapably alive. Artistic failure or not, its second-line validity rescues it. It is inadequate expression of art, but it succeeds as expression of the artist.

The directing artist is the one link binding the diversities of this book into a serviceable unity; he forced into it a concentration of one overpowering mood. The saving consistency of temper is sustained from the beginning to the end, and it is able to uphold the unevenness for long enough to avoid the more serious consequences of the obvious defects. The prevailing mood is set right away, ironically, in the title of the book and the name of the steamboat. *The Confidence-Man. Fidele.* Trust. The power in the episodes springs from the bitter conviction in the author's mind that informs them all—that in the hard context of contemporary civilisation no man is to be trusted. Looking back in the light of this belief along these bewildering manœuvres, the reader is brought up with a start against the one purely dramatic fact of the book—that all these plausible pilferers and swindlers are in reality one man only, who moves in a series of disguises through the steam-boat, leaving behind him the echoes of a confident, reassuring voice and a trail of willing or unwilling dupes. The almost complete success of his enterprises is Melville's uncompromising comment on that American world that he had been facing squarely ever since writing *Moby Dick*; a world in which high tragedy no longer had place, where fools and knaves, preyed on indiscriminately by the cleverest rogue of the lot, voyaged down river in ignorant and self-seeking complacency. *The Confidence-Man* is the spontaneous, almost artless outcry of an affronted spirit against the enormities of the new materialism. Because it is artless it is not a part of literature; but because it is spontaneous it is a part of life. The spontaneities of a writer like Melville are worth ten times the fastidious artificialities of lesser artists.

The medium which he chose—or rather, which chose him—to express his indignation is an unusual one, and it has on that account been misunderstood and misrepresented. This is important, for much of the obscurity in which this novel has been lingering is due to misreadings of that medium by otherwise responsible critics, who have taken it for a satire and blamed it for an unsuccess-ful one. John Freeman, one of the most capable of Melville's biographers, followed this very course. "This novel," he remarked, "showed, so surely that you might think it deliberate, that the writer of the noblest of prose epics was the writer also of the vainest of satires." Such detailed criticism as he allows to the book is conducted on the basis of the incredibility of incident and character, and he stresses its superficial parallelisms with *Martin Chuzzlewit* in its American sequences, an unfair comparison on any count, the more so as Melville was not attempting Dickens' technique at all. "Here is a novel," he goes on, "laboured out to the extent of a hundred thousand words for the vain purpose of exposing the hypocrisy and assertiveness of passengers on a steamship"—an elementary solecism which he qualified later, though not early enough to avoid the conviction that he saw the book through the wrong end of the telescope. And he proceeds to examine the origins of Melville's satiric temper in a paragraph as dogmatic as it is mysterious.

"Meanness there is none," he says, "nor any petty exultation, but nevertheless one cannot help seeing that Melville's basis for satire is not philosophical; it is rather the sense of personal failure. The author of *Moby Dick*, conscious of its uniqueness— the supreme privilege of authorship—was conscious also that he could not live by producing masterpieces; and this, the last of his disillusionments, dictated the mood of *The Confidence-Man*, and made the book an abortion.''

This is a remarkable conclusion to come to about a writer who had so lately shown in Hunilla, in Bartleby, even in Israel Potter, the stoical strength and nobility to which pettinesses of the kind Freeman postulates are utterly foreign. Freeman's conjecture is without evidence or warrant; to deny to this one book the magnanimity he was willing to allow to all the other tragic tales of this phase seems arbitrary and capricious. We have found no concrete cause that we can assign to Melville's lapse into despair, and Freeman has done him no service by electing, in this important instance, to venture a random guess at one. If a great writer lapses from standard, there are two places in which to look for the cause; the writer himself, or his subject. Freeman looked no further than the writer; but in this case there is little need to go beyond the subject.

The subject is mid-nineteenth-century America, on the full tide of business prosperity. To a reader who understands only a fraction of what that meant, it will no longer seem odd that a close contemplation of it drove a sensibility as delicately-balanced as Melville's into an unusual desperation of spirit. Faced with the glaring rapacities and discordancies of the social scene in the ten years prior to the outbreak of the Civil War, we have no need to unearth visionary inadequacies in Melville's own nature. *The Confidence-Man* is a baffled, disgusted recoil; the involuntary outcry of the honest idealist brought into sharp contact with the daily commonplace of dishonour. The deterioration of innocence, in the sequence of Melville's previous novels and stories, had never yet involved its own annihilation. It may have been assailed and injured, driven in upon its own final resources of courage, defeated and despised—all these; but never yet ignored as if it had never existed. Where there is no innocence there is no nobility. Even in the jaws of *Moby Dick*, in the stark fanaticism of Ahab, there had been cleanness, even integrity. There was at least a supreme dignity in the evil with which Ahab strove. Again, the fate of Pierre was stagey and unconvincing, but it was at least within the territories of tragedy. In *The Confidence-Man*, since there is no innocence, there is no tragedy; simply the stale brassy cynicism of the street-corner, knowing and furtive and as commonplace as Hell. Of that rancid bitterness was begotten this strange prose-poem, the work of a man who in *Moby Dick* had commanded epic and dramatic qualities unmatched in his own nation.

Moreover I believe it to be a mistake to regard it as a satire. It contains satiric elements, no doubt; but the bemused fascination with which Melville's affronted sensibility looked on the spectacle of his commercialised continent was utterly alien to the detachment necessary to the satiric temper. The book is no more a satire than its greater predecessor is the plain record of a whale-hunt. It is the embittered utterance of a bewildered mind expressing its bewilderment by bewilderment, just as the kindred imagination of Franz Kafka half a century later was to embody his own spiritual predicaments in strange unfolding symbolisms just as subtly revealing. It is as inept to lecture Melville on the failure of a satire he never conceived as it would be to condemn *The Trial* on the score of the inaccuracy of its legal terminology or the discursiveness of its narrative technique. It is more valuable to compare Melville's challenge with quite a different literary phenomenon, bred of the same age and the same society—the popularity and success of his contemporary Mark Twain. The story of this great but compromised talent is a warning of the dangers implicit in a ruthless materialist society, and of the reluctant absorption of a fine artist into its corruption. He could not refuse to co-operate with it, for his talents suited its limitations and its limitations suited his talents; he was neither profound enough nor independent enough to withhold himself from it. Courting popular favour, he frittered away his rare gifts in a medley of catchpenny trivialities and gross tastelessness; whereas Melville chose to outface compromise, turning scornfully to communion with his own distaste. "Something further may follow of this Masquerade," he says crisply at the end of the book, and lapses, so far as his prose fiction is concerned, into a sardonic silence a generation long. There has been a good deal of conjecture about this mysterious remark. Did he intend a sequel? If so, did he write it and destroy it, or did his disillusioned and exhausted imagination recoil from the effort? On the other hand, did his words imply a continuation at all?

"Something further may follow of this Masquerade." It is an enigmatic comment, but Melville ended his book with it, and a writer of his power and capacity does not set sentences in strategic positions for nothing. The lack of a sequel suggests to me one unexplored possibility outside the usual ones; which is, that the statement refers to forces entirely outside his own creative purposes. Suppose that the "something further" that was to follow was not another book of Melville's like *The Confidence-Man* but some social or historical phenomenon consequent upon those very processes of which Melville knew his book to be merely the imperfect symbol. In the light of this possibility the sudden ending of the book takes on almost an oracular quality, as Melville hints laconically of the decline into chaos of the very civilisation he has been at pains to present in all its horror. Evil was to continue beyond the bounds of Melville's book. Melville knew it and recorded it and retired.[1]

It has been justly pointed out that *The Confidence-Man* lacks the stable equilibrium of a character or a set of embodied precepts by whose standards the prime eccentricities of the theme are to be measured or judged. Thus it represents a philosophic attack which is entirely destructive; and any correctives have necessarily to be provided from outside the book, almost it would seem from outside Melville's own range. This is damaging to the book as a piece of literature; but it cannot detract from its value as a personal document as well as a criticism of a civilisation. In fact, Melville has consciously or unconsciously supplied a kind of corrective in his numerous implicit and explicit references to the Bible. The great texts in *Corinthians* are clearly displayed at the very beginning; and the strange symbolic darkness that descends like an inky curtain over the last few paragraphs of the book settles down over an abortive religious discussion in which the Bible itself is brought in, only to be discarded. Nevertheless the sanction of the Bible, and particularly of the New Testament, is never far from Melville's active and curious cerebrations in this the strangest of all his allegories. It is far from the final words, and counts little for comfort, but it stands in the background as a saving grace never finally repudiated.

[1] Cf. a curiously unrelated couplet in *Clarel*, Part IV, section XIX,

" *House your cattle and stall your steed,*
Stand by, stand by for the great stampede! "

The Confidence-Man shows a decided narrowing of Melville's creative range. Shakespeare, who was much in his mind during the greater part of his creative life, had experienced himself a dim and difficult progress into tragedy, and through it to serenity. His progress towards *The Tempest* involved partial failures like *Timon* and *Troilus*, miscarriages of mood in which the savage misanthropy of Melville's darker moments finds a helpful parallel. Melville recognised Shakespeare's greater capacity for creative sympathy, for serene comprehension of good and evil,[1] but he had not the power to compass it in his own person. His art was circumscribed by his preoccupations as Shakespeare's never was; when he wrote *The Confidence-Man* his scope had dwindled to the wits of Autolycus and the philosophy of Thersites. The result is not a great book; but it is the aberration of a mind unmistakably great— a work inspired by an honesty, a generosity, a charity, that created it but themselves remained aloof from it.

---

[1] See the poem called "The Coming Storm" in *Battle-Pieces*:

> *No utter surprise can come to him*
> *Who reaches Shakespeare's core;*
> *That which we seek and shun is there,*
> *Earth's final lore.*

CHAPTER XV

The Poems

AFTER *The Confidence-Man* Melville's output of prose virtually ceased. A few months later he set out on another journey to Europe, one that took him this time as far as Palestine. It is a journey into which a good deal of suppressed symbolism has been read; not without justice, for Melville's travels throughout his life have the curious appearance of according closely and faithfully with the adventures in his mind, and it was no mere chance that took a deeply-exercised spiritual curiosity on a voyage to the birthplace of Christianity. On the way he stopped at Liverpool and met Hawthorne once more; the renewed contact pleased him, but left him dissatisfied. Melville went off to the East, and they did not see each other again. On his return to America he spent some years in deciding what best to do, for he was now convinced that his books were becoming steadily less saleable and that there was little chance of a permanent living that way. He did some lecturing with only moderate success; tried again for the inevitable consular appointment, once getting as far as an interview with Lincoln, but not further. It is not very clear how he employed himself until 1866, when he took a subsidiary job in the Customs office which he was to hold for the next twenty years. The crowded prolific output of the previous decade shredded down rapidly to occasional essays, reviews and poems. The nature of his literary vocation seemed to change abruptly, and he ceased to attract popular notice. For the rest of his life he worked in an obscurity in which criticism has until lately felt justified in leaving him. There has been much talk of his thirty-five years of silence; the withdrawal into misanthropic sullenness after the failure of *The Confidence-Man* is a ready and plausible story.

But the facts do not warrant it. By the evidence of the productions themselves which are the fruits of these "barren" years, the vital activity of his mind continued quite unabated. The work of this period fills three considerable volumes in the Standard Edition of his writings; the Journal of his voyage to Palestine accounts for yet another complete book. It was only that he chose a new and unfamiliar medium for which, at first at any rate, he had but an amateur's aptitude, that has effectively prevented the important development that he underwent during these years from being given its due critical consideration; and it has to be admitted that until he returned to prose at the very end of his life he was never able to reproduce quite the authority of the finest achievements of his prime. Unluckily for the critic, a key point in his spiritual development is embedded in the long period when he expressed himself only in verse; and the deterioration of the quality of his art is a dangerously effective cloak for what is in fact the simultaneous, and surprising, rebirth of his imagination.

Therefore it comes about that the work of these obscurer years has to be examined with a specialised care. More than in the prose works, the shortcomings of his choice and achievement of form and expression must be steadfastly overlooked, and the product criticised less as a contribution to literature than as the painful expressions of a solitary mind with important decisions to chronicle. There is little point in guessing the reasons why he gave up prose, for he never explained them himself. He was by now facing, and accepting, a steady decrease in his sales. At the same time he realised that his main preoccupations fitted less and less easily into the symbolic life of his fiction, and he turned to lyric as a form of expression which taxed his stamina far less, and yielded a quicker. more personally satisfying return. Possibly he found that he could no longer sustain to book-length the creative impulses which now alternated with the metaphysical speculations occupying the greater part of his mental energy. *The Confidence-Man* is evidence enough of the dangers of overloading with cerebration a symbolism that could not carry conviction because it lacked the necessary re-inforcement of imaginative power. Perhaps he found that the creative mood now operated best, conveyed his responses most faithfully, within unambitious and restricted limits only. Hence the success of some of the short stories and sketches; hence, too, the recourse to lyric poetry—a form which he clearly enjoyed, for numerically his output of poems is high.

Melville is not at all an easy poet to appreciate with fairness, for he attempts a lyric form with the slenderest of lyric equipment. His ear was poor, his rhythmic sense uncertain, his taste by no means infallible. An unduly large proportion of the poems he wrote is slack with cliché and inconspicuous for originality of thought or expression; and many of them are presented in a metrical setting inappropriate to the content. But when all this has been admitted there remains in nearly every poem a sense of deep penetration into the heart of the chosen mood. That this penetration was very frequently an intellectual rather than emotional one merely accentuates the metaphysical bent of Melville's matured mind and his somewhat irregular ability to co-ordinate his intuition with his intellect in the process of artistic expression. The result is often the production of a poem conventional and commonplace in form but concealing an intellectual power not fully realised in its individual context. Thus there are few anthology-pieces; but the collective impact is a formidable one.

Melville took to verse almost as soon as he returned from his Palestine trip. In 1859 his wife reported in a letter that "Herman has taken to writing poetry", adding a hint that this was not to be generally known at present. It seems that many of the poems which he wrote at this time were hawked round the publishers without success in 1860, and did not reach print until 1891, when the *Timoleon* volume included a section entitled *Fruit of Travel Long Ago*, which may account for some of this early work. In 1862 he himself spoke of his "doggerel", and there is evidence that in these years he was actively and closely at work on his lyrics; while the long labour of *Clarel*, though it did not find publication until 1876, is so intimately concerned with his journey to the East that it is difficult to believe that it was not composed over the first decade, rather than the second, that followed his actual travels.

Nevertheless the first book of poems that he published came from Harper's in 1866, the volume entitled *Battle-Pieces*, in which he

collected a series of lyrics on the Civil War and which was presumably
ventured by the publishers more on the strength of its topicality
than of the sales-value of an author already lapsing into obscurity.
It is by its very nature cohesive; the only collection of Melville's
verse which can be grasped as an entity; and this essential homo-
geneity helps to give it a moving authority to which it is easy
to respond.[1] *Battle-Pieces* contains relatively few of Melville's
really striking lyrics, but there is a quality of spiritual calm and
strength underlying all the poems in this book that comes as a
curious relief after our last farewell of Melville as he suspended at
his pleasure the savage masquerade of *The Confidence-Man.*

It is important to try to seek out the source of this apparent calm;
especially as it is possible to infer that it was only illusory, or at best
partial. He wrote in a foreword to the poems that, with few exceptions, the pieces in this volume originated in an impulse imparted
by the fall of Richmond, and were composed without reference to
collective arrangement. Now the Confederate capital did not fall
until 3 April 1865, Lee capitulating at Appomattox less than a week
later; it follows that Melville's urgent little lyrics, commemorating
heroes and incidents of the war from Harper's Ferry to the death
of Lincoln, were for the most part retrospective. On the face of it
the proposition seems impossible; responding to the carefully-
isolated little scenes, the detached skirmish-incidents, the glimpses
of famous or forgotten faces, the reader cannot believe in the notion
of such a made-up collection of show-pieces of the war as Melville's
preface implies. The explanation must lie in the unusual intensity
with which Melville had experienced, back in New York, the
endless fluctuations of the war. The mood of pity for doomed
innocence aroused in him by the sight of the first volunteers,
marching to the massacre of Bull Run in the first summer, lasted
freshly and poignantly as long as the war lasted. The collection
called *Battle-Pieces* is a record of a host of such closely-pondered
moments in the long national crisis; if we are to take Melville at
his word and assume that in the composition of these pieces he
simply yielded (like the hackneyed Aeolian harp, the image he
himself uses) to the compulsion of an unusual variety of moods,
then allowing eighteen months at most between the fall of Richmond

[1] It is interesting to note the appeal of these poems to such a man of action as
T. E. Lawrence, who declared in a letter that "One of Melville's finest works is
Clarel, in verse; but it isn't as fine verse as his War Stuff. That's magnificent.
Melville was a great man."

and the publication of his book it argues not only an astonishing fertility but a remarkable use of re-creative memory. It testifies in fact to a depth of sympathetic emotion towards the fact of the Civil War which is not superficially apparent in the poems themselves.

More than one great writer has owed to the Civil War his first or most conspicuous opportunity to shape his art round a productive symbol. With Melville this was not historically so, as he had already found full satisfaction in his voyages and in the whale; but the experience came to him none the less as a badly-needed occasion for concentration and synthesis. This experience he shared (without being conscious of it, for their paths never crossed) with Whitman. Whitman naturally felt it far more profoundly, for he was engaged deeply, body and soul, a tireless hospital attendant who had none of Melville's philosophic aloofness. For such a theme this aloofness was a serious handicap; to attain the degree of sympathy which converted Whitman's natural humanity into a universal tenderness, Melville would have had to go outside his nature and overcome this almost pathological reticence. Thus Whitman's total spiritual immersion in the common agony of his nation gave his utterances a sublimity to which Melville's more impersonal reflections could not attain. But Whitman was simpler-souled than Melville. Overpowered by the injury which the war had wreaked upon humanity, he devoted himself to the generation of a recompensing love, seeing his duty plan, unambiguous, imperative.

> —*Learning inures not to me,*
> *Beauty, knowledge, inure not to me—yet there are two or three*
> *things inure to me,*
> *I have nourish'd the wounded and sooth'd many a dying soldier,*
> *And at intervals waiting or in the midst of camp*
> *Composed these songs.*

To reconcile was all Whitman's self-set task; his greatness lies partly in his complete abandonment to it. He saw and performed this duty in an extraordinary mystical vision bred of a deep sensuousness and a high social idealism which gave him an unusual power of self-identification with mankind in the mass. The Civil War embodied for him both physically and mentally the essential glories and agonies incident to man's attainment of universal love; therefore he embraced the horror mystically while he repudiated it, called out of himself the extremes of physical devotion to his mundane duty and his emotional ideal, until only his glowing integrity saved him from sentimentality, and his simplicity from emotional perversion.

I sit by the restless all the dark night, some are so young,
Some suffer so much, I recall the experience sweet and sad,
(Many a soldier's loving arms about this neck have crossed and rested,
Many a soldier's kiss dwells on these bearded lips.)

This almost tactile sensuousness prolonging the mood was utterly alien to Melville. Just as he was never, as Whitman was, closely involved in the ugly business of the war or its after-effects, so his personal attitude was by one significant remove the less engaged. But like Whitman he seeks in his Civil War poems to resolve a paradox, though it is not quite Whitman's paradox that he sees or resolves. Where Whitman saw only the physical hates, Melville saw the intellectual ambiguity behind the physical one— the problem of the warring idealisms compelling the action that both he and Whitman knew to be meaningless. He would have agreed with Whitman on the utter inconclusiveness of the act of war; but unlike Whitman he was not content to stop when he had expounded it. As always he saw both sides; and as he saw the Civil War, the tragedy was less in the slaughter than in the idealistic conflict necessitating it. Not the deaths but the dilemmas exercised Melville.

Therefore the war arrived, in a sense, opportunely for him. Parted from his symbols, he drifted in a waste of metaphysical speculation, losing direction as his acute and pertinacious intelligence chased every ambiguous implication of his theme and left the main topic stranded. The war provided at last a symbol to unite his intellect and his imagination once more in a context of significance as well as stability. The war spoke to the condition of every American, and especially to Melville's, since in the bitter paradoxes of civil strife he found an image of his own inner conflict. For one thing, it represented his own lifelong parable of America, enacting in stark reality the doom he had prophesied for it. The allegory of *Mardi*, the broader nationalist symbolisms of *Moby Dick*, *Israel Potter* and *The Confidence-Man* all project themselves forward into the fact of the Civil War, and the Civil War itself confirmed

Melville's prophetic insight sooner than he could have expected or desired. For another thing, and this is fundamental, the distressing complication of loyalties involved answered most aptly the kindred state of speculative dissatisfaction in which Melville had abandoned prose. The fight for the Union typified clearly to him his own life-long fight for an answer to the ambiguities which had so obsessed his imagination. The title of one of the early poems in the book is "The Conflict of Convictions", expressing the doubts and fears which spread through the minds of thinking people during the last few months before the attack on Sumter. "Death, with silent negative" is the gloomy conclusion of speculation, yet the whole poem is rounded by a gnomic verse which might stand as epigraph for the temper of the entire collection:

> *Yea and Nay—*
> *Each saith his say*
> *But God He keeps the middle way.*
> *None was by*
> *When he spread the sky;*
> *Wisdom is vain, and prophecy.*

Melville, too, though his sympathies were wholly with the North, and though he identified the cause of the Union, without qualification, with the Right, kept throughout the book as near the middle way as a human could. Feeling that wisdom and prophecy were for the moment vain, he fell back as he had fallen back before (in Hunilla, Bulkington, Bartleby and the rest), upon courage. This is a variant upon the reticence which at the end of his prose period had been his only retreat from the oppression of destroying fate and destructive humanity; here it is coupled with action, which gives it dramatic as well as philosophic quality, and it is a constant theme repeated in one form or another in nearly all the *Battle-Pieces*. The innocent bravery of the volunteers before Bull Run and Ball's Bluff,

> *(No berrying party, pleasure-wooed,*
> *No picnic-party in the May,*
> *Ever went less loth than they*
> *Into that leafy neighbourhood.*
> *In Bacchic glee they file toward Fate*
> *Moloch's uninitiate),*

is grimly contrasted with the picture, two years later, of the prematurely aged veteran who had been one of the glad youth in the earlier time:

> *A still rigidity and pale—*
> *An Indian aloofness lones his brow:*
> *He has lived a thousand years*
> *Compressed in battle's pains and prayers,*
> *Marches and watches slow.*

If we mark that "Indian aloofness", the fruit of the deadly experience, and recall the great and lonely heroes of Melville's middle period, the strong symbolic affinity between the War itself and Melville's personal conflicts becomes plainer. The Typee innocence duplicates itself before Bull Run, whereas the weary conclusion of the war engenders a resignation akin to Hunilla's. There can be little wonder that this fortuitous parallelism provided a genuine liberation. And in their smaller, more occasional contexts, the poems recounting some of the battles and incidents of heroism which stood for the very experience that turned innocence into Indian aloofness, are most effective and moving records. The long piece describing the siege of Fort Donelson is an unforgettable glimpse of desperate conditions and human endurance, told with a brilliant obliqueness which makes the receipt of the news of the battle as dramatically painful as the battle itself; and the evocation, in "The Scout toward Aldie", of the ambiguous terrors of a woodland country infested by rebel partisans, is at one and the same time a further commentary upon courage and a striking (perhaps unconscious) allegory of philosophic doubt. Less complex in form or implication are the more conventional tributes to named heroes of the war: the romantic, dictatorial McClellan, Sheridan of Cedar Creek, the stoical Nathaniel Lyon, all have their lyric tributes; but it is the great Southerner Stonewall Jackson who enforces Melville's deepest admiration and represents in his own person the most suggestive paradox of his theme.

> *Earnest in error, as we feel,*
> *True to the thing he deemed was due,*
> *True as John Brown or steel. . . .*

So deeply did Melville feel the inadequacy of any partisan judgment on Jackson (and implicitly, the inadequacy of any partisan judgment on the war as a whole) that he set two poems on his memory side by side, the one as from a Northerner, the other as from one of Stonewall's own followers.

> *O, much of doubt in after days*
> *Shall cling, as now, to the war;*
> *Of the right and the wrong they'll still debate,*
> *Puzzled by Stonewall's star.*

Melville's only recourse, out of the bitter wrangling of his conscience, was to that finer refinement of courage and contemplation, pity; a thing which he had found in Launcelott's Hey with young Redburn so many years ago but in the tumult of disillusioning experience had somehow lost again. But the pity he recovered in the Civil War was not of the same order as the tender Samaritan kind of Redburn's or as Whitman's almost maternal grieving over shuddering, palpable flesh. It had full measure of the Indian aloofness; it was rooted in the imagination, but had enough of the intellectual cast to render it contemplative rather than dynamic. It can perhaps be best compared with Thomas Hardy's;[1] deeply sympathetic, and relating the bitterness of the tragedy to causes beyond the control of the individuals most closely involved; able to offer no recompense save understanding and wisdom, and occupied more in the search for the latter than in vain eulogy or elegy. I believe this central store of pity to be Melville's chief acquisition from the War; temporarily, at least, it acted as a palliative. It informed what is perhaps the most delicate and moving lyric of the collection; in which the contemplation of the bloody affray at Shiloh, where a full quarter of the hundred thousand combatants died in heaps in a two days' vicious battle, induced a mood of calm resignation which is Melville's rarest gift to poetry. By good fortune, too, it called out his dormant lyric talent in a gentle felicity he did not often achieve:

> *Skimming lightly, wheeling still,*
> *The swallows fly low*
> *Over the field in clouded days,*
> *The forest-field of Shiloh—*
> *Over the field where April rain*

---

[1] I find that John Freeman has already made this comparison; but I feel that it is too just and illuminating to refrain from repeating it on that account.

Solaced the parched ones stretched in pain
Through the pause of night
That followed the Sunday fight
Around the church of Shiloh—
The church so lone, the log-built one,
That echoed to many a parting groan
And natural prayer
Of dying foemen mingled there—
Foemen at dawn, but friends at eve—
Fame or country least their care:
(What like a bullet can undeceive!)
But now they lie low,
While over them the swallows skim
And all is hushed at Shiloh.

The swallows fly over the dead; and Melville takes the swallow's-eye view; in this lovely poem it is the swallows we see first and last, like Hardy's Spirit of the Pities. The men are pitiable, but the men are dead. In Indian aloofness there is nothing that can be done but record the final reconciliation of death; and this reconciliation is the nearest that Melville attained, during these obscure difficult years, to the peace that had always eluded him.

Where Whitman translated the war into terms of personal relationship unaffected by political dogmas or duties, Melville saw it in terms of philosophical principles tragically embodied in individual lives. One result of this was that as the war drew to its close, he tended to believe in the reconciliation of the two ideals even then typified in the warring forces, of whom one imposed and the other submitted to the reconciliation demanded by circumstance. Melville's intellect would never for a moment have believed that the conflicts inherent in human nature could be as readily resolved as a four years' war; but his imagination which had seized upon it as a symbol was led by the imminence of peace to suggest to him (as it could never have done to the Melville of *The Confidence Man*) the possibility of reconciliation. The tone of the later poems in the book is unmistakable and urgent—a call for leniency and forbearance on the part of the victors, a strong reprobation of vengeance or prolonged hatred. The long poem "Lee in the Capitol" in which the defeated General is imagined as making a formal plea for national wisdom and enlightenment before Congress, is eloquent of Melville's deep concern for spiritual as well as political unity.

It is echoed, remarkably, in the prose Supplement which Melville supplied to the book, in which he discards once and for all the ironic bitterness of the personal philosophy betrayed in such of his recent prose writings as *The Confidence-Man* and *Israel Potter*, and pleads for a new co-operativeness and a general readiness to forget the rancour of the war years. This Supplement is alight with wisdom and charity, in the passionate urgency for forbearance as well as in the clarity of the argument that prove that forbearance necessary. He argues specifically for Christ and Machiavelli, as he says; benevolence and policy alike demand generosity. Level-headed, modest, civilised, this impressive little document reveals a Melville stripped of all his own warping prejudices, a wise man seeing, as keenly as Lincoln saw, the ultimate necessity and a part of the ultimate meaning of Union. "Let us pray that the terrible historic tragedy of our time," he concludes, "may not have been enacted without instructing our whole beloved country through terror and pity." The protestations of this prose essay, the diffidence with which Melville added it to his book of verse at all, suggest his own impression that the ideas expressed in it might be considered unacceptably revolutionary. Today they seem transparently sensible, carrying a magnanimity native to Melville;[1] in those days they would seem to have been a unique utterance, leading Mr. Ellery Sedgwick for one to compare them in quality and in courage with Lincoln's celebrated Second Inaugural. Without attempting any such comparison, it is enough to remark the assured sanity and nobility that gave them expression.

Because the poems are united around the common image of the war, *Battle-Pieces* can be more compactly dealt with than the remainder of Melville's verse, which is spread indefinitely enough over more than thirty years of his life. Apart from the very long separate poem *Clarel*, the rest is comprised in two published volumes, *John Marr and Other Sailors* and *Timoleon*, both printed late in his life, and in a number of uncollected pieces that remained unknown until the Standard Edition presented them to the public in 1924. It is not possible to trace a coherent sequence in what seem to have been rather arbitrary arrangements of unrelated

[1] Typical of "The Hamiltonian extremes against the Franklin mean"—Stephen Vincent Benet, *John Brown's Body*. Lauding some of the old Southern characteristics that died with the Civil War, this excellent modern poet made this side-criticism of Franklin's utilitarianism with which Melville would have heartily concurred.

pieces produced at wide intervals; but close examination can reveal the general philosophical temper that unites them and at the same time provides, along with *Clarel*, the only guide to Melville's obscurest years.

They are largely apart from the concentrated mood of pity and reconciliation which impregnated the reflective *Battle-Pieces*, but they have their links with its central atmosphere, which is traceable chiefly in two of the Civil War poems a little removed from their fellows. The Civil War was primarily an affair of the land forces; but Melville would have been the last to ignore the facts of the sea-blockade, the fights of the monitors and ironclads, the ocean-transports and the discipline of warfare at sea.

> *The discipline of arms refines,*
> *And the wave gives tempering.*

Several of the *Battle-Pieces* commemorate naval occasions; and in particular these two, the "Requiem for Soldiers Lost In Ocean Transports" and the ode "Commemorative of a Naval Victory", revive his instinctive sympathies with all activity by sea; the first with a decorative nobility that in certain passages recalls "Lycidas", and the other conceived as a muted eulogy of the sailor's character, but grimly insistent both on the dangers he dares and his courageous awareness of them—the reference in the last line to the shark that "Glides white through the phosphorous sea" raising once again the old terror that had glimmered in his consciousness throughout *Moby Dick*. This obsession never left him entirely; he elaborated it in one of the poems printed later in the *John Marr* collection, "The Maldive Shark", in which with a sort of fascinated horror he describes the busy little pilot-fish in alert attendance upon the murderous ravener of the seas, ever guiding him to the prey they never share. So the elegiac mood of *Battle-Pieces* shades down into a grimmer and sharper emotion; if not of fear, then of an awareness of peril as acute as fear.

> *Come out of the Golden Gate,*
> *Go round the Horn with streamers,*
> *Carry royals early and late:*
> *But, brother, be not over-elate—*
> All hands save ship! *has startled dreamers.*

It is clear that the beautiful revival of compassion which led Melville to invoke reconciliations in *Battle-Pieces* had not wholly exorcised this elemental terror, although it rescued him from final submission to it. The immanence of a hostile Fate haunted him for years. Chronology is not a trustworty guide, and it is not possible with the scanty evidence provided to decide which poems precede which; and it is particularly dangerous to make assumptions to fit comfortable theories. It might be useful or reassuring to assume that the poems which seem to qualify or contradict the mood of enlightenment were all composed far back in the stoical period of *The Encantadas*, say, before the Civil War had provided an emotional conflict and a provisional resolution of that conflict, but it would not be warrantable to take this for granted. What is certain is that all his published and unpublished collections contain poems of striking force which owe that force to the vividness of the stoical, not the optimistic, vision. The magnificent vision of "The Berg" replaces the shark as image of the common enemy by the iceberg that remains utterly indifferent and unmoved even though a great ship foul herself on it and founder.

> *Hard Berg (methought) so cold, so vast,*
> *With mortal damp so overcast*
> *Exhaling still the dankish breath—*
> *Adrift dissolving, bound for death;*
> *Though lumpish thou, a lumbering one—*
> *A lumbering lubbard loitering slow,*
> *Impingers rue thee and go down*
> *Sounding thy precipice below,*
> *Nor stir the slimy slug that sprawls*
> *Along thy dread indifference of walls.*

"Le silence éternel de ces espaces infinis m'effraie," said Pascal; and with Melville the silence was as appalling; its monumental indifference rivalled the white hostility of Moby Dick or the pallor of the murderous shark. In face of this elemental aloofness there could be no ready reconciliation; and it was perhaps as well that this visionary horror of his was not a permanent or even a constant mood. It had its productive variants, as the random variety of the poems shows—from the simple friendly nostalgia which drew him back in the *John Marr* poems to rough artless songs of old sailor-companions, to sardonic moments of irony expressed in gnomic little quatrains reminiscent of Blake—and out of these variants it is possible to trace constant patterns of thought that, though they may not all rank with the horror in intensity, yet range beyond it and suggest possibilities of overcoming it. The sad realisation that the advent of man's higher knowledge was restricting rather than liberating him had been noted once memorably in *Battle-Pieces*, where the deadly mechanization of once-heroic war was given bitter notice—

> *War yet shall be, but warriors*
> *Are now but operatives; War's made*
>   *Less grand than Peace,*
> *And a singe runs through lace and feather.—*

—and in one of the nostalgic addresses to his old companions, he echoes the melancholy truth in a couplet:

> *Well, Adam advances, smart in pace*
> *But scarce by violets that advance you trace.*

And much of his occasional verse suggests that his contemplation of the sons of Adam held out for him little hope of a more enlightened advance:

> *In bed I muse on Teniers' boors*
> *Embrowned and beery losels all:*
>   *A wakeful brain*
>   *Elaborates pain:*
> *Within low doors the slugs of boors*
> *Laze and yawn and doze again. . . .*
>
> *Sleepless, I see the slumberous boors,*
> *Their blurred eyes blink, their eyelids fall:*
>   *Thought's eager sight*
>   *Aches—overbright!*
> *Within low doors the boozy boors*
> *Cat-naps take in pipe-bowl light.*

—A poem of which it would be unwise to make too much, but which is an amusing demonstration of his sense of the contrast between his own uneasy speculative mind and the indifferent sluggishness of the majority of his fellows.

> *Tired of the homeless deep*
> *Look how their flight yon hurrying billows urge*
> *Hitherward but to reap*
> *Passive repulse from the iron-bound verge!*

This sense of frustration, implicit in nearly all his best work, is expressed with astonishing power in the poem from which that quatrain is taken—a long, passionate and unusually personal revelation of the sensual conflict which he confesses had at times dominated his nature. "After the Pleasure Party" is a poem of tormented sincerity, referring back without doubt to the Mediterranean journey of 1857, and indicting with all the iron Puritanism which lay at the roots of his nature the treacherous revenges that the flesh can take over the spirit.

> *For, Nature, in no shallow surge*
> *Against thee either sex may urge*
> *Why hast thou made us but in halves*
> *Co-relatives? This makes us slaves.*
> *If these co-relatives never meet*
> *Selfhood itself seems incomplete*
> *And such the dicing of blind fate*
> *Few matching halves here meet and mate.*
> *What cosmic jest or Anarch blunder*
> *The human integral clove asunder*
> *And shied the fractions through life's gate?*

The poem concludes with an appeal to the goddess of Love for power to unify the sensual and the spiritual urges; and a comment, final and unsparing, that the appeal will be in vain. It is Melville's most impressive revelation in lyric form of the personal conflict which he had always been at such pains to suppress or at best to universalize: the sex-obsession standing both literally and symbolically for the destructive torment of the sensitive man.

For the moment he has no answer but a steadfastness that I believe (in spite of the almost hysterical note of certain passages in *The Confidence-Man*) never broke. The firm spirit which accompanied him through the dizzying instabilities of the period following *Moby Dick* never seems to have abandoned him entirely.

Each burning boat in Caesar's rear
Flames—No return through me!
So put the torch to ties though dear
If ties but tempters be.
Nor cringe if come the night;
Walk through the cloud to meet the pall,
Though light forsake thee, never fall
From fealty to light.

A sterling precept that he was to elaborate in *Clarel*; it is time now to take up this long poem and watch its extensions of the hints, dropped in the lyrics, into the presages of a new and stable philosophy. But meanwhile it is difficult to abandon the poems (beyond the *Battle-Pieces* collection which had its own separate synthesis) without the feeling that here again he has been driven back upon the lonely defiance of Bulkington or Bartleby, the lonely submission of Hunilla. In only one of the poems from the later collections, "The Night March", does there appear a hint of a serenity that can be bestowed from above the individual spirit rather than imagined from within it; the first glimpse (in a form clearly suggested by the *Battle-Pieces* imageries, and exquisitely adapted) of the Christian myth as it touched Melville's lyric responses. A measured dignity and beauty, linked with an impalpable sense of awe, have given this lyric a perfection both of mood and form that Melville's random Muse seldom achieved.

With banners furled, and clarions mute
An army passes in the night
And beaming spears and helms salute
The dark with bright.

In silence deep the legions stream,
With open ranks, in order true;
Over boundless plains they stream and gleam—
No chief in view!

Afar, in twinkling distance lost
(So legends tell) he lonely wends,
And back through all that shining host
His mandate sends.

CHAPTER XVI

Clarel: the Spirit above the Dust

CLAREL deserves from students of Melville much closer consideration than it is usually given. It is handicapped by its great length, its unattractive and partly misconceived form of presentation, and its consequent inaccessibility. It is yet another of those unhappy experiments of Melville's whose failure was more damaging to his intention than he could ever have realised. Its popular condemnation on artistic or aesthetic grounds has resulted in its being ignored as an expression of the development of his faith; consequently it has tended to throw out of perspective not only the little-known work which accompanied or succeeded it, but also the familiar accepted material which had come before it. *Clarel* is nothing less than the most sustained and significant attempt that Melville's considerable intellect was ever to make to rationalise and resolve the paradoxes which his intuitions had bred in his imagination. It is not itself primarily a work of imagination, in spite of the poetic form in which he cloaked it; rather it is a remarkably thorough intellectual exercise which conceals by its very use of poetic form the nature of the effort Melville was making. Moreover the fact that the gravelly Hudibrastics in which it is written are quite unsuitable to the theme and contrive to appear derivative and archaic, even when they are used with uncommon skill, helps to suggest that Melville was working over old ground when in fact the whole poem is a clarion testimony to his courage in adventuring upon new.

It is fascinating to watch the unerring directness with which all Melville's instincts sent him, in his moments of deepest doubt, back to the emotional securities that had satisfied his Puritan forebears. His literary training had been chiefly among the Elizabethans, and the form of his maturest prose-poetry had been determined partly by Shakespeare and Webster, partly by Fuller and Browne. On the other hand he was never, save in his love for metaphysics, emotionally akin to the Elizabethan temper; his father was of Scottish ancestry, his mother of Dutch, and the two strains united in a common Presbyterianism that coloured Melville's spiritual preoccupations all his life. Therefore his continuing obsession with the Holy Land ranks side by side with his adoration of Shakespeare as a formative influence upon his later work; and clearly he knew Shakespeare no more thoroughly than he knew his Bible. *Clarel* from the very nature of the poem is saturated with Biblical reference, with that significant preponderance of interest in the Old Testament over the New which marks out the Puritan fundamentalist from the more sophisticated and elaborate degrees of Christian belief. This instinctive bias may be remarked in many seemingly casual (and probably unintentional) allusions in all parts of his work; one curious instance being his choice of Old Testament names for many of his characters—Ishmael, Ahab, Gabriel, Elijah, Bildad, Jonathan, Israel, from the novels; Nathan, Nehemiah, Ruth and others from *Clarel*, where admittedly this feature is not unexpected. The point need not be laboured, but the symbolic power of the Holy Land over Melville's imagination is plain—implicitly in *Moby Dick* at the height of his creative enthusiasm, where again and again in the "prophetic" passages not only the characters' names but a part of the quality of their Biblical originals show through the romantic texture of the overlay; and explicitly in the Journals and in the subject and purpose of *Clarel*, which was created out of the material of the Journals. Adrift on a sea of metaphysical speculation, Melville hankered for the Holy Land as an ideal representation of a secure and primal dogmatism in which he might find spiritual consolation and at least a presage of the permanence that the doomed flux of Western materialism denied him. Therefore it is no surprise to find him, after the inconclusive pessimism of *The Confidence-Man*, making the physical pilgrimage to Palestine which he had so

P

often contemplated. The journey took him some months; the poem probably some years. It did not appear until 1876, and then only through the generosity of Melville's uncle Peter Gansevoort, to whom Melville paid grateful tribute in the dedication. It was never issued in England at all until the Standard Edition of 1924 presented it in two large volumes now very difficult to obtain—another reason for the absence of perspective in the popular appreciation of Melville on this side of the Atlantic. The commercial unsaleability of *Clarel*, its superficial unwieldiness, its lack of poise and pace, its insistent preoccupation with sectarian dogma, are all factors which must be taken into account, and which make it unlikely that editions of the poem will ever be available in great numbers. It only remains for the critic of Melville to realise, and insist, that if justice is to be done to Melville's work it is as important to appreciate *Clarel* as it is to appreciate *Moby Dick*.[1]

The setting of *Clarel*—for 'setting' is a more appropriate word than 'story' in a narrative where significant action is cut to a minimum and serves as little more than the bare framework on which an elaborate pattern of argument is traced—is nineteenth-century Jerusalem, with its maze of traditional association, its hordes of merchants and tourists, and its strange mingling of the primitive and sophisticated; a microcosm of Melville's wry assessment of modern civilisation, a kind of comparison between the acceptance of tradition and the exploitation of it, in which ancient faiths have been distorted and corrupted and yet manage to survive. Clarel, a young American and ex-student of divinity, is discovered alone in Jerusalem on just such a pilgrimage as Melville himself had made; and here he makes the acquaintance of a young Jewish girl, Ruth, daughter of an American who had espoused the Jewish faith and the Jewish way of life many years before. The young man falls in love with the girl, and when her father is killed on his farm by marauders he seeks to comfort her, but is rigidly excluded by the practice of her religion from access to her during the mourning period. To counter his impatience he joins a party of travellers who are starting on an expedition, part pilgrimage, part sight-seeing

---

[1] John Freeman's study of Melville condemns the poem on artistic grounds, rightly enough, and attempts no analysis of the intellectual processes which inspired it; and in this way he renders the first English criticism of Melville dangerously lopsided. American critics have shown more forbearance; but Mr. Ellery Sedgwick's analysis in 1942 was the first to allot the poem its true significance, and remains the best available study of it yet published.

trip, through the desert plains in the southern valley of Jordan. They ride for some days through the mountainous wastes and along the shores of the Dead Sea, the company constantly changing by the way; and this journey through the Wilderness, with its few interpolated days of sojourn at the monasteries of Mar Saba and Bethlehem, comprises the bulk of the poem, with its detailed recitals of creed and dogma, debate and commentary, and its slow but sure evolution for Clarel of the kind of faith that alone can satisfy his own deeply-dissatisfied spirit. On returning to Jerusalem, his faith receives a sudden and crippling test when he hears the news that Ruth has died of grief while he has been away, and the poem ends with his attempt to meet this sorrow stoically, to reconcile himself with the bewildering principles of life which have baffled him throughout and have now dealt him such a cruel blow. The eloquent Epilogue to the poem suggests, contrary I think to the philosophical drift of the main action, an optimistic solution.

The poem is divided into four main books, each of which in turn is split into short sections each presenting a scene, a conversation, an incident, a mood, sometimes an almost unrelated lyric. Melville's choice of the cursive octosyllabic metre does not accord very happily with the contemplative conception of the whole poem, and although the partition into short sections was necessary if monotony was to be avoided, the total effect is one of a series of head-long rushes coming each to an unexpected end, rather than the intended one of a cumulation of selected scenes built into an ordered and inevitable sequence controlling the central force of the work. These are serious faults and no ambitious poem could overcome them; but when all that has been said, there is a great deal on the credit side that has never had adequate stress. Even in the finest of his prose Melville had always tended to rely on a rich vocabulary and a natural eloquence rather than on a selective taste; here he bound himself down to a metrical scheme of unaccustomed rigour. The results are sometimes unexpected. A precision of imagery is often accompanied by a new intensity of expression, without any sacrifice of his natural colour and range. For he found in the discipline of this verse an economy to which prose never compelled him; and he often contrived to pack into half a dozen lines the essence of whole paragraphs of prose narrative. Here he succeeds as Browning succeeded—by refusal to subjugate the concreteness of his image to the superficial necessities of euphony; and he is often only less brilliant than Browning because his setting is deliberately deprived of the Renaissance panache which wins for Browning so much of the attraction that his metaphysic might otherwise lack. And where Melville finds abstract argument too intricate to carry a vivid imagery he avoids the feverish pyrotechnics into which Meredith retreated when his own restless intellect tried his poetic imagination similarly hard. Readers who find no difficulty in Browning or Meredith, or alternatively find the difficulties of these poets no essential obstacle to an appreciation of their poems, should not find *Clarel* the weary vain discussion, the facile chat, the unwieldly and prolonged versification of a personal journal, that critics have been so ready to dismiss. The very texture of the verse, knotted, irregular, nervous, indicates the presence of a mind electrically vital behind every phrase. So far from being the otiose production of an imagination burned out with its early activity, it is the sustained, perhaps over-elaborated, attempt of an unusually vigorous intellect at an elucidation of the deepest spiritual problems of his age, and of his own life.

Instinctively perhaps, Melville made his poem the microcosm not only of his age but of himself, a subject he knew well by this time to be honeycombed with every possible complexity. By starting his narrative in Jerusalem and following his hero's wanderings around nearly all the most celebrated spots in Biblical history—the Holy Sepulchre, the Mount of Olives, the Gate of Palms, the road to Emmaus, as well as countless *loci classici* out of both Old and New Testaments—he founded it most significantly upon a basis of tradition. Tradition was his first objective; to examine the past and its influence upon the present, his own national, ancestral, and hereditary backgrounds in their relations with his own living and perplexed individuality; to test first of all the reliability of the known before the adventure of compassing the immediate unknown could be faced. It is the tale of *Mardi* over again, with the holy places of Palestine for the islands, Clarel for Taji, the young Jewish maiden for Yillah, and the conflicting voices of the pilgrims for the dialectical strife of Media and Babbalanja. Yet here he is nearer to the roots of his own and his age's history; for the Christian imagery has a deeper and closer sanction than the self-created fantasies of the islands, and a test of the Christian tradition is a test of civilisation's intuition, not merely of Melville's.

It is not surprising that the lonely student Clarel, oppressed like his creator with the loss of his early faith, finds little comfort in the haven where he has sought for it. His very first impression repels him:

> *And at the last, aloft for goal,*
> *Like the ice-bastions round the Pole,*
> *Thy blank, blank towers, Jerusalem!*

And in the thronged diversity of the life which hustles through the narrow streets, the chief impression recorded in his mind is of the bewildering lack of unanimity in. faith and creed. Even the Sepulchre itself cannot impose a reconciling unity; childlike faith is confronted by scorn and cynicism, profound acceptance is answered on the one hand by materialist indifference and on the other by reluctant doubt. The calm and ancient faith of the Jews is rivalled by the romantic turbulence of Islam as well as by the innumerable factions of Christendom—

> *Yet going he could but recall*
> *The wrangles here which oft befall*
> *Contentions for each holy place,*
> *And jealousies how far from grace:*
> *O bickering family bereft*
> *Was feud the heritage He left?*

It is a distracted city, in which the traffic of modern commercialism and the attacks of scepticism are swamping the authority of the faith which had sustained it through the centuries and which seemed to exist now as an irrelevant survival. The simplicity of primitive Christianity has been lost; when it makes an appearance, in the person of the aged votary Nehemiah, it is remarkable enough to attract attention and even ridicule—

> *Pestered he passed through Gentile throngs*
> *Teased by an eddying urchin host,*
> *His tracts all fluttering like tongues,*
> *The fire-flakes of the Pentecost.*

Nehemiah's evangelistic enthusiasm touches no response in Clarel's wary reticence. He can do no more than recognise his sincerity; aware of deeper complexities than the saint's naïveties ever plumbed, he cannot rest until an answer may be supplied adequate to meet these. There is a strange encounter with a lonely Italian named Celio, whom they meet in the desolate valley of Gihon, the place of tombs, revealing in his overheard mutterings that even a tomb lacks reassurance for him. Here we meet for the first time in the poem an objective sketch of a "Melville man". Reserved and solitary, embittered by a hunchback's deformity, he had lost the Catholic faith of his family and, like Clarel, journeyed to Jerusalem in search not so much of faith as of re-establishment in tradition. Feeling himself outcast, he sought desperately for an older Past than the civilisation that he felt to have disowned him.

> *Blue-lights sent up by ship forlorn*
> *Are answered oft but by the glare*
> *Of rockets from another, torn*
> *In the same gale's inclusive snare,*

is Melville's comment on the strange affinity between Clarel and Celio—travellers who mutely recognise each other's likeness and yet through reticence or uncertainty never acknowledge it. Each withdraws into his own defensive meditations, Clarel back to Jerusalem, Celio to a fierce self-tormenting vigil (in which he up-braids the name of Christ for holding out to imperfect man the promises of perfection that he may never attain), and ultimately into solitary wanderings ending in lonely death; but not before Clarel in his loneliness had realised, by understanding of Celio's profounder loneliness, something of the nature of his own malady.

> *A second self therein he found*
> *But stronger . . .*
> *   . . . Here in press*
> *To Clarel came a dreamy token:*
> *What speck is that so far away*
> *That wanes and wanes in waxing day?*
> *Is it the sail ye fain had spoken*
> *Last night when surges parted ye?*
> *But on, it is a boundless sea.*

The *Mardi*-imagery is still there in all its potency; Clarel is still in most essentials the lost wanderer Taji; his boundless sea is the endless sea over which pursuers and pursued fled on beyond the

limits of that haunting allegory. The old voyage-symbol is inescapable for Melville. *Clarel* is a poem of miles of wanderings on dry
desert land, but when Melville pauses for a metaphor or a simile he
returns without incongruity and with complete appropriateness to
the sea. At times it seems as though his deep-rooted mariner's
instinct automatically converted the prospect of the heaving mountains of Moab into the even more menacing mountains of the Pacific
waves—

> *" See ye, see?*
> *Way over where the gray hills be:*
> *Yonder—no, there—that upland dim*
> *Wreck ho! the wreck—Jerusalem!"* [1]

His insistent recourse to the live metaphors of sea-faring adds
untold vitality to the narrative of his land-voyage; and more it links
it still closer with the spiritual voyage which he had so long ago
begun among the islands. Clarel is thus not only Melville of the
time of writing; he is an autobiographical record of all Melville's
past personifications—not so specifically of the early innocences
like Redburn, but certainly of the first confrontation of disillusionment. The primitive desperation of Taji and the more stoical
resignation of Ishmael are fused by Melville's maturer intellect into
a studious cultivated despair, that is the more pitiful at the outset
for the failure of the intellect to ameliorate it. The poem *Clarel*
accordingly declares itself at the outset as a contemplative recapitulation of all Melville's imaginative life; an impressive intellectual
attempt to impose order upon the distresses into which hitherto his
incompletely controlled imagination had led him.

The episode of Ruth is less integral to the purpose of the poem,
being an artificial contrivance designed to give emotional point to a
plot which does not at any time seem organically controlled by it.
Its most valuable contribution to the poem is the short study of
Ruth's embittered father Nathan; again a variation upon the Celio
theme and another of Melville's numerous *alter egos*, he stands for
the apostate Christian American who has made his pilgrimage to the

---

[1] Compare also the wonderful description in Book III, section XXIX, of the
ravines as if they were ocean-waves:

> *—And far as eye*
> *Can range through mist and sand which fly*
> *Peak behind peak the liquid summits grow.*

Holy Land by the most uncompromising method possible—conversion to the Jewish faith and doubly zealous observance of it. In search of a haven he has simply created a discipline harsher than the exile he fled; and his foreshadowed, and later accomplished, death is Melville's curt comment on his misplaced zeal. The renunciations of Bulkington, Plinlimmon, even perhaps Bartleby, had been in essence liberating; but Celio's and Nathan's were not of that kind. Their malady was lack of faith; it was faith, of an unusual kind perhaps but still profound and creative, that upheld the strange solitudes of Bulkington and Bartleby and compelled the lasting admiration of Melville. Clarel might perhaps have divined, from Celio's and Nathan's failures, that a broken faith cannot be regrafted on to an alien root; that he did not do so may argue that Melville never felt the heritage of the Holy Land to be altogether alien. These failures drove him inevitably towards the pilgrimage that was to symbolise the minutest examination that he was ever to give to the origins of the religious culture into which he had grown.

The death of Nathan enforces ritual mourning upon his household, and Clarel is excluded from all communication with Ruth. If we care to read symbolism into every twist of the story, we may argue that where the Jerusalem of the first section of the poem represents the dogmatic tradition on which Melville based his examination of religion and from which he started his survey, the Wilderness of the second part, into which the pilgrim party travels out of the Holy City, stands for the intellectual doubt which marks the first stage on the progress of scepticism. Subtilising even further, it is not too much to read the arbitrary restrictions of the ritual mourning, which were the means of starting Clarel upon that journey, as the last insult of sectarian dogmatism which finally drove the sensitive seeker away from the confines of religion. At any rate, this is all implicit in the story; and the company that sets out into the desert is patently representative of all the facets of intellectual and imaginative curiosity that engaged Melville's mind during this the most deeply speculative period of his life.

In Melville's context this is a significant change of policy. Until this moment he had always conformed as far as he could to the familiar practice of the poet or novelist in embodying his idea in a symbolic character and pursuing the character rather than the abstraction to such conclusion as seemed appropriate to it. He examined each problem, therefore, romantically, relying upon his instinctive sense of fitness or inevitability to guide his personified theme, and content to accept the answer it gave him in the process. Inescapably, character became the key element in his diagnosis of life, the individual attitude predominating in importance over collective social or historical principles. This is the natural bias of the imaginative artist and it is no surprise to find Melville's work as much affected by it as the crudest of romantic dramatists. The surprise, and the revolution, of *Clarel* is the substitution for the dramatic treatment of the historical, even dialectical, approach. The 'characters' encountered by Clarel on the journey into the wilderness are not characters as Ahab or Jackson or Bulkington had been, evolving from close observation of humanity into representative figures of tragedy; they are 'types', exhibited at full stature after close observation of principles which they are designed to represent. They are static where the others were dynamic; they are animated heads of discussion, drawn from a careful analysis of the degrees of nineteenth-century belief and doubt. The main action of the poem is not the journey at all, but the intellectual and spiritual progress resulting from the analysis of conflicting principles; and it speaks much for the underrated skill of Melville that the characters themselves are for the most part well-differentiated, credible, individual men speaking doctrine that echoes individual character as well as established dogma. Moreover, he is not entirely without success in infusing into this prolonged and elaborate debate a dramatic vitality of its own. In a different context and with very different tools Peacock had performed something of the same task for the early decades of the century; and Pater in *Marius the Epicurean* was soon to achieve success in a setting and with a purpose much closer to Melville's. Their aims were not far different. Peacock, by satirising the eccentric, sought to isolate the desirable mean; Pater, by examining the relative values of the predominating creeds in terms of the aesthetic experiences they offered, to find a spiritual haven in that which might contain the greatest potentialities for beauty; Melville, by deploying in discussion the spiritual faiths and follies of the modern world, to create a dialectical conflict whose catastrophe might point to the most creative solution. The success or failure of this manoeuvre is the success or failure of *Clarel*.

The party is strangely assorted and a little unwieldy. Melville at first had the Canterbury parallel in mind and embarked on

descriptions whose elaborate and lively detail recalls, without notice-
ably emulating, the *Prologue*; but he did not persevere with the
analogy throughout the poem, although he was at pains to make the
chief members clear in every particular. Clarel, the central character,
is the least positive of them all, the melancholy receptive vessel for
every alternating creed or opinion which the argument puts forward.
So retired does he seem at times that he is submerged under the
more thrustful personalities of his companions and forgotten: yet
it is in his mind that the chief conflict is to be fought out, and he
stands indisputably as the main representative of Melville's own
most studious mood. Ranged before him in a number of curious
disguises are other, just as recognisable, aspects of Melville's
character—the sturdy impetuous Rolfe, a man who had lived a life
of energetic travel,

> *—A genial heart, a brain austere . . .*
> *Though given to study, as might seem*
> *Was no scholastic partisan*
> *Or euphonist of Academe,*
> *But supplemented Plato's theme*
> *With daedal life in boats and tents,*
> *A messmate of the elements;*
> *And yet, more bronzed in face than mind*
> *Sensitive still and frankly kind—*

Rolfe is the Melville of the bygone South Sea travels. His
reveries, while full of supple speculation, keep returning to the
idyllic days of old when he was worshipped as a god by innocent
Polynesian natives; he combines, as Weaver was later to record
that Melville himself combined, the tough but sensitive experience of mariner and mystic. Melville, completing the self-portrait,
wittingly or not, calls him

> *Sterling—yes,*
> *Despite illogical wild range*
> *Of brain and heart's impulsive counterchange.*

Side by side with Rolfe is the mysterious reticent figure of Vine.
This figure is purposely kept in shadow, a silent watchful character
who recoils from the eager arguments of the other members of the

party, and who, if he experiences deeper visions than they, chooses
to cherish them in solitude rather than to share them. In Gethsemane, for example,

> *Wistful here Clarel turned towards Vine,*
> *And would have spoken; but as well*
> *Hail Dathan swallowed in the mine—*
> *Tradition, legend, lent such spell*
> *And rapt him in remoteness so.*

Ellery Sedgwick sees in Vine an idealised portrait of Hawthorne.
This is possible, and there is no need to set about disproving it;
I see rather an attempt to remind readers, and even himself, of
Melville's own inscrutable reticences. The oracular solitude of his
latter years, to which such few of his contemporaries as knew him
all testify, answer to Vine's characteristics rather than to any other's
in the *Clarel* company; and even Melville's insatiable curiosity
and readiness to examine it publicly could not cover the whole of
his imaginative range. There were deep and necessary silences in
Melville, silences like the depths of the ocean whose surface turbulence he chronicled so completely; and those silences, so essential
to the contemplative poet for which he must certainly be recognised, are suggested in Vine as nowhere else in Melville.

> *Like to the nunnery's denizen*
> *His virgin soul communed with men*
> *But thro' the wicket . . .*
> *It seemed his very speech in tone*
> *Betrayed disuse. Thronged streets astir*
> *To Vine but ampler cloisters were.*
> *Cloisters? No monk he was, allow;*
> *But gleamed the richer for the shade*
> *Above him, as in sombre glade*
> *Of Virgil's wood the Sibyl's Golden Bough.*

Over against these are set the worldly merchants, treated broadly
as Chaucer would have treated them, the dignified Moslem guides,
and the completest, perhaps most masterly individual portrait
in the poem—the affable English churchman Derwent, a superb
blend of Bishop Blougram and Archdeacon Grantly, ready-witted,
intelligent, optimistic, Broad Church, liberal, and damningly

superficial. Derwent is a brilliant piece of satirical criticism of all those fashionable trends in nineteenth-century perfectibility that made the Church of England at once so powerful, so attractive and so deeply suspect to those outside it who distrusted its readiness to compromise. Melville, the least compromising of all contemporary novelists, clearly detested all that the good man represented; yet he had the fairness and the charity to present him neither as a knave nor a fool. He knew he was no pretentious charlatan like Chadband or hypocrite like Tartuffe; and he paid him the compliment of bestowing on him a culture and intelligence quite foreign to Trollope's preferment-chasing clerics. Profoundly antipathetic to the woolly liberalism that pervaded the Church of England in the nineteenth century from Charles Kingsley to James Mavor Morell, Melville had yet restraint enough to recognise the honesty of purpose and genuine humanitarian principle that made Derwent a worthy companion on the pilgrimage. Yet Derwent's is the idealism that he most distrusts; and because Derwent broadly approves the progress of the century, sees in it the fulfilment of the Christian purpose and the facile answer to the mysteries of the ages, it is through Derwent that he delivers his strongest assault upon it. The crisis in the relationship between Clarel and Derwent comes in the late section entitled "In Confidence" where the priest seeks to soothe the student's nagging dissatisfactions with fair optimistic platitudes that can satisfy no serious seeker after the truth. It is as Clarel had suspected; Derwent's "easy skim" over the superficialities of life made a professional evasiveness the simplest attitude of all. Says Derwent,

> " *Alas, too deep you dive.*
> *But hear me yet for little space:*
> *This shaft you sink shall strike no bloom;*
> *The surface, ah, heaven keeps* that *green;*
> *Green, sunny: nature's active scene,*
> *For man appointed, man's true home.*"

In Derwent is the culmination of Melville's contempt for all the pretensions of Christian liberalism that he had first attacked in his own Mr. Fallsgrave in *Pierre*; and he was not slow to provide more characters in his narrative to share the assault with him. The two crabbed solitaries Mortmain and Ungar are both of Melville's mind; they do not appear together, since the first after a strange and wayward pilgrimage dies on the journey and is buried in an unmarked grave, while Ungar only joins the company towards the end. It was Mortmain who turned angrily upon Derwent's bland optimism and snapped

> " 'Twas Shaftesbury first assumed your tone,
> Trying to cheerfulize Christ's moan,"

and later in an access of anguished eloquence, cries

> " Cut off, cut off! Canst feel elate
> While all the depths of being moan?"

Mortmain is one of the strongest influences upon the progress of thought in the poem—a natural rebel, with the double slur upon him of bastardy and (high-principled) treason, a frustrated idealist schooled in the debates and intrigues of mid-nineteenth century Europe;

> That uncreated Good
> He sought, whose absence is the cause
> Of creeds and Atheists, mobs and laws.

In the tangle of vicissitudes that hamper and encourage rebellion and revolution, Mortmain had been exiled into the company of his own bitterest thoughts.

> He, under ban
> Of strange repentance and last dearth
> Roved the gray places of the earth,
> And what seemed most his heart to wring
> Was some unrenderable thing . . .
> Not thwarted aims of high design;
> But deeper—deep as nature's mine.

Mortmain is the scornful rebel who has failed, and whose faith loses its substance through that failure. He sees bitterly but clearly through the academic pretensions of the theorist or the hedonist. Hs is a more intellectual, more disillusioned Bulkington; a man who has first chosen the way of idealism and found it insubstantial, and next the way of detachment and found that no better. He asks no more than oblivion, and oblivion is all he gets. He is dynamic enough in this nihilistic role in his dramatic place in the poem, savagely counteracting Derwent and rendering even Rolfe in his restless curiosity and the old pilgrim Nehemiah in his devoutness, colourless and unmeaning. But much more is he significant if we regard him as a direct picture of Melville's own renunciations. He is the final recantation of the idealisms which had sustained him through all but the bitterest moments of his life. Of those bitterest moments Mortmain himself is perhaps the least diluted record; the grim and empty embodiment of the craving for death that lurked beneath the stern independence and deliberate non-attachment of Bulkington and Plinlimmon.

Ungar, his spiritual successor on the pilgrimage, is designed as a closer representation of Melville's attitude to contemporary history —of which we have already had more than a hint in *The Confidence-Man*, which proclaimed his distrust of the tendencies which were rapidly destroying his early nationalist aspirations. Ungar, a late arrival in the poem, was evidently conceived after the end of the Civil War, for he alone of the pilgrims springs alive from contemporary America rather than from a theoretical conception of a slightly earlier Europe. Ungar is an American from the South, self-exiled after the War, steadfast in loyalty to his cause though personally opposed to slavery. While believing that slavery was an evil thing, he believes still more that the Civil War was worse, that it betrayed the principles of justice by demanding life-and-death fealty on matters of personal conscience and opinion. Here are Melville's own deepest scruples dramatized once more; and Ungar's desperate exile symbolises only in a higher degree the spiritual exile into which Melville felt himself driven by the very same events. We have seen from *Battle-Pieces* and their Supplement that he had succeeded himself in dredging out of the wreck a saving pity; this resolved his dilemmas where it was unable to resolve Ungar's. Hence Ungar's contribution to the running symposium is reinforced throughout with a rasping pessimistic bitterness; and in one of the most direct indictments of the deterioration of his once promising nation that even Melville ever delivered, Ungar is made the mouthpiece of a terribly accurate prophecy:

> " *Your arts advance in faith's decay*
> *You are but drilling the new Hun*
> *Whose growl even now can some dismay;*

Vindictive in his heart of hearts,
He schools him in your mines and marts,
A skilled destroyer."

Rolfe, his interlocutor, protests, but Ungar beats him down;

" *If be a people which began*
Without impediment . . .
Even striving all things to forget
But this—the excellence of man
Left to himself, his natural bent,
His own devices and intent;

And if, in satire of the heaven
A world, a new world have been given
For stage on which to deploy the event;
If such a people be—well, well,
One hears the kettledrums of hell!"

America, entrusted with the highest idealisms of the human race, has signally betrayed them, is his meaning. The whole of this long section ("Ungar and Rolfe", Part IV, Section XXI, of the main poem) should be read with care and appreciation; Melville's unusually clear understanding of the direction of contemporary developments was never more shrewdly in evidence.

"*Know,*" he continues,
" *Whatever happen in the end,*
Be sure 'twill yield to one and all
New confirmation of the fall
Of Adam. Sequel may ensue,
Indeed, whose germs one now may view:
Myriads playing pygmy parts
Debased into equality
In glut of all material arts.
A civic barbarism may be
Man disennobled—brutalised
By popular science—atheised
Into a smatterer . . .
Dead level of rank commonplace:
An Anglo-Saxon China, see,
May on your vast plains shame the race
In the Dark Ages of Democracy."

There can be few people to-day who would care to question the appositeness of the picture, drawn in obscurity and unpopularity in the middle of the great perfectionist century of Progressive Man. It is curious, and yet it comes as no surprise, that in Melville's tormented quest for a hand-hold of reassurance in the shifting scene of decay and desolation the only institution on which he can lean with any sense of security at all is the Church of Rome. The Oriental religions are impressive, they teach a remarkable stoicism, yet temperamentally the Westerner is an alien to them and they can afford him courtesy but never comfort. Rome always has her answer ready, is never evasive like Derwent or embittered like the wandering visionaries who in turn represent the roving, restless spirit of Melville himself. Seeing the failure and betrayal of revolutionary idealism, Melville is thrown more and more into the shelter of a discipline against which his whole hereditary and imaginative nature cries out in distrust. In his native Protestantism his honest speculative examination finds, to its bitter disappointment, nothing but compromise with the materialist degradation of society. Just as modern commercialism is spurning the great idealisms of the past, so modern Protestantism is ready to jettison the substance of the truth by which she has her ultimate sanction.

> *The Past she spurns, though 'tis the Past*
> *From which she gets her saving part—*
> *That Good which lets her Evil last.*

(He is speaking of latter-day Democracy, but the two are closely associated in his mind.) By its refusal to abide by the established traditions of the original church, and by its readiness to make terms with the most iconoclastic innovations of Science, Protestantism seems to have lost cogency. The amorphous goodwill of Derwent is, in Melville's eyes, Christianity without purpose and without force; and against it he ranges, unobtrusively but unmistakably, the authority of Rome. The young Dominican encountered on the journey, the friar who conducts them round the church at Bethlehem, even certain of the pilgrims themselves, particularly Rolfe, all bear eloquent testimony to the sinewy power of Rome, its ready adaptability to new conditions:

> *Rome being fixed in form*
> *Unyielding there, how may she keep*

> *Adjustment with new times? But deep*
> *Below rigidities of form*
> *The invisible nerves and tissues change*
> *Adaptively . . .*

Rome emerges from Melville's prolonged dialectical disputation with nearly all the honours.

> " *Man's heart is what it used to be*
> *And hence her stout persistency,*"

says Rolfe of the refusal of Rome to dissociate itself from man's innermost passions and emotions, its attachment to the heart contrasting with Protestantism's traffic with the things of the mind (an arid pursuit, creating nothing and leading nowhere, Melville implies.) By thus allying his sympathies with an institution that all his instincts and all his traditions would normally have led him to abominate, Melville is perhaps not so much proclaiming his approval of Catholicism as underlining a new realisation that was only now forcing itself upon his meditations—that no faith can be effective and no philosophy have sanction without a firm discipline to enforce it. Protestantism he regarded as flabby with the lack of it; Judaism as perhaps tyrannical with an overdose of it; but Rome he saw for the time as providing just that necessary blend of regulation and rapture that could illuminate an individual without rendering him either unsuitable for contemporary society or too readily corruptible by its compromises. Rome, I must emphasize, symbolized this discipline only, did not necessarily represent it. Melville did not turn Roman Catholic; merely had the perception to invoke on behalf of his rarest visionaries a discipline that their own hearts could not provide alone, but for which they would be forced to turn to a tradition outside their own contexts. This I believe to be one of the most important stages in his spiritual progress. Once admit as essential the submission to a discipline not his own, and the tragic hero advances a step further from the stage reached by Bulkington, Israel Potter, Plinlimmon. Melville's gallery of the great and dispossessed, now swelled by Rolfe and Vine, Mortmain and Ungar, must now reckon with a new profundity in their creator's vision. It is no accident that *Billy Budd* contains no figure of a kind that can be added to these. As I hope to show, the principle of discipline, by the time *Billy Budd* came to be written, had at last tamed the "landlessness", the roving impetuosity, of the Melville man. And it is through such discipline that the innocence, which experience had driven into solitary and independent ways and for the time had seemed to defeat, can be re-established.

This is, in the main, the lesson of *Clarel*. It records, and recommends, an act of faith rather than any panacea for general doubt. The Epilogue, a sudden and inspiriting fanfare of trumpets, proclaims a triumph that the inconclusive debate and minor tragedies of the superficial narrative itself do not seem to warrant. The triumph is in fact not Clarel's but Melville's. The student's bewildering conjecturings had shown him the kind of faith that he had sought in vain all his life.

> *Unmoved by all the claims our times avow*
> *The ancient Sphinx still keeps the porch of shade,*
> *And comes Despair, whom not her calm may cow,*
> *And coldly on that adamantine brow*
> *Scrawls undeterred his bitter pasquinade.*
> *But Faith (who from the scrawl indignant turns)*
> *With blood warm oozing from her wounded trust,*
> *Inscribes even on her shards of broken urns*
> *The sign o' the cross—the spirit above the dust!*

The Epilogue gives a telling lyric utterance to the culmination of a quest that had been bravely sustained through great tracts of weariness and despair; and the Epilogue is as much a recapitulation of Melville's emotional history as the whole long poem of *Clarel* is of his intellectual progress. In his own despairing period he had scrawled his own bitter pasquinades across the brow of the statuesque riddle of life—*Moby Dick, Pierre, The Encantadas, Bartleby, The Confidence-Man*. In his turn he was to experience as *Clarel* suggests, a resurgence of faith; and faith alone could give him restoration.

"Science the feud can only aggravate," he says in the Epilogue, tacitly condemning once more the truckling of his native Protestantism to this intrusive vandal. New knowledge has brought new fear, materialism is suffocating the new opportunities for enlightenment;

But through such strange illusions have they passed
Who in life's pilgrimage have baffled striven—
Even death may prove unreal at the last,
And stoics be astounded into heaven.

Therefore, he says, take less care of the conflicting bewilderments of the intellect; the key to the conflict is the heart, for the heart of man and not his intellect is constant and reliable. It was the heart that had guided Rome to her enduring authority, and only the heart could guide humanity towards the faith that alone could preserve it.

Then keep thy heart, though yet but ill-resigned,
Clarel, thy heart, the issues there but mind;
That like the crocus budding through the snow—
That like a swimmer rising from the deep—
That like a burning secret which doth go
Even from the bosom that would hoard and keep;
Emerge thou mayst from the last whelming sea
And prove that death but routs life into victory.

I do not make claims for the distinction of this lyric; it is splendidly invigorating, but its epithets are commonplace, recalling some of the more vaporous passages of Shelley, and it has a flavour of wishful revivalist emotion. Nevertheless it accentuates very clearly what from now on will distinguish Melville's work—the insistence upon the heart and not the mind, the abrogation of the scolding intellect in favour of the receptive imagination. To Melville now, even Plinlimmon, Bartleby, Israel Potter, the landless Bulkington, were heartless; they followed towards chaos the dictates not of their natures but of a twisted satirical intelligence of the same order which had once been Melville's own. In Hawthorne's fantasy the heart of Ethan Brand resisted the fire as long as the bones of his skeleton, leading the lime-burner to the conclusion that his heart was made of marble. We know now that Ethan Brand was not Melville, but the likeness was at one time sufficient to make the mistaken belief of identity common; the later Melville in *Clarel* was repudiating just that image of his earlier years. Out of the conflicts of tradition and the deserts of intellectual speculation he had forced himself towards a new faith. The setting of the action of *Clarel* in desert waste is as appropriate as it is often monotonous and occasionally deeply impressive.

> *'Tis a land*
> *Direful yet holy—blest tho' banned.*
> *But to pure hearts it yields no fear;*
> *And John, he found wild honey here.*

The accent is, as always, upon the compensating element; the honey in the wilderness, the spirit above the dust. *Clarel* is accordingly a poem of acceptance, not of rejection; its conclusion is tragic enough yet it ends on a note of comfort. *Mardi*, its early counterpart, had ended upon the racing tide, with Taji bound into the unknown at the mercy of the elements, with the avengers close behind. *Clarel* is the return journey; the hero is a mourner but he is re-established among his fellows, and he is given the hint of a faith he will not reject as Taji rejected Serenia. For the experiences of Clarel have accentuated not his defiance but his humility; they leave him as desolate as the tragedy of Mardi left Taji, but he salves his desolation in community and not in solitude. He has reached a point where it is no longer in his nature to reject.

CHAPTER XVII

Billy Budd and the Victory of Innocence

CLAREL points forward to a potential but untried faith; *Billy Budd*, composed probably more than twenty years later, is proof that Melville had tested it and absorbed it into his vision. Because *Billy Budd* is a record of experience and not an imaginative adventure into a mysterious unknown, it stands apart, in quality and atmosphere, from the greatest of his other work. As none of his other conceptions are, it is a calm and authoritative revelation; the doubts which had tormented his most vigorous and productive moments have by years and years of unrecorded wrestling, both of intellect and imagination, been resolved. There is nothing between *Clarel* and *Billy Budd* to reveal the intricacies of the process; merely occasional glimpses of his unpretentious life in New York, the daily walk to the office, the routine in which he absorbed the whole of his common energy and which perhaps acted as a stabiliser, freeing his mind from preoccupations and giving it space to carry on its conjectures upon the lines he had hinted for it in *Clarel*. In 1885 he finally retired from the Custom House, and continued to live quietly at home with his wife and family, genial and lovable with his grandchildren but indifferent to the society of his contemporaries. It was recorded of him at the time of his death that he would never talk of his own works. In November 1888, when he was sixty-nine, he felt himself prepared for a final expression of the vision to which the contemplative years had obscurely guided him; and he wrote the first rough draft of *Billy Budd* in six months. He seems to have taken far more pains with the detailed construction of this one story than he ever did with any of his previous writings; and short though it is in its final version, it occupied him in rewriting and revision until the April of 1891. By this time he had been engaged on it for a little under two and a half years; and when he finally put a date to it on 19th April, with the words "End of Book", the pencilled manuscript was in an unusually crabbed and illegible condition which needed all Professor Weaver's patient scholarship to unravel and present it. Melville died in September 1891; and it was 1924 before it reached print.

"Towards the end," said Auden at the beginning of his deeply perceptive poem on Melville, "he sailed into an extraordinary mildness." This is well said; the clarity and the serenity of this last work are the most conspicuous elements in its detailed and precise presentation. They are conspicuous because in the context of the familiar Melville of the novels and poems they are unexpected; in the making of *Billy Budd* the old ingredients of doubt and fear have, almost mysteriously, disappeared. There had been nothing, even in his most recently-published work, to foreshadow this amazing alleviation. The Epilogue to *Clarel* was a pious, even empty, hope by the side of this reality. Only in the short lyric, "The Night March", from the *Timoleon* collection, which I have already quoted in full, is there anything approaching the intensity of the mood of resolute acceptance in which the complete story of *Billy Budd* was to be conceived, although certain of the later poems, composed probably almost as late as the story itself, carry evanescent hints of an enlightenment for which nearly the whole of his life's considerable production had been the exhausting search. Here in *Billy Budd* comes, at last, the answer; and the disproportionate labour which Melville is known to have expended on its composition is evidence of the care he took to make its expression final and unmistakable.

Melville the hereditary Puritan and Presbyterian, who had set his philosophic courses away from the conventional dogmas of his fathers and forced himself through scepticism into nihilism and a state of mind that at one time seemed to herald spiritual disintegration, had come home triumphant to the certainties which he had thought to lose for ever. He had never, throughout his whole life, been estranged from the Christian context of thought and image, though clearly he had for very long and important tracts of it lost all sense of communion with its tradition and had ceased to believe in its efficacy. But even in his most desperate distresses he had retained its original standards of judgment. Hunilla in her desolation eyed the jointed workings of the ass's armorial cross; the sordid traffic on the Mississippi steamboat had been balanced at every turn against the great maxims from Corinthians. Clarel's frustrated and querulous wanderings were upon the very soil in which Christian history and tradition were rooted. It is not an exaggeration to describe Melville as fascinated throughout the whole of his life by the work and character and (most of all) symbolic significance of Jesus. Yet Melville, when he returned to Christianity, returned to it by the hard way.

The prodigious repetition of the old slogans and symbols by authors whose Christian faith was stronger than their imagination resulted in the last century in the flooding of the market and the consequent devaluation of a once precious coinage. Any Tom, Dick or Harry who was moved to hymnology played ducks and drakes with the superb Biblical imagery until the lovely imaginative structure lay scattered like rubble, and through being forced to do duty for second hand ideas lost its power to communicate the genuine inspiration with its old compulsion. The Bible itself was drained of all virtue save a residual mumbo-jumbo sanctity, and, in certain circles a repressive police authority which has hardly vanished yet. Dinned into ears which were severally frightened or indifferent, the resounding Elizabethan prose frittered away into tags, hung on in the language as a permanent cadence only, finished as ready common coin of speech to be rubbed smooth. The Christian symbol began to lose all value.

Creative minds of the first order occupied by religious problems had two courses left to them. One was to pursue the personal, living Christian faith into regions where only the profoundest psychological and spiritual conflicts could exist. For those few who can follow this course there can be nothing but admiration, unless it be reverence. To trace the intensities of the spiritual progress of a major artist like Hopkins is a deeply enriching experience. Nevertheless it is possible to find still more impressive the records of those other minds who have felt themselves obliged to track out of accepted Christian courses altogether and to seek integrity in an honest substitution of inward and individual values for outward and communal ones. And it can be the most rewarding experience of all to watch, not a conflict within the bounds of a faith, but the dramatic and barely voluntary return to it by a great and troubled imagination that has begun by embracing a permanent exile from it. Taji's return to Serenia is a more wonderful story than his early renunciation of its shelter.

I do not mean to suggest that such a return is conclusive; it may be less of a fact than a symbol. An artist's life is lived in symbols, and Christianity may be to the tired but resolved wanderer the handiest workable image of the peace to which he has attained. If great artist after great artist has made this return it speaks as much for the nearness of the Christian vision of truth to the artistic vision of truth as it does for the operation of moral judgment upon the artistic conscience. It proves the validity of the artist's creative vision; it proves the essential aptitude of the Christian myth as a symbol of imaginative artistic fulfilment. In the teaching and life of Jesus is the perfect symbol of truth—moral and spiritual— attained through the abandonment of the selfhood. Hence its arresting significance in the hands of an artist who has not always professed the Christian faith, who has in fact implicitly abandoned the Christian faith at a crucial moment of his life, and whose integrity and imaginative power have proved themselves, without its help, in far other courses.

Melville was one of these; and here it is useful to recall his affinities with a greater artist. By now it is all but a commonplace of criticism to equate the period of his one supreme masterpiece and its immediate successors with the tragic period of Shakespeare. I have already had cause to remark the obvious parallelisms between *Moby Dick* and *Lear*, *Pierre* and *Hamlet*. Melville's innumerable references to Shakespeare in his novels, poems and letters are further evidence of the very close influence that the plays exerted over his conscious and unconscious mind. Atmospherically as well as thematically, the correspondences between Melville and Shakespeare, at their period of crucial development, are real and convincing. At the source of *Moby Dick* and *Pierre* as at the source of *Hamlet* and *Lear* is a recognisably common perplexity, urged in each case by the dynamic imagination of the poet into a barely reconcilable conflict of values. The complexity of the symbols, best exemplified in the elaborate whaling metaphors of *Moby Dick* but extraordinarily potent in *Pierre*, *The Confidence-Man* and the contemporary short stories, is merely a surface indication of the complexity of the intellectual and spiritual problem. In Melville, a lesser artist than Shakespeare and in less complete control over his medium, the difficulties are accentuated. Scale down the artistry of *Lear* and *Hamlet* to the level of *Timon* and *Troilus*, and we have a closer parallel—the artist perplexed in the extreme, perplexed even out of his capacity to shape his artistic symbolism aright.

But if the keynote of the Shakespearian tragedies is perplexity, that of *The Tempest* is surely simplicity; simplicity of the most matured and resolved order, sure and unhurried and composed. Shakespeare left a record, enigmatic and spasmodic it is true, but traceable, of his journey to the ultimate consummation; and by the time we reach *The Tempest* we have been eased without strain or surprise into its wonderful atmosphere of reconciliation. Tchekov's illuminating little note in his journal, on the theme of listening to music, is apt in the contest of this sublime play where the isle is full of noises—that when one listens to music everything has a meaning; "the avalanche even is no longer meaningless, since in nature everything has a meaning. And everything is forgiven, and it would be strange not to forgive." That is the central keynote of *The Tempest*; it is a palpably Christian atmosphere on Prospero's island; and in recent years the detailed studies of Professor Wilson Knight of the imagery of this play and its immediate predecessors have revealed unmistakeably the alignment of the imaginative haven, to which the poet had won, with the heaven-haven of the Christian myth. Dostoevsky, struggling through from Stavrogin to Alyosha Karamazov, trod something of the same path. The power of these imaginative creations is such that whereas Bunyan seems to have seen Christian's journey as plain as Bedford jail, Dostoevsky and Shakespeare, each in his own bedevilled solitude, seem to have travelled it.

And so did Melville. To describe *Billy Budd* as his *Tempest* is another platitude; but that is what it is. And although he reaches in this book a destination which is not quite unexpected after the yearnings of *Clarel*, there is no record to be gleaned from Melville's later years, as there is from Shakespeare's, of the manner in which his spiritual conquest was attained. Therefore *Billy Budd* enjoys a curious isolation. It describes a resolve of which there has been no detailed contemporary record. Knowing Melville's early habit of breaking in his ideas and images on paper, we are led to profitless conjectures about what he may have written in the intervening years and destroyed. Here is an artist markedly faithful to the intuitive man's motto, *solvitur ambulando*; in the nature of things it seems unlikely that he could hatch out a new imaginative process in silence. If he did, *Billy Budd* is a *tour de force*, a recollection in tranquillity with few parallels in the language.

The story, austere and economical, is by now familiar—of Billy the honourable and innocent sailor falsely accused of mutinous tendencies in his captain's presence by his enemy the master-at-arms, whom he incontinently and involuntarily strikes dead and for whose homicide he suffers due execution. Into this moving and tragic series of incidents—based on fact, as so much of Melville's fiction is—Melville infuses a great part of that same imaginative vitality and power that created *Moby Dick*; and that is as much as to say that every concrete symbol carries a load of overtones and suggestions that must be sought out and understood if the full significence of the tragedy is to be appreciated.

Billy is the Handsome Sailor, without vice, beloved of his shipmates, the cause and centre of their common peace and good-will. "A virtue went out of him," says the reproachful captain of the merchantman from which he has been pressed into the Navy, "sugaring the sour ones. . . . you are going to take away my peace-maker". Innocence is his prime characteristic—a paradisal and prelapsarian innocence which has led authorities of the calibre of Matthiessen to establish him as a symbol of Adam before the Fall, though it is of the kind of dynamic pervasive innocence credited to Jesus rather than the savage kind appropriate to Adam. Read with reference to his death, these spiritual qualities fall more readily into place; for the sentence is technically legal though equitably unjust, and the execution scene, presented with supreme dignity and skill, reveals the central figure of the Hanged Man against a background of the rising sun—"The vapory fleece, hanging low in the East, was shot through with a soft glory as of the fleece of the Lamb of God seen in mystical vision." The symbolism here is too deliberate to be ignored. It hardly needs for corroboration the additional details of this curiously meticulous likeness. There is the last spoken phrase before execution, "God bless Captain Vere!", an echo of the great cries from the Cross; there is the tracing by the sailors of the spar from which Billy was hanged, from ship to dockyard and back again to ship, so closely reminiscent of early Christian hagiography that Melville's own comment that to them it was as a piece of the Cross is less necessary than he realised; there is the gradual apotheosis of the Handsome Sailor, epitomised eventually in the doggerel broadsheet, a repetition of the growth of the Christ-legend and the ultimate composition of the Gospels themselves. The ironic touch that Melville could not forgo, the report in the naval chronicle in which the facts and conclusions of the story are grossly distorted, has perhaps a parallel in the common ill-repute in which the early Christians and the memory of their founder were held even in the writings of so enlightened a man as Tacitus. But perhaps most striking of all the parallelisms is Billy's vigil between the guns, during which his innocence is confronted for the first and last time with the full knowledge and understanding of evil and, by resolving the universal tension, achieves a reconcilation. This Gethsemane was strictly enacted in two parts, the first with the captain in his cabin, an interview to which we are not admitted but at which the tension, says Melville, was first broken, and the second in the solitary night watch during which that tension is recapitulated and overcome for ever. And although the ship's chaplain is no Iscariot, and his kiss is an obeisance before a greatness he can never attain himself, he is sufficiently indequate to the spiritual intensity of the context to make his kiss a significant reference to that other.

Billy himself is a lay figure charged with life from the power of the symbolism surrounding him; against him Claggart the master-at-arms opposes a more individual vitality. Twice before in his major work Melville had attempted detailed sketches of the essentially evil-natured individual. In Jackson of *Redburn* he had recorded a vital venomous malignity which inspired and communicated a sense of fear and hatred through all his shipmates; while in *White Jacket* the figure of Bland, the master-at-arms, is invested with a certain silky fascination which accentuates rather than conceals the depravity of his nature. Physically, Claggart recalls Bland most strongly; it is possible that for these two men Melville may have drawn on a common source in his own naval experience. It is perhaps a result of Jackson's superior dramatic vitality that it is Jackson and not Bland with whom Claggart has been most often compared. In Claggart Melville has set himself a subtler task than he attempted in Billy; he is at some pains to create a recognisable and coherent psychological type, and up to a point he has succeeded. Yet the novel is a consistency; and Claggart has his universal symbolisms too, as significant in their less obvious way as the striking Jesus-symbols of the central character. Handsome and distinguished in feature, with dark curls clustering over a faint amber pallor, without human antecedent or adherent, Claggart is at once repellent and attractive, a figure of character and purpose, defined against the level perfection of the handsome sailor with an almost refreshing clarity. Because he is complex, Melville has a difficult task with him. Melville's great tragic period, when complexity and ambiguity were the air he breathed, had now been superseded by an era of simplicity, of allegory. Here mixed motive was not in question, but sheer stark Evil had to be present, to be confronted and refuted. Consequently Claggart is given devilry in plenty but is not allowed complexity; Melville's ranging imagination conceives the former and with considerable skill withholds the latter, modelling the man into an embodiment of evil that must necessarily conform to an almost primitive pattern of simplicity. For the reinforcement of the intensity of the drama his depravity has to be anatomised at some length; and in a long and thoughtful passage Melville calls in aid, only to reject, the Hebrew prophets as guides; and by a passing reference to the Calvinistic theory of natural depravity, leads up to an analysis of his "phenomenal pride" and his instinctive hatred of his spiritual opposite. Disdain and distrust of an innocence, that he would have shared if he had had the power, even of redemptive remorse, in his contemplation of the unconscious Billy is a subtle touch absent from Shakespeare's far fuller conception of un-regenerative evil in Iago, but rather closely reminiscent of another supreme fallen figure.

> *And care*
> *Sat on his faded cheek, but under brows*
> *Of dauntless courage and considerate pride*
> *Waiting revenge. Cruel his eyes, but cast*
> *Signs of remorse and passion. . . .*

And Melville by quoting as epigraph to the section introducing Claggart the half-line "Pale ire, envy and despair" from the scene of Satan's approach to Eden, explicitly confirms the reference. Accepting it, we must accept a further reckoning along with it; that the Puritan tradition still lay closely upon all New England culture, and that in its context, Milton's powerful imagination had successfully grafted his own colossel myth on to Old or even New Testament legend. Consequently the Devil against whom the common run of Puritans strove was the Devil in the likeness of Satan of *Paradise Lost*, and therefore a reference to him carries with it in the nineteenth-century New England atmosphere[1] many overtones of Christian association which elsewhere might not be implied. Accordingly in the conflict of Claggart and Billy there is a new embodiment of the conflict imagined in *Paradise Regained*; though not here confined to the Temptation (another episode in the Jesus story lightly symbolised in *Billy Budd* in the sporadic incitements to mutiny) but played out in the larger symbolic and religious context of Redemption through Sacrifice.

Over the two central protagonists presides the calm, dignified but aloof and even mysterious figure of Captain Vere. The touch of remoteness in his nature is cleverly pointed by Melville's adoption of the epithet "starry" from Andrew Marvell's poem, and further insisted on by the elaboration of his aristocratic antecedents and upbringing.[2] In him the symbolism is extended to the very name itself—the Truth; and what is implicit in the name is explicit in his condition and conduct, a being compact of Melville's most admired qualities—nobility, honour, courage, justice, and above all the old aloofness seasoned with the new discipline. In Vere's consciousness the whole piteous dilemma is wrestled into resolution; for to him only is it presented as a direct war of alternatives, on him only is laid the responsibility for the ultimate decision, and to him only is the tragedy a consciously controllable, rather than a predetermined, series of actions. Thus Claggart's evil is predestined, like Satan's; he obeys his destiny with just that touch of regret that adds poignancy to his character and situation. Thus too Billy's fate is out of his control; what sublimates his tragedy into a triumph is his ready and imaginative acceptance of it. Vere on the other hand is beholden to no law save eternal justice; and his is the prerogative of the fateful decision which shall uphold it. He does not

[1] Melville was not in fact a New Englander, but the whole culture of nineteenth-century America was so coloured and dominated by that region that a generalisation that embraces New England is almost certain to affect a writer who found all his literary friends and contacts there, and was not far away himself.

[2] It is a quaint coincidence that he shares his Christian names—Edward Fairfax—with another great symbolic figure of nineteenth-century fiction, Mr. Rochester. This has little significance except perhaps as evidence of some involuntary thought-transference in Melville's mind from one symbol of power to another.

hesitate, even though it involves the destruction of one in whom by now he has recognised an implicit sonship, as Billy has recognised in Vere an implicit fatherhood. There are hints in the text—the insistence on Billy's noble antecedents and the equal stress on Vere's nobility of birth—that leave room at least for the implication that Billy was Vere's actual as well as spiritual son. There is no definite textual warrant for this, but the unusual accentuation may not be fortuitous. Melville carries analogy no further than a reference to the Abraham-Isaac relationship; but the profounder reference, to the God the Father of the Christian Trinity, will stand even closer examination.

Equipped with the supreme symbolism of God the Father decreeing the sacrifice of his incarnate Son in the redemption of innocence from the powers of the Arch-Enemy, Melville achieved this unique and unforgettable allegory. Mr. William Plomer sees it as Melville's final protest against the nature of things, saved from despondency only by his zest for physical energy and beauty and for all the varieties of human goodness to which even advanced disillusionment could not blind him. It may be so; his guess is as good as mine. But with Melville the symbol is everything, and Mr. Plomer has not taken the symbol into account. It is the symbol that surprises. Read alone, *Billy Budd* is a masterly and moving story. Read as it must be, as part of Melville, that colossal and still imperfectly understood adventurer of the imagination, it is the symbol that stuns.

For Melville is and was Ishmael, tossed from the security of his whaleboat to watch the whirlpool engulf every soul of his ship's company. After *Moby Dick* his course had been bitter and difficult; material no less than spiritual circumstances had given him only too concrete cause for despair, and in his hunger for truth he seemed to have looked too far into its complexities to have been capable of a coherent account of it. Melville, like idiot Pip, saw "God's foot upon the treadle of the loom, and spoke it; and therefore his shipmates called him mad." But the quotation proceeds, it will be remembered, "Man's insanity is heaven's sense; and wandering from all mortal reason, man comes at last to that celestial thought, which to reason is absurd and frantic; and weal or woe, feels then uncompromised." The progress from *Moby Dick* to *Billy Budd* is a record of just such a wandering. In *Billy Budd* Melville achieved a projection of an imaginative state that enunciated familiar and all but outworn truths with the delight and freshness of a newly-discovered solution to the years of scarifying troubles; and this achievement speaks more for the ultimate validity of the Christian vision than all the vanloads of hymnbooks and moral pocket-handkerchiefs with which the nineteenth century had sought to bolster its tired creeds.

Billy's last words, as he stood with the rope round his neck an instant before being swung lifeless from the yard-arm, were de-livered, says Melville, "in the clear melody of a singing-bird on the point of launching from the twig". In this sublime sentence, ir-radiating the sombre context as the sacrifice behind the Crucifixion irradiates the tragedy itself, Melville epitomises the imaginative mood which had begotten this late masterpiece. He has returned at last to "that celestial thought, which to reason is absurd and frantic", the conviction of the ultimate victory of innocence, in all the conflicts which experience can wish upon it. It was the hope which had been with him all his life from the moment when he embodied his own youthful ardours in the naïvetés of Tommo and his yearnings for a peaceful basis for social relationships in the primitive lotus-eating Typees. He had seen his innocence assailed and traduced and insulted, and finally, it seemed, defeated. *Pierre* sees that primal innocence out, and for the moment can offer no substitute. Only the hero-worshipping memory of Jack Chase, and the eager, ultimately frustrated, pursuit of Hawthorne, sustained Melville over those middle years whose most enduring creation was the "Melville man", the resigned solitary aware of the shark beneath the wave and the certain implacability of Fate. Bulkington, Plinlimmon, Bartleby, one by one retired from the hopelessness of the search, and made do with a hermit-integrity of their own. Melville seemed to approve; he stressed the destructiveness of society and civilisation too heavily for misapprehension. It was in swarming London, not in desert wastes or trackless seas, that Israel Potter was submerged in poverty for forty years. In Melville's eyes, as in Yeats' many years later, the ceremony of innocence was drowned. He himself retired, like Plin-limmon, into an obscurity like Potter's. In this, it may be, his in-stinct was right, and only in an untrammelled contemplation was there any chance of preserving, or rather re-discovering by pro-longed self-analysis, the original hope. In the desert John found wild honey; the pilgrimage to the Holy Land and the aftermath of sustained speculation both testify to an act of faith on Melville's part which may have been born of desperation but which had in it a grain of prophetic genius. For here Melville found wild honey too.

In brief, he rediscovered the virtue in the lost innocence. In *Billy Budd* the innocence is no less vulnerable to the attacks of a malevolence with which Fate too often conspires to combine; and the tragedy of Billy is really far less acceptable than the tragedy of Pierre, since it is Pierre's defects that turn his fortune in the direction of death, while Billy is caught in a deadly vice by forces he cannot humanly control. Nevertheless the state of innocence which Melville was able to imagine at the end of his life was altogether maturer and profounder than either the childlike simplicity of the Typees or the defensive simplicity of Hunilla or Bartleby. The story of Billy Budd is a triumph and not a tragedy for the reason that the reinforced innocence of Billy can accept the tragedy and thus transcend it, as Prospero accepted and transcended his. *The Tempest* and *Billy Budd* are alike in conveying the reader into spheres in which even the colossal forces of tragedy are rendered impotent. Shakespeare was reconciled to life because he found mercy in it. Melville could not see so far; yet his acceptance of an order in which mercy was denied carries a nobility as admirable as Shakespeare's clearer vision.

The secret of the reinforcement of the old spontaneous innocence can perhaps be found in the implied conclusions of *Clarel*—the suggestions never too definitely pressed but enduring so far beyond the actual reading of the poem that they stand out in the memory as its most complete declaration; that without a carefully established order to guide it through the indifferences and hostilities of materialist society neither imagination nor religion can survive. Derwent's indolent idealism stands 'for the inadequate translation of amiable Typee innocence into the terms of modern civilisation; and Melville has little but condemnation for it. On the other hand, though he has more respect for the rootlessness of Mortmain and Ungar and the unsatisfied curiosities of Vine and Rolfe, he cannot give them full approval because nothing in their philosophy can give anything but a negative answer to his own problems. In his consciousness of their inadequacy is his acknowledgment of the uncreative nature of the defensive mood of Bulkington and Bartleby; although for very many years he had identified himself with the order of solitaries, he had recognised by the time *Clarel* was done that indisciplined rootlessness led only to disintegration. It is the ordered faith (not specifically Catholic or Islamic, though these in their turn represent it) that comes nearest in that poem to resolving for Melville the quandaries in which first inexperience and next escapism had plunged the best-intentioned men. Just as he had had to wait for the historical fact of the Civil War to help in the unification of his straying symbolism, so he had to wait for the philosophical conception of order to help in the unification of his vision. *Billy Budd* is the clearest proclamation he ever made of the necessity of an ordered discipline to the attainment of either spiritual contentment or imaginative enlightenment.

The character of Captain Vere is the incarnation of this new conception of discipline. Confronted with the dilemma of the fact of a killing and the utter innocence of the killer, Vere's decision is conclusively upon the side of the rule of law. Even though the killer is the angel of God, yet the iron laws of discipline demand that the angel must hang. In the broader contexts of humanity the sentence is unbelievably harsh; at the historical moment at which Vere is called upon to decide (a few months after the mutinies in the British Fleet, when the slightest deviation from strict duty might precipitate disaster) Vere has material excuse on his side. Nevertheless it is not only the material excuse that determines Vere; he is of the kind that would never resort to it alone. "For the law and the rigour of it we are not responsible," he says. "Our vowed responsibility is in this—that however pitilessly that law may operate, we nevertheless adhere to it and administer it. . . . The heart is the feminine in man, and hard though it be, she must here be ruled out." For the heart alone, as Melville's profound experience had proved, is capricious without a guide. It cannot be allowed to flout the natural laws; without those laws innocence is defenceless, but under their protection it can overcome the world. Accepting the omnipotence of natural order, Billy Budd accepts the adverse verdict in love and understanding, and with his last breach forgives the instrument of his own destruction. Indeed, it is not a forgiveness, since he recognises nothing for which forgiveness is necessary. More properly it is an acknowledgement that he and Captain Vere alike, the representative of natural goodness and the representative of natural justice, are each content to play their allotted parts in a design which they gladly accept. This element of assured acceptance, resulting from Melville's recognition of order as an essential in nature, stamps *Billy Budd* as the sign of the completion of an

R

imaginative quest with few parallels in literature. The Christian conception of love, which partakes not only of understanding and forgiveness, but of acceptance of evil which transcends and converts that evil to creative good, has at last been absorbed into Melville's imaginative vision. It marks the final victory of innocence, before which all assailants are powerless and all distractions vain. At one stroke Melville has rendered all his previous work out of date, but all the more precious for the imperfections and discords which are now superseded. Moreover, comparison between the obscure and tormenting greatness of *Moby Dick* and the luminous greatness of *Billy Budd* illustrates the important axiom that the unravelling through art of a state of spiritual bewilderment requires complex symbols for its expression, whereas a state of assured resolution needs no more than the simplest rudiments of form. It may be argued from this that an inclination towards the primitive is expressive of a refined spiritual vision rather than a retrogressive timidity; but this is a generalisation that must be fortified in each instance by a close examination of the individual artist. It cannot be doubted that Melville's experience and achievement endorse it.

The implications range wider than the limits of one writer's work. That the answer to the tragic experience that has overwhelmed the primal innocence is simply a reaffirmation of the truth of that innocence, is not the whole story. The answer must rather be that the early, unfledged vision of beauty was genuine but incomplete; that the late recognition of the saving simplicity of the natural order is neither a retreat from experience nor a proclamation of the spiritual superiority of the child over the man. For the early simplicity was instinctive and ignorant, like the Typee savage; the late simplicity was experienced, responsible and assured, Billy's responsiveness allied to Vere's unerring sense of justice. The late simplicity contains in itself, and has successfully mastered, the complexities of experience; the expression of it is not therefore a reaffirmation of an earlier state of being, but a fresh discovery of a new one. It is the discovery that the love which has come to be recognised as the guiding principle of the universe can only exist co-extensively with its opposite, hate; that a love which does not comprehend hate is a rootless and unenduring love; and that even hate carries with it the seeds of redemption since it provides the reality upon which love can exercise its creative power. Claggart is as essential to nature as Vere or Billy; and only the sentimentalist can deny it. In *The Confidence-Man* Melville had embodied an earlier glimpse of this truth in the curious little inset episode of Colonel John Moredock, the Indian-hater, the man in whom implacable hatred towards the Indians was combined with a rigid integrity and self-abnegation. "In short," says Melville, "he was not unaware that to be a consistent Indian-hater involves the renunciation of ambition, with its objects—the pomps and glories of this world". In the conception of Colonel Moredock is hinted the reconciliation of opposing elements that *Billy Budd* was to ratify; and in the later book the baffling paradox was to be made plain at last.

In the process Melville made trial of two altogether different kinds of imaginative expression; for the statement of his bewilderments he found intricate and ambiguous symbolisms corresponding to the intricacies and ambiguities of his dilemmas; for the statement of his ultimate serenity, the austerest of allegories. The success of both these attempts can only be called an achievement of natural genius, the instinct leading him right where in similar case his intellect so often misdirected him into clumsiness. At his supreme moments, as in the composition of *Moby Dick* and *Billy Budd*, a rare artistic tact controlled all his natural vagaries; at less-inspired periods he was led into disastrous by-ways of tedium, where neither the facetious jollities of *Mardi* nor the tireless cerebrations of *Clarel* can compensate for the pedestrianism of the one or the misbegotten metre of the other. Yet with no pretensions to scholarship or style, he attained greatness; never more than a literary amateur, by the best standards of the prevailing conventions, he put the existing novel-form to tests which no contemporary professional would have dared impose upon it, and when it survived under his hand it survived to endure.

Melville unashamedly bent art to his own ends. Dissatisfied with experience, he used his considerable gifts to force his way to the roots of his dissatisfaction, and thence if he could contrive it to the roots of the universal mystery. Of the common sophistications of art he was quite careless; they stood in his way. Although in the intensity of his creative power he can be said to have extended the scope of the novel in *Moby Dick*, his influence upon the art of fiction, considered purely as art, is not permanent. Like *Wuthering Heights*, a novel of similar imaginative power and eccentricity, Melville's masterpiece is the triumph of its author rather than the triumph of an art. All his talents, whether co-ordinated or not, were absorbed in the translation of his own spiritual conflicts into a form which, either at the point of creation or at some later time, might serve to illuminate the common stock of experience. His responsiveness, his curiosity, his sanity and his courage were combined with an unusually vigorous narrative talent and a creative imagination of great power to make his stock of books a treasury of spiritual rather than literary achievement. Yet for all the defects of his art he advanced nearer to the creative understanding of the human situation than any of his countrymen; for the myth he made from his chosen symbol was more than the myth of a maturing society, or of a civilisation struggling with its own deadly products for its own survival. It was at once more intimate and less parochial than these; it included both these elements without confining itself to either; and it traced the progress of man's individual soul through its inevitable frustrations to an ultimate resolution in acceptance and love. No other purely American writer, of Melville's own time or indeed of any other, has attempted either the scope or the profundity of the task that Melville set himself. In a young and expanding literature, reinforced by the ambitious self-consciousness which marks a society whose sophistications are outrunning its spontaneous artistic development, Melville stands out as the first great poetic artist in whom the national genius attained universal stature. American literature is still awaiting a successor to him, not in his technical achievement since that was imperfect and subject to limitations which many lesser writers have easily overcome, but in his imaginative kind, in which he commands a power and a vision that there are few to share with him and none to express in language as memorable as his.

LIST OF REFERENCES

In APPENDING a list of books on Melville that I have found helpful,
I should make it clear that it is in no sense a complete bibliography,
but merely a selection that can be recommended with confidence to
anyone wishing to study his work closely.

BIOGRAPHICAL AND CRITICAL STUDIES

Raymond Weaver: Herman Melville, Mariner and Mystic. 1921.

John Freeman: Herman Melville (English Men of Letters series). 1927.

Lewis Mumford: Herman Melville. 1929.

William Ellery Sedgwick: Herman Melville: The Tragedy of Mind. 1944.

Howard P. Vincent: The Trying-Out of *Moby-Dick*. 1949.

Pierre Frédérix: Herman Melville. 1950.
The only existing biography in French, since the unfortunate destruction by fire during the war of the complete edition of the long Study by M. Jean Simon (1940).

Newton Arvin: Herman Melville (American Men of Letters series). 1950.

Richard Chase: Herman Melville. 1951.

William H. Gilman:	Melville's Early Life and *Redburn.* 1951.
Leon Howard:	Herman Melville. 1951.
Eleanor Melville Metcalfe:	Herman Melville: Cycle and Epicycle. 1953.
Harrison Hayford and Merton Sealts:	Melville's *Billy Budd, Sailor.* 1962.
A. R. Humphreys:	Melville (Writers and Critics series). 1962.
Jay Leyda:	The Melville Log. 1951; 1969.
Howard P. Vincent:	The Tailoring of Melville's *White-Jacket.* 1970.

ESSAYS

D. H. Lawrence:	Studies in Classical American Literature, 1919. (Essays on *Typee* and *Omoo* and *Moby Dick.*)
John Middleton Murry:	Discoveries. 1929. (Essay on *Billy Budd* entiled "The End of Herman Melville".)
Yvor Winters:	Maule's Curse. 1938. (Essay on Melville.)

HISTORICAL AND GENERAL

F. O. Matthiessen:	American Renaissance. 1941.
Van Wyck Brooks:	The Times of Melville and Whitman. 1948.
W. H. Auden:	The Enchaféd Flood, 1951, (containing some illuminating chapters on the imagery in Moby Dick.)
James E. Miller:	A Reader's Guide to Herman Melville. 1962.

The Works of Herman Melville

Novels and Stories

Typee 1846

Omoo 1847

Mardi 1849

Redburn 1849

White-Jacket . . . 1850

Moby Dick . . . 1851

Pierre 1852

Israel Potter . . . 1855

The Piazza Tales . . 1856

The Confidence-Man . . 1857

The Apple-Tree Table and other Sketches (*written at various dates: published 1922; contains the essay on "Hawthorne and his Mosses".*)

Billy Budd (*written 1888–91; published* 1924).

Poems

Battle-Pieces . . . 1866

Clarel 1876

John Marr . . . 1888

Timoleon . . . 1891

Weeds and Wildings, *and other unpublished verses*, 1924.

Journals

Journal of a Visit to London and the Continent, 1849–50.

Journal up the Straits, 1856–7.

INDEX

265